Professor, mentor, author, disability advocate—around the world—Dr. David Anderson corralled his many talents and worldwide experiences to author this important book. The volume should prove invaluable to Christians concerned about disabilities, especially teachers. Without flinching, Dr. Anderson tackles the tough issues: How could a good and benevolent God permit disabled children? Are disabilities the result of sin? How does a Christian teacher of the disabled differ from secular counterparts? Especially helpful is his emphasis on the reflective teacher integrating faith and learning. Certainly this is a volume that belongs on the bookshelves of anyone concerned with disabilities.

Steven A. Kaatz PhD, Graduate Programs in Special Education, Bethel University, St. Paul, MN.

I have had the privilege of traveling with Dr. Anderson as he has taught the concepts addressed in this book to educators, pastors, and parents in a variety of countries. I've seen the material "come alive" as leaders discover the importance of thinking Christianly about disability. This book has the potential of impacting all readers in similar ways. Dr. Anderson challenges all of us to come to grips with a biblical worldview and then to live it out within our spheres of influence. *A Theology of Special Education* thus encourages all readers to think Christianly about disability. Such thinking will then motivate us to care with God's care and to serve with God's concern for justice and compassion.

Dr. Richard Schoenert, Pastor Emeritus, Calvary Church, Roseville, MN.

# TOWARD
## A THEOLOGY OF
### *Special Education*
#### INTEGRATING FAITH AND PRACTICE

DAVID W. ANDERSON, ED.D.

WESTBOW
PRESS
A DIVISION OF THOMAS NELSON

WestBow Press books may be ordered through booksellers or by contacting:

WestBow Press
A Division of Thomas Nelson
1663 Liberty Drive
Bloomington, IN 47403
www.westbowpress.com
1-(866) 928-1240

ISBN: 978-1-4497-7251-2 (hc)
ISBN: 978-1-4497-7249-9 (sc)
ISBN: 978-1-4497-7250-5 (e)

Library of Congress Control Number: 2012919873

Printed in the United States of America

WestBow Press rev. date: 10/26/2012

# Contents

Foreword................................................................vii

Acknowledgments ...................................................xi

Introduction..........................................................xiii

Chapter 1: Why a *Theology* of Special Education? ............1

Chapter 2: Biblical/Theological Themes That Inform
          Special Education..........................................17

Chapter 3: Special Education as Practical Theology.........45

Chapter 4: Theology and the Character of Special
          Education Teachers ....................................77

Chapter 5: Special Education as Spiritual Warfare .........107

Chapter 6: Special Education as Reconciliation .............123

Chapter 7: Inclusion and Interdependence: Students with
          Special Needs in the Regular Classroom.................141

Chapter 8: Biblical Hospitality and Inclusive Education..............163

Chapter 9: Biblical Justice and Inclusive Education .....................185

Chapter 10: Special Education as Spiritual Formation.................205

Moving Forward.......................................................231

References .............................................................239

# Foreword

Central to the mission of Calvin College, where I have worked to prepare teachers of students with disabilities, is the task of learning through the eyes of faith. Many students choose a Christian college because they want to know what difference it makes to learn about special education, or any field, from a Christian perspective. And so we explore that together, critiquing professional literature and best practices, analyzing what we do and why we do it, looking for congruence with a Christian view of persons, society, and schooling. Together we search the Scriptures and the growing canon of works that illuminate a theology of disability and apply that to our work in schools.

In the last several years, the writing of Professor David W. Anderson has emerged to help us. While he is not the first to apply biblical themes to thinking about disability, Anderson is one of few authors to use the lens of faith to think specifically about the education of students with disabilities. Professor Anderson correctly discerns that special education is a ministry to which one can be called. He also helps us see clearly that biblical themes such as justice, reconciliation, and hospitality have direct bearing on how we view persons, the purpose of schooling, the culture of schools, and the ways in which we teach. To have such thinking, some of it published previously in article form, collected in one place and expanded upon, is a gift to all who want to extend the Lordship of Jesus Christ to this square inch of creation. It will be useful especially to teachers in preparation at Christian institutions of higher education. For Christian students at secular colleges and universities, this book will guide their thinking in ways their professors may not.

To be clear, the focus of this book is not narrowly on the education of students with disabilities in private, Christian schools, though what Anderson has to teach us can certainly be applied in such settings. The book's broader focus is on helping Christian people—be they teachers, parents, school administrators, board members, or others—think Christianly about the education of children who learn in diverse ways, about the broad purposes of schools, and about the communities in which learning takes place. In doing this, Anderson goes beyond the medical model, which dominated the field of special education for many years, and beyond the social constructivist model that today dominates discussion of disability in special education and the burgeoning field of disability studies. Anderson's distinctly biblical focus has great potential for moving educational practice for all children in new directions, reforming and re-energizing schools.

Particularly compelling are Anderson's arguments that go beyond appeals to Constitutional principles such as "equal protection" and "due process" and beyond notions of individual rights. For him, the more salient concepts are those of biblical justice and reconciliation, and he presents a communitarian vision of life together in schools and elsewhere. Among other things, Anderson argues that both unnecessary segregation and mindless integration can be ways of treating students unjustly. In situations such as those, reconciliation is necessary in order to establish healthy relationships between people—parents and children, children and teachers, parents and educators, children and children. Living out justice means resolving conflict so that people may experience harmony and gracious living in community. As Anderson says, "Reconciled relationships and belonging are hallmarks of the type of just community we seek to establish in our classrooms."

Inclusive educational practice arises from more than the principle of biblical justice. Professor Anderson also illuminates ideas such as interdependence and *shalom*. His thinking provides guidance to those who wish to create inclusive schools, faith communities, neighborhoods, and places of work and play. He argues for a deepened view of inclusion that is more than physical and temporal and pedagogical. Deep inclusion envisions solidarity within community and imagines school, church, and other cultural arenas free from alienation and characterized by mutuality. He asserts that this way of living together is part of God's design for the way things are supposed to be.

Though Dr. Anderson focuses on an area of human difference commonly referred to as *disability*, his ideas can be applied readily to any area of human diversity, be it ethnicity, language, gender, social class, sexual orientation, or others. He humbly invites others to add insights to the work he has begun. While the strength of his book is its perspectival approach, additional writing is needed in which classroom practice is pushed to embody the principles elucidated here in practical, applied ways. Nonetheless, readers of this book will be challenged as well as given critical tools for doing that work. Few could have written this book, which is at the nexus of faith, disability, and education. Anderson goes a long way in helping us to rethink and remember who we are as God's people.

Thomas B. Hoeksema, Ph.D.
Professor of Education, Emeritus
Calvin College
Grand Rapids, Michigan

# Acknowledgments

As I reflect on how I reached this place in my life, many people deserve to be acknowledged, because their lives and teaching or their written works have had a significant influence on my development and thinking, both personally and spiritually. To attempt to name every person whom God has used to shape me or to contribute to my intellectual and professional development would be problematic both in terms of the space it would require and because, inevitably, someone might be overlooked. So I will mention those who have had the most direct influence, principally my wife of 48 years, Florence, and our three daughters, Jennifer, Melissa, and Amy. All have been immensely supportive over the years. Without their love and encouragement, my life would have been greatly diminished.

I must also acknowledge God, whose grace and forgiveness, presence and provision, continue to amaze me. The journey on which he has taken me is one I had never envisioned, but one that has brought joy and opened the world to me—or perhaps more accurately, has opened me to the world.

It would be remiss of me not to mention Dr. Mel Stewart who served many years ago as youth director at Chestnut Hill Baptist Church in Philadelphia, and his wife, Donna. Without their love and life witness, I might never have been introduced to Jesus.

I must also acknowledge Dr. Thomas Hoeksema for his encouragement and for taking time to write the foreword for this book; my former colleague at Bethel University Dr. Steven Kaatz for his friendship, his participation on the board of directors for Crossing Bridges, Inc., and for his help in editing some of the content; and Dr. Richard Schoenert for his friendship, his long-time service as senior pastor at my home church, and for his review of the manuscript.

I also want to acknowledge the disabled children at the Center for Empowerment of Females with Disabilities in Cameroon for all that they have taught me through their example of joy despite dealing with the struggles of being disabled in a developing nation, where individuals with disabilities are yet marginalized and disrespected.

Thanks also to Maggie D. England and the editorial staff at WestBow Press for their assistance through the development of this project. Finally, thanks to the editors of the *Journal of Education and Christian Belief,* the *Journal of Religion, Disability, and Health,* and the *Journal of the International Christian Community for Teacher Education* for permission to reproduce some of my articles.

# Introduction

A theology of special education is not something on which most Christians who teach children with special needs have given serious thought. For most, being a special education teacher is seen simply as a career, a way of earning a living that seems to match their temperament. Some may refer to a "calling" when they refer to being or becoming a teacher of children with special needs, but they have generally given little thought to what that actually means. Reflecting theologically on how their faith informs special education—or on *being* a special educator—is not something at the forefront of their thinking.

We live in a culture that tends to define people by what they do rather than by who they are. Questions of purpose or meaning to life is frequently either shallowly considered or not pondered at all until reaching a later stage of life, when many begin to question whether they have made a difference or contributed to the world in some way—or until something happens that significantly alters their life and affects their career, such as becoming seriously ill or disabled. Most are too caught up in making a comfortable and secure life for themselves and their families to reflect on the significance of their life choices.

By no means do I question the genuineness of anyone's faith, but it is important to acknowledge the spiritual divide commonly seen in many Christians today. Thinking theologically about one's life and career is a challenge for many Christians (even those who have been involved in a profession for many years). One might think of theology as meaning simply *doctrine* and assume that exploring it is the responsibility of a professional minister or theologian rather than any given layperson's. But let's suppose that theological considerations touch all of us. Darrow Miller (1998) holds that many of today's Christians have split personalities: "Their lives are divided into compartments: the *religious*—what they do when attending church or a Bible study—and the *secular*—their jobs, recreation, and education" (p. 44). Miller referred to this as *evangelical gnosticism*, the result of never being challenged to be consciously Christian in their daily lives (p. 45). In the same way, Christian teachers often practice *operational secularism*, separating their faith from practice in their academic discipline (Robinson, 2010).

When studying to become a special educator, one's focus is on understanding the causes and effects of disabilities on an individual's development and functioning; legal issues surrounding assessment and the provision of an appropriate education; and strategies, methods, and teaching accommodations. The student's immediate focus is on the need to satisfy course requirements and obtain passing scores on state or national examinations to secure a teaching license or certification, and the challenge of finding employment. Once employed, attention is directed toward putting into practice what they have learned; effectively managing the classroom; interacting with parents and professionals and resolving potential conflicts; balancing teaching and the requisite paperwork with its time-constraints; being accepted into the educational community, where some general education teachers may still resist including students with special needs in their classrooms; and having a life outside of school. Even well-prepared teachers will continue to upgrade their skills, seeking and learning new methods for teaching students with special needs, especially students with autism or learning disabilities. All of these demands leave little time and energy—or even inclination—to wrestle with the larger issue of a theology of special education.

As a professor of special education in a Christian university, it was my hope not simply to give my students the basic knowledge and skills necessary to becoming a good teacher but to encourage them to think about how their faith integrates with the discipline. My colleagues and I sought to prepare competent teachers, the objective measure of which would be their academic grades, successful student teaching or practicum experiences, and passing scores on the state competency exams. But we did not view our task as simply to present research-based ideas and practices—some of which could actually be in conflict with biblical teaching or implications. Rather, we hoped to help students think biblically and critically about the discipline of special education.

University professors recognize the power of education to shape how people think. But often education does more to conform us to the world than to promote transformation toward Christlikeness and "taking every thought captive to obey Christ" (2 Corinthians 10:5, NIV). The Apostle Paul claimed that believers have "the mind of Christ" (1 Corinthians 2:16). The Greek word *nous* (mind) means thinking, understanding, or insight. In the context of that passage, Paul specifically addressed understanding of spiritual things. But since Jesus is Lord of all, and all truth is God's truth, having the mind of Christ also applies to seeing all creation and all bodies of knowledge as related to him who "existed before anything else" and who "holds all creation together" (Colossians 1:17). To have the mind of Christ means to share his views, understanding, and even his feelings toward the world and toward people affected by disability. As Arthur Holmes (1985) explained,

> To bring our every thought into captivity to Christ,
> to think Christianly, to see all of life in relationship
> to the Creator and Lord of all, this is not an optional

appendage of secondary importance, but is at the very heart of what it means to be a Christian. (p. 11)

In my own case, studying special education at a secular university certainly did not encourage me to consider how my faith integrates with the discipline. From the very beginning of my studies I sensed there was something inherently Christian about special education, though at that time I could not express that relationship. I suspect that many faculty in Christian colleges and universities, when asked to write about how their faith integrates with their discipline, find this a daunting task, despite having greater knowledge of their academic field and despite their being mature and maturing Christians. For junior faculty, this may be the first time they have wrestled with such an idea. Given the challenge faced by many professors to write about faith-learning integration, how can students entering this field of special education be expected to integrate their faith with the academic knowledge and skills they are struggling to acquire, especially since they may be of lesser spiritual maturity than their professors (at least in terms of the integration of faith and life)?

Marsden (1997) asserted, "In order to have Christians who take seriously their calling as Christian scholars, we must first have scholars shaped by deep spiritual commitments" (p. 107). Our role in the formation of Christian teachers includes challenging them to reflect deeply on their core values, their curriculum area, and society in the light of biblical truth. We must help them realize that Christian perspectives have great significance in any academic discipline, especially when it comes to the "big questions" of greater meaning (Marsden, 1997). Their vision must be transformed from focusing only on self and career goals to their role in the world as salt and light (Matthew 5:13–14).

My professional life has centered on special education and disability studies; hence, what follows reflects my own spiritual journey in understanding the relationship of Christian faith and special education. Since there is no specifically Christian teaching method, and since the factual knowledge in any academic area is the same for Christian and non-Christian teachers (e.g., 2 x 2 = 4 no matter what religious or faith base a teacher professes), my reflections center on how Christian faith informs the discipline and practice of special education at a deeper level—the level of what Wolterstorff calls "control beliefs" (1976).

> To do scholarship Christianly, then, is to consciously allow our faith to direct our studies.... One doesn't become a 'Christian student' simply by applying biblical texts of Christian theology to his or her discipline.... We need to develop ... a theoretical framework ... which is sensitive to and rooted in the biblical world view. (Walsh & Middletown, 1984, p. 172–173)

Special education and disability studies draw heavily from developmental and behavioral psychology, medical science, sociology, and cultural studies, as well as pedagogical studies (from regular, remedial, and special education). However, in contrast to mathematics or history, which focus on facts, the content of special education studies is individuals who are affected by disability, and their unique needs. When reflecting on how my faith informs the discipline of special education, I have found it more productive to begin with biblical/theological themes about how Christians are to be, about the world, and about persons with disabilities.

I view special education as a legitimate Christian ministry focusing on reconciliation and healing—not *curing*, as in the miraculous, but an awareness of God's healing presence, an acceptance of who we are as God's creatures, and the experience of the peace of Christ. Elements of God's sovereignty in creation, spiritual warfare, biblical justice, compassion, and hospitality are crucial informants to special education in that they provide both reasons for and motivation to be involved in special education. My basic control beliefs include this being God's world, people being created in the image of God, God's love for all individuals, and the principles of stewardship and servanthood, among other biblical teachings.

The curriculum for training special education teachers includes such elements as theoretical and methodological issues; understanding causes and effects of disabling conditions and their teaching implications; legal aspects related to provision of special education; technicalities of assessment, collaborative teamwork, and IEP development; and advocacy. This is no different whether one teaches in a Christian or a secular university. But there are clear biblical principles related to human interaction—humility, grace, forgiveness, reconciliation, human worth, etc.—which are relevant to these elements of special education practice. These biblical principles provide greater incentive for why special educators do what they do than simply legal requirements. Recognizing biblical principles may keep Christians who are involved in special education from feeling overwhelmed by the task and experiencing the burnout that continues to plague the field. There is a sense, then, that the point of intersection between faith and the discipline is most clearly seen in the area of attitude or character—things which we may not consciously teach and which are not usually measured by the required state competency tests, but which clearly address the preparation of caring, competent teachers.

The primary audience for this text comprises Christians directly involved in special education, either as teacher-trainers, university students preparing for a career in special education, or individuals currently providing direct service to students with disabilities in the schools. The goal is to help them acquire a deeper meaning of special education—both its significance to God's ongoing kingdom-building activity and their role in it. My desire is to frame special education as a ministry that is rooted in biblical concepts and practical theology. The ideas developed in this book can also inform Christians who work in other professional capacities besides special education with persons who have a disability, such as social workers, psychologists, counselors, therapists, Sunday School teachers, family pastors, or para-church ministries specifically oriented toward disability. Even families affected by disability may find the ideas helpful in their struggle to understand what God is taking them through. The book may also serve as a model for those engaged in other aspects of education as an approach to the integration of their faith and their discipline.

I have titled this book *Toward a Theology of Special Education: Integrating Faith and Practice.* What do I mean by this? How can the study of God be applied to special education? I think that not only can it be, but for Christians, it must be. Because just as God is relevant to our lives, so is theology. Paul claimed in Acts 17:28 that God is not far from of us, for "in him we live and move and exist" (NLT). In this verse, Paul acknowledges each person's dependence on God who has given us life, sustains our life, and gives us the strength necessary to *do* life. Hoekema (1986) said it plainly: "We cannot lift a finger apart from God's will" (p.5).

The Greek verb *esmen,* translated as *exist* in the NLT, comes from *eimi,* which carries the idea of *being* (as it is translated in the NIV) or *belonging to* (as in 1 John 3:19). Paul was tracing our dependence on God from the very beginning of our lives "to the highest powers of action and of continued existence" (Barnes, n.d.). Having existence—or being—has an everyday ring to it. I take this to imply that, whether we acknowledge it or not, God is always in some way involved in our lives—even if we are unaware of it at the moment. Paul shows the practical significance of this by teaching that whatever we do, in word or deed, it is to be done in the name of the Lord Jesus (Colossians 3:17). "In the name of" implies *identification* (we belong to God) and *authority* (we represent him and act on his authorization). Paul's teaching in 1 Corinthians 10:31 is somewhat parallel—our responsibility is to glorify God in all that we do. Paul is referring specifically to eating and drinking in that passage—and the possibility of offending others by the way we employ these actions. He highlights the believer's responsibility to promote the edification of others. But the timeless principle beneath his teaching goes beyond cultural or religious dietary restrictions to the admonition that our behavior carries as much of a message as our speech. We must be watchful, therefore, lest we do or say anything that could potentially cause our neighbor (or for our purposes, our students) to stumble. Paul's statement cuts to the bottom line: Everything we do should be done so that God will receive glory.

These two passages (Colossians 3:17 and 1 Corinthians 10:31) underscore the importance of theology to life. Knowing God is necessary if we are to appropriately respond to our commission and calling. Theology is an ongoing search for the truth of God (Migliore, 2004). It must not be thought of as an encyclopedic body of knowledge found in a book or debated by scholars of arcane matters. Rather, theology is embedded in our life and practice as Christians and, as such, is legitimately applicable to the life and work of special educators. To my mind, special education is practical theology, reading "Scripture into the context of ministry" (Anderson, 2001, p. 4). In the following pages, we will consider the interplay of theology and special education and make clear the relevance of theology in the context of special education. Moreover, I suggest that our work with students who have disabilities is a powerful way to learn more about God and his world.

One disclaimer: This book does not claim to be *the definitive* theology of special education. Through my own involvement in special education and disability ministry, God continues to reveal more from Scripture that bears on disability issues. For me, it is difficult to read Scripture and *not* see something that relates to disability issues. So this book is incomplete in that sense; the subject is alive and ever-expanding. But it will, hopefully, encourage others to reflect on theology and special education, thereby continuing the discussion.

## CHAPTER ONE

# Why a *Theology* of Special Education?

When serving as director of graduate programs in special education at a midwestern Christian university, part of my responsibility was to interview applicants to our program. This afforded me the opportunity to get to know them as individuals, to learn of their previous education and experience, and to understand their career goals. It also gave me the opportunity to explain our program more fully and to determine with each one whether there was a good match between what our program offered and the prospective student's interest. As part of the interview, I would ask about their reasons for wanting to study special education and why they thought they would be an effective teacher of students with special needs.

Some shared their experiences as a teacher's aide, tutor, or camp counselor working with students who had disabilities, or as a care-provider for a family member or neighborhood child who had a disabling condition. The applicants generally reported personal satisfaction from their work with these children, and nearly all expressed a caring attitude. Some even used *calling* in reference to their desire to become a special education teacher (although a few may have thought this would be helpful to their being accepted into our program of studies).

However, when I would bring up the issue of how they saw their faith relating to being or becoming a special educator, the relatively blank expressions on their faces suggested that this was not something they had ever considered. Few could expand on what they meant by having been called to special education. (In fairness, this is not something on which I could have spoken with much clarity when I first began my studies in special education either.) Clearly, the question of how one's faith might inform the field of special education was not something about which these students had thought, let alone a *theology* of special education. For that reason, to lay the foundation for our discussion, let's explore the idea of calling.

## Calling

Christian faculty in teacher-training programs often speak of teaching as a calling. Many special education teachers view their calling as involving advocacy in social justice, as well as teaching, and enabling their students to access appropriate learning opportunities beyond the classroom (Thorsos, 2012). But my experience with undergraduate and graduate students seeking to enter the field of special education suggests that for the majority this perception of their calling is something that developed during or as a result of their college training, rather than as a reason for entering the field.

Special education teacher-preparation programs generally address legal issues and the historical conditions that led to the passage of the federal mandate that schools provide an appropriate education to all students with disabilities[*]. This aspect of their coursework gives them

---

[*] Public Law 94-142, *The Education of All Handicapped Children Act* passed in 1975 and each amendment leading to Public Law 108-446, *The Individuals with Disabilities Education Improvement Act* passed in 2004.

an understanding of the social injustices students with disabilities have experienced (and may yet experience), while reinforcing the need to provide an appropriate education to students with disabilities, including their placement in regular classrooms whenever possible and to the extent befitting their needs and abilities. The changes in the delivery of special education required by these laws were largely the result of civil rights arguments and a shift from a medical-model to a social-model of understanding disability. Although today some sense the movement to include students with disabilities in the regular classroom may be waning (see Smith, 2010), my point is that students' exposure to these events and the intent of the law to "right past wrongs" may shape their thinking as they actively enter the field, but may not be something that predates their preparatory studies. Calling seems to be used more to describe their intent—a goal that has assumed a priority in their professional life, sometimes spilling over into their personal life and their efforts to work toward dismantling discrimination against persons with disabilities.

I suggest that this view of one's calling is more secular than biblical, connoting simply vocation or occupation—a job and a paycheck. If asked about the origin of their call, some might respond, "God," but this does not necessarily signify any real concept of being called by a higher being, let alone the personal God revealed in Scripture. Nor does it suggest that they have reflected biblically on special education or disability issues. Their interest in this field of study and endeavor may be more charitable than Christian, per se.

## What Is God's Call?

Does our calling as Christians link to a specific academic discipline or profession? How does our involvement in any particular field of study and practice relate to God's calling in our lives? Os Guinness (1998) wrote that "God calls us to himself so decisively that everything we are, everything we do, and everything we have is invested with a special devotion and dynamism lived out as a response to his summons and service" (p. 4). God's call, then, is much broader than a call to a particular occupation. It is a call to God, a response to God, and a service to God. It is God's claim, not just on what we do for a living, but on our lives. "Our primary calling is to a living and dynamic relationship with God" (Hillman, 2008, p. 198).

This goes beyond an invitation to accept Christ into our lives; it is a complete surrendering of our lives to God. It is realizing—actualizing—the full implications of the Apostle Paul's teaching in Galatians 2:20, where he says, "It is no longer I who live, but Christ who lives in me," and in 2 Corinthians 5:17–21, where Paul describes those who are in Christ as "new creations" to whom the ministry and message of reconciliation have been given such that we are now Christ's ambassadors. Christians are described as "[God's] workmanship, created in Christ Jesus for good works, which God prepared beforehand that we should walk in them" (Ephesians 2:10). The Greek word translated as "workmanship" is *poiema*, from which the English word poem is derived. Some modern English versions of the Bible translate the word as masterpiece. Paul's reference is not, however, limited to church-related activity (preaching, Sunday school, youth ministry, evangelism, etc.); it applies to all who claim to be Christ-followers. Since our primary call in life is to glorify God, all our work—all our life—is spiritual work. This encompasses works of service and compassion—such as working as a special education teacher to help students with disabilities realize their potential. Conversion is not the end goal; it is the beginning—the beginning of our lives as believers and the beginning of our transformation into Christlikeness. The "good works" Christians have been created to do become a visible attestation of the reality of our salvation, and because we are God's workmanship, these good works are tied to his design of each one of us, proving we are equipped to walk and work in this world as Christians, so that we can "join [Jesus] in the work he does, and the good work he has gotten ready for us to do" (Ephesians 2:8–10, MSG).

## Calling and Vocation

Quoting again from Guinness,

> We are not primarily called to do something or go somewhere: we are called to Someone. We are not called first to special work but to God. The key to answering the call is to be devoted to no one and nothing above God himself. (1998, p. 23)

Hillman described this primary call as "the umbrella under which we function as believers" (2008, p. 198). In service to this primary calling is what Hillman termed a functional call, which alludes not to our occupations, but to how we relate as Christians to our family, serve our neighbors in Christian love, function in the local body of Christ, and serve the greater society in stewardship and mission. Hillman's point is that everything that brings us into relationship with others is a part of our functional call.

Hillman held that vocation or career is subsidiary to this functional call and warned against confusing the two. "Every rightful human task is some aspect of God's own work: making, designing, doing chores, beautifying, organizing, helping, bringing dignity, and leading. Our work, then, is to reflect God's work" (Hillman, 2008, p. 201). Similarly,

Smith (1999) spoke of a primary or general call that supersedes a more specific vocational call, which is unique to each person, yet in concert with God's mission.

We can say that God's call is the same for all Christians: a call to him and to honoring and discovering God in and through our discipline. I suggest that our professional role is more related to our gifting. Given that God has "created [us] in Christ Jesus for good works, which God prepared beforehand" (Ephesians 2:10), it is not unexpected that God's forming us includes our temperament and specific interests, talents, and abilities that he intended for us to use. These, along with the Holy Spirit, serve to guide us into certain professions and away from others. "God normally calls us along the line of our giftedness, but the purpose of giftedness is stewardship and service, not selfishness" (Guinness, 1998, p. 46). Whatever field we end up in will be related to God's gifting, and will be the place where we can best serve God and his mission. If we are unhappy or uncomfortable with the profession we have chosen, it is likely that we have *mis*-heard God's call. As Zacharias (2007) said, God's call "is his beckoning, but it is more. It is God's vital purpose in positioning you in life and giving you the location and context of your call to serve him with a total commitment to do the job well" (p. 59).

The Christian teacher's calling, thus, is not, strictly speaking, a call to teaching. It is a call to *be* Christ, to demonstrate in and through his or her life the heart of Christ. Wherever we live and work is the place where God has called us to represent, encourage, and further the kingdom of God. To enable us to do this, God has gifted us—some as preachers, some as healers, some as artists, some as mechanics, and some as teachers, etc. God has designed into us talents, interests, aptitudes, abilities, desires, and even experiences that enable us to fulfill our calling to be Christ in the world. Whereas we sometimes struggle to understand where God would have us serve in his mission,

God's perspective is different. He is not seeking a place for us to use our gifts; rather, "God has created us and our gifts for a place of his choosing—and we will only be ourselves when we are finally there" (Guinness, 1998, p. 47).

## Serving in God's Kingdom

> [T]hrough God's special, saving grace Christians have been given a fundamental, dispositional commitment to *embrace* God's truth; yet in our actual experience the lingering effects of sin hinder us from consistently thinking God's thoughts after him. (Johnson, 2002, p. 87, emphasis in original)

Darrow Miller's book, *Life Work: A Biblical Theology for What You Do Every Day* (2009) critically examined the separation Johnson described between embracing God's truth and actual experience. Focusing on the false dichotomy between the sacred and the secular, Miller's book directs his readers toward recovery of a biblical worldview of purpose, calling, vocation, and ministry. Miller stressed that we have been called *by* God *to* God—called into his kingdom and given unique roles in manifesting and extending that kingdom.

The Greek word *basileia*, translated kingdom, signifies authority and the rightful exercise of royal power. Rather than referring to a place, as *kingdom* is commonly used today, the biblical word describes "the time when God puts forth his royal power to end injustice and oppression by the world's evil powers and to establish his rule of righteousness, peace and joy for humanity" (Beasley-Murray, 1992, p. 19). Jesus said that the kingdom was "near" (Mark 1:15; Luke 10:9, 11) or "is in the midst of you" (Luke 17:21), that is, in the person of Jesus and in the reign of God manifested in Jesus's ministry. Jesus's claim in Luke 4:17–21 marked the inauguration of the kingdom and made clear the characteristics of his kingdom:

> [T]he scroll of the prophet Isaiah was given to him. He unrolled the scroll and found the place where it was written, "The Spirit of the Lord is upon me, because he has anointed me to proclaim good news to the poor. He has sent me to proclaim liberty to the captives and recovering of sight to the blind, to set at liberty those who are oppressed, to proclaim the year of the Lord's favor...." And he began to say to them, "Today this Scripture has been fulfilled in your hearing."

In other words, through the ministry of Jesus, the kingdom (authority) of God powerfully broke through into the world. The miracles Jesus performed gave proof of his authority over nature (Matthew 8:27), disease (Matthew 8:1–4), disability (John 5:1–9), Satan (Matthew 12:22–29), unclean spirits (Mark 1:27), sin and forgiveness (Mark 2:1–12), and death (John 11:43–44). Jesus's authority and service in the kingdom did not end with his death and resurrection; it continues in the Church, working by the aid of the Holy Spirit (Beasley-Murray, 1992, pp. 29–30). Jesus authorized the Church to continue his ministry in his name (Matthew 28:18–20).

The Church's charge to manifest and extend the kingdom is something to be actively pursued in our daily lives and work. Manifesting and extending does not mean just "winning people for Christ" with a view to a future, heavenly kingdom. Jesus inaugurated the kingdom and called us to life in that kingdom—a life lived under his Lordship, committed to kingdom ethics being actualized in our lives (Matthew

5–7), and committed to continuing Jesus's ministry of bringing freedom and release, breaking bonds of oppression and injustice. The kingdom continues to grow and will not be complete until Jesus returns to consummate God's plan. In the interim, Christians are "called to be a 'sign' of God's tomorrow in the world today" (Glasser, 2006).

If we are to demonstrate our citizenship in God's kingdom (Graham, 2003), to serve Jesus, and to witness to the character and values of his kingdom (Snyder, 2004), then biblical and theological teaching must work itself out in and through our life. Our life must demonstrate the spiritual transformation that God is bringing about as we mature in Christ, so that we are no longer conformed to the thought patterns and actions of this world (Romans 12:2). This transformation and renewal results in a new way of *seeing* and *being* in God's world—to "see the world through God's eyes," as Swinton (1999) said.

God created and designed us to work for his honor and glory. He has been shaping us through our schooling and experiences, even before we decided to follow Christ, to prepare us to serve him. To grasp the spiritual significance of our work as special educators we need to ask how our work reflects God's work. How is being a special educator in concert with God's will? How can the discipline be shaped to serve God's purpose or mission? What relationship is there between our involvement in special education and our life and mission as Christians? How does "having the mind of Christ" relate to our being a special educator? How does our Christian faith function integrally to our work? These and other questions will be addressed in the chapters which follow.

## The Ministry of Special Education

Most people involved in special education probably have not thought of it in terms of ministry. That word is generally thought to mean "church work"—being a pastor or serving as a missionary, for example. *The American Heritage Dictionary* (1982) defines *ministry* as "the act of serving others" (p. 800). This definition is in accord with the meaning of the biblical word *diakonia*, variously translated in the English-language Bibles as minister, ministry, ministration, service, or serving. The word is used in the New Testament of Jesus (Luke 3:23), of the Apostles (Acts 6:4), of Paul (Acts 12:23; Romans 15:16), and of believers in general (2 Corinthians 5:18; Ephesians 4:12). The word indicates "the investment of self for another's advancement, whether in relation to God or other human beings" (Ryken, Wilhoit, & Longman, 1998, p. 558).

Diakonia (ministry) is focused on bringing glory to God, whom the minister represents, not bring glory to the one doing the ministry. Ministry involves the quality of work and worship offered to God (Ryken et al., p. 559). Worship, not meaning Sunday morning meetings, but life, includes all types of service motivated by the desire to honor the Lord, such as caring for persons, meeting physical needs, giving, building up others through education (Christian and basic), and encouraging and empowering others. As Shults and Sandage (2006) stated, "To be a Christian is to be 'in' ministry—to be ministering to (serving) others, which is how the Spirit of love is manifested in the community for the 'common good'" (p. 120).

Special education is ministry, then, because its goal is to help students who are affected by disability to flourish as human beings. Special education teachers are concerned with the total development and functioning of individuals who have an impairment, disability, or disorder. Special education is a legitimate Christian ministry, one which focuses on reconciliation and healing. We may not be equipped to bring physical healing to the disabled as did Jesus, but we can help students who have a disability grow within the limitations of their bodily or intellectual capacity (perhaps even beyond what those limitations are perceived to be), and to view their handicapping condition as simply one aspect of their personhood, but which in no way lessens their value as human beings.

With children and youth who have emotional problems, the healing ministry is similar to counseling, or even to the pastorate, since the teacher's concern is with more than academics. Certainly, biblical teaching on living and loving; on relationship with God and with others; on sin, grace, and forgiveness, all have direct relevance to the special education profession. Thus, in training college and university students to become teachers of children with emotional, physical, intellectual, or sensory impairments, we are training people for ministry. I am obviously not referring to the academic content of the discipline, but to the *why* and *how* of special education—the character of the special educator.

Nouwen (2003) made this comment:

> Education is not primarily ministry because of what is taught but because of the nature of the educational process itself. Perhaps we have paid too much attention to the content of teaching without realizing that the teaching relationship is the most important factor in the ministry of teaching. (p. 11)

Any discussion of individual purpose must not be divorced from consideration of God's larger, eternal purpose in and for the world, of which our call plays a part.

> The Scriptures reveal that, having been called into the kingdom, we each have a unique role in manifesting and extending the kingdom.... As citizens of the

kingdom of God and members of the body of Christ, we are called to put feet, hands, and imaginations to the prayer "your kingdom come, your will be done on earth as it is in heaven." (Miller, 2009, p. 137)

In preparing special education teachers, we need to help our students see all that they are studying, not as simply related to a profession, but to our total life-response to God. Although we study theories developed by secular educators, philosophers, and psychologists, it is essential that these ideas be evaluated from a Scriptural, Christian perspective. Recognizing that all truth is God's truth, our students need to develop an attitude of responsible stewardship in the use of their own minds and talents, as well as stewardship over the things that God has given them in his world. This includes the students with a disability whom God has brought into their classroom, helping them grow academically and to discover and develop their God-given talents and abilities. We need to help our students understand how being a special educator serves to extend God's kingdom, especially if they teach in a public school, where direct presentation of the gospel's call to repent and believe is prohibited by law. Miller appropriately reminded us that Christians are called "to extend that kingdom into the world by bringing truth (the biblical metaphysic), justice (the biblical ethic), and beauty (the biblical aesthetic) into all of life, through our faith and our vocation" (2009, p. 118).

The gospel that Jesus preached was not limited to giving an invitation to accept Christ as Savior. Though he did ask people to "repent, for the kingdom of heaven is a hand" (Matthew 4:17), Jesus's only direct invitation was to "follow me" (e.g., Matthew 4:19; Luke

9:23; John 1:43). But to his disciples, including his modern-day disciples, Jesus gave a direct commission. As Christians in education, we have a responsibility not just to serve our students but also to serve that commission (Tucker, 1996).

Exactly what is our commission? Matthew 28:18–20 is, perhaps, the best known Scripture containing a commissioning of Christ's disciples. That commission "is a comprehensive mandate that goes to the ends of the earth, penetrates culture, and brings good news for all creation" (Miller, 2009, p. 208). It is theologically linked with God's promise that through Abraham all the families of the earth will be blessed (Genesis 12:1–5). The command of Jesus in Matthew 28:19–20 is not to make converts but to make disciples (followers of Jesus) from all nations, "teaching them to observe all that he had commanded." This does not just mean retelling Jesus's lessons, but also "repeating" the actions and the attitude of Jesus.

With this commission, Jesus transferred his mission to his disciples (then and now) who are to continue his mission by modeling Jesus, his concerns, and his broad definition of the gospel as reflected in his "inaugural address" at the synagogue on Nazareth, where Jesus claimed fulfillment of the prophecy of Isaiah 61 in him and his ministry: to proclaim good news to the poor, liberty to captives, recovering of sight to the blind, liberty for those who are oppressed—a proclamation that the year of the Lord's favor had begun with Jesus's coming (Luke 4:18–19).

As his followers, we are commissioned to continue Jesus's ministry of restoration and reconciliation not just in terms of sin, but in all relationships—with God, with others, and with creation itself. Miller (2009) reminded us that the call of God encompasses the entirety of our being: heart, mind, soul, and strength. And God's call also involves our relationship with God, our neighbors, and creation.

That our commission as Christ-followers continues Jesus's work of restoration, release, and reconciliation (beyond simply freedom from sin and judgment) is clear from Paul's teaching in 2 Corinthians 5:18–19 that God has entrusted to us the message and the ministry of reconciliation. We will more fully explore the concept of special education as reconciliation in chapter six, but let me suggest here that Matthew 25:40 can be understood as a commentary on that commission and on our ministry as special education teachers: "As you did it to one of the least of these my brothers, you did it to me."

## God's Call to Special Education

The entire Bible records God's story of "redeeming his creation and rescuing humanity from captivity to sin *and its effects*" (Shelly & Miller, 1999, p. 153, emphasis added). Disability, especially as negatively viewed by many, is one of the "captivating" effects of sin (this will be developed in the chapters which follow). From the biblical point of view, the history of humanity is moving toward a goal which is outside of itself. It is moving toward the accomplishment of God's purpose—the "purpose and potential he instilled in us when he created us in his image" (Miller, 2009, p. 137).

As was said previously, God's call is to him. Our draw to a particular profession, such as special education, is built on that foundation. Within this call is God's desire that we extend his kingdom. Smith (1999) pointed out that,

> All vocations are sacred because the kingdom is not merely spiritual. God is establishing his kingdom on the earth as the whole of creation comes under his divine authority. To that end, God calls and enables his children to be his kingdom agents within every sphere of life

and society. Each vocation reflects but one avenue by which God, through word and deed, is accomplishing the establishment of his kingdom. (p. 25)

"Every call that honors God's purpose for life is a sacred call" (Zacharias, 2007, p. 64). The special educator's goal of helping students who have a disability develop to their potential and learn skills to successfully integrate into community life; to promote reconciliation between those with disabilities and their able-bodied peers; to help parents find needed community services; and to support the parents in their desire to secure an appropriate education for their disabled child—all honor God's purpose for life.

# CHAPTER TWO

# Biblical/Theological Themes That Inform Special Education

## Preliminary Thoughts

Readers may ask: Is there a reason for our involvement in special education beyond simply educating students who have a disability? Why do we do this? Why do we care about individuals who are disabled?

Job responsibilities, especially for new teachers, often do not allow time for deep reflection on the integration of faith and special education. For others, the question of integration of faith and learning may seem meaningless, or at least superfluous. Some may see special education simply as a "job," having no eternal significance. I suggest, however, that special education and concern for equality of education for students who have a disability without a theological basis is merely activism, defined by Miller (1998, p. 279) as "action without reflection" (cf. Hazle, 2003).

Theology must not remain a static body of encyclopedic knowledge; the Bible is not just a theological or historical textbook. Theology must be *living*. Though God may work in new and different ways today than centuries before, God himself does not change. We must read God's Word to learn what he revealed about himself through actions and events in the past, and we must examine our lives and situations to discover God's activity in, through, and around us today. In a sense, we personalize theology as we seek to discover God in our present-day life context. Though theology *proper* may not change, the Holy Spirit can lead us to see instances where its application or implications go beyond our preconceived, and perhaps limiting, notions. There may be nuances that are new to us as we learn more about God through study and experience. The many implications of theology for our professional activity as special education teachers must be clear in our minds.

Perhaps what is missing is not so much integration of faith and learning related to the discipline of special education, but an integration of faith and life. Our lives, both personal and professional, should be organized within a framework of consistent biblical theology and worldview. "To follow Jesus, to understand who we are and what we have been created and called to do, we need both a relationship with the living God and an increasing understanding of the biblical worldview" (Miller, 2009, p. 73). Worldview refers to the conscious and unconscious assumptions we hold about the essential makeup of our world—how we understand, explain, and define the world (Miller, 1998; Sire, 1997). It deals with questions of God, truth, reality, purpose, morality, and evil. Worldview is the lens through which we understand the world and relationships. It structures how we see our life's purpose and bears on our career choices. Everyone has a view of the world that consciously or unconsciously informs their decisions, plans, and opinions and, as Miller (2009) pointed out, is really theological (though not necessarily theistic). For the Christian, however, that worldview must be biblical.

It is necessary that our theology be demonstrated in relationship between ourselves and God and between ourselves and others, because it is within relationship that we are able to examine values, beliefs, and behaviors that emanate from our theological convictions (Stevens, 1992). A Christian worldview is a legitimate framework from within which to understand the meaning and practice of any profession (Cooling, 2010). In this chapter, special education will be brought into "critical and creative conversation" with a biblical/theological framework, focusing on what Scripture teaches about God and about humanity.

## Integration of Faith and Learning

Van Brummelen (1997) asserted that Christian teacher-education programs must be transformative, vital, and transcendent. To be *transformative,* there must be a biblical sensitivity to social injustice that provides a basis for compassion, integrity, and the search for workable solutions to social problems. The focus of the programs must not be simply on understanding theories or developing skills; it must be *vital*—connected with, or essential to life. A life-affirming program recognizes God as creator of the world and humankind as created in God's image, and acknowledges that God has revealed himself and certain eternal precepts that bear on everything we undertake. Programs must also be *transcendent,* going beyond what is learned in the classroom, to apply knowledge and experience gained in the university in unique and personal ways as God enables us to do so. This necessitates that Christian faculty consciously seek to integrate the theological content or significance of their faith with the curriculum and vocational content, and encourage their students to do the same.

### But what is involved in this integration?

To integrate our Christian faith and learning within special education, we do not just place Scripture atop special education ideas, or simply give praise to God for the subject matter, or open a class with a devotional that may or may not be related to the topic being discussed—a sort of doxological integration (cf. Moreland, 1999). Nor would we be seeking scriptural support for what is currently considered best practice—a proof-texting approach, which seeks to sanctify special education by finding Scripture verses that somehow seem to relate. And integration of faith and learning does not mean simply showing excellence in our work as Christian teachers, in response to Paul's teaching that whatever we do, in word or deed, should be done in the name of the Lord Jesus (Colossians 3:17) and to the glory of God (1 Corinthians 10:31). These may all be helpful practices, but they fall short of the integration we seek.

The difficulty faculty and students in Christian colleges and universities often have in explaining how their faith integrates with their discipline results from an artificial divide between faith alone (the traditional evangelical view) and an emphasis on social outreach (traditionally associated with liberal theology). Borrowing Stearns's (2010) wording, we can say that this discord between faith and the academic discipline reflects not only a "hole in our gospel," but a hole in our teaching.

To consider how special education fits with the view of the world and redemptive history as revealed in Scripture requires a consciously Christian worldview, one that is inclusive of all persons—disabled and non-disabled—a worldview that addresses who people with disabilities are and why we should be concerned about them; one that speaks to the question of how a sovereign, righteous, loving God can allow disabilities to exist. It requires that we ask what biblical assumptions about persons and relationships fuel our approach to teaching, and how "having the mind of Christ" relates to our professional activity. It is also important to recognize that integrating faith and learning is an ongoing process. As we develop spiritually, as biblical teaching becomes more deeply a part of our daily life, God's Spirit will enable us to recognize more clearly the connection between theology and our commitment to special education.

Borrowing terms from psycholinguistics, we can speak of the *surface structure* of teaching to refer to the design of our teaching and the specific procedures selected to help our students achieve a desired outcome. And then there is the *deep structure* of teaching, which draws upon both our understanding of the discipline itself and our beliefs about God, human beings, relationships, interdependence, and so forth (cf. Smith, 1999). We need to consider whether the particular technique or approach being taught (surface structure) meshes with our conceptualization of humankind (deep structure).

For example, a behavioral approach is often taught in special education teacher-training programs. But is such a view compatible with a biblical view of humanity? It is at this deep structure level where integration of faith and learning is sought. This deeper level is concerned not so much with how God fits into special education, but how special education fits into God's design, God's purpose. The desire is to understand how involvement in special education connects with our life and mission as believers. This chapter will focus on theological issues that inform the deep structure of special education.

## Biblical/Theological Themes and Special Education

Walsh and Middleton (1984) said that "Christ calls us to submit everything in our lives, including our studies, to his lordship" (p. 35), and pointed out that "to do scholarship Christianly ... is to consciously allow our faith to direct our studies" (p. 172). There are several biblical themes we can draw from to develop a Christian worldview that includes disability and disabled persons, allowing us to formulate a theology of special education. In fact, as I read through Scripture in my

21

own study times, or when a pastor shares from various passages from the Bible, God often shows me a way in which that passage relates to working with people who are affected by disability. Consequently, the following discussion is not intended to be a comprehensive, exhaustive exploration of doctrinal teaching on God and mankind. Rather, it will highlight principles that touch on disability and special education. Our focus in this chapter is on two primary areas:

- The Bible's teaching about God as sovereign Creator, particularly as it relates to God's *design* of human beings, and to certain characteristics of God—righteousness, immutability, and goodness.
- The Bible's teaching about humanity, specifically our being created in the image of God, the meaning of life, and stewardship.

## The Nature and Character of God

### God as Sovereign Creator

A Christian worldview acknowledges God to be the Creator of all that is and Sovereign Ruler of the universe. The first words of the Bible—"In the beginning God" (Genesis 1:1)—not only speak of God's eternality but, in introducing the creation account, encapsulate the Bible's teaching of God's sovereignty. Romans 11:36 tells us that all things are "from him and through him and to him," and implies that all is done in order to bring him glory. In Job 38 and 39, God gives his own explanation of his sovereignty as the One who laid the foundation of the earth and all that is. That God created and actively sustains the world, directing events toward the fulfillment of his eternal plan, is the clear teaching of the Bible.

Genesis 1:1 also underscores the reason that seeking a biblically informed worldview and its connection to special education is necessary. God is intimately involved in the lives of his people (cf. Colossians 1:16–17). With regard to disability, the question becomes whether the birth of a child with a severe disability challenges Scripture's view of God as sovereign and loving. Scripture clearly teaches that God is involved in the creation of every child. We read that God "made everything beautiful [appropriate] in its time" (Ecclesiastes 3:11), and that "children are a heritage [gift] from the Lord" (Psalm 127:3). In Psalm 139:13–16, David beautifully describes God's involvement in the creation of each individual:

> For you formed my inward parts; you knitted me together in my mother's womb. I praise you, for I am fearfully and wonderfully made. Wonderful are your works; my soul knows it very well. My frame was not hidden from you, when I was being made in secret, intricately woven in the depths of the earth. Your eyes saw my unformed substance; in your book were written, every one of them, the days that were formed for me, when as yet there was none of them.

David's conclusion that we are fearfully and wonderfully made makes references to the awesomeness of mankind and our distinction above the rest of creation. That our frame was "intricately woven" by God has reference not just to our physical body or skeleton, but to our entire being—intellect, emotions, talents, abilities, and interests as well. We are individually designed and pieced together by God. David's words also explain that God had determined our "days"—indicating not just the length of our lives but, in light of Ephesians 2:10 and

Philippians 2:12–13, also the tasks that God has planned for our undertaking, plans that come from a loving heart and have our best interest in view, as well as his own glory (Wiersbe, 2004).

How do we reconcile these truths of Scripture with the presence of a child born with disabilities? Is the child an exception to the rule? Did God make a mistake or lose control? Did God cause this to happen? If he did not cause it, why did he allow it to happen? Questions such as these, and the uncertainty they reflect, are natural reactions when faced with a disability, given our human tendency to want to make sense of our experiences and maintain some sense of order in our lives. Understandably, these are questions that families directly affected by disability may have, but they are also issues that Christians who are involved in special education should consider—not only because they may have occasion to respond to inquiries from the parents, but because disability is *real* and could happen to them, thus challenging their own view of the world and of God.

In trying to understand these issues, it is important to maintain our belief that God is infinite, eternal, and unchangeable in all his attributes, even when a child has a disability. Most disabling conditions are ultimately a natural consequence of living in a sinful, fallen world. God's sovereignty and goodness are not in question because of disability. We have no reason to assume that God was absent when a child is born with a handicapping condition or becomes disabled through illness or accident. The Bible does not tell us exactly how God is involved in the creation of each child, nor why God does not intervene in the embryonic or fetal development to correct or overrule a genetic defect or prenatal insult, or to prevent an illness or accident from leaving a person disabled. In truth, God may do this more often that we realize but, in his providential wisdom, God chooses *not* to intervene in every case. However, any notion that God has made a mistake, which would bring his sovereignty and wisdom into question, must be dismissed.

Also to be rejected is the thought that God punishes people for their sin by disabling their child. This would be to accuse God of acting arbitrarily rather than righteously, and implies that a non-disabled person is of greater value or worth to God. Some Christians incorrectly understand Scripture to be teaching that God's typical *modus operandi* is to bless those who are righteous and to punish those who are sinners, leading them to conclude that being or becoming disabled confirms that either the person or the parents have sinned, resulting in God's judgment. This line of reasoning is reflected in the arguments of Job's counselors in claiming that Job's suffering was the result of unconfessed sin, and of the disciples in John 9 who asked Jesus whether the man was born blind because of his own sin or that of his parents.

The faulty logic of these assumptions is challenged by the Scripture's assertion that we are all sinners, that no one can claim to be righteous on the basis of his or her own merit (Isaiah 64:6–7; Romans 1:18–2:1, 3:23). If disability (or suffering) is causally connected to sin, we would need to account for why all people are not disabled (or suffering). Moreover, it was while we were "dead in our trespasses" that God, in grace, mercy, and love, saved us (Ephesians 2:4–10). In Exodus 4:11, God asks Moses, "Who has made man's mouth? Who makes him mute, or deaf, or seeing, or blind? Is it not I, the Lord?" This is God's declaration that he honors persons with disabilities: "His point is that He makes all people, regardless of abilities or disabilities. He loves them equally and claims them equally as His special creation" (Palau, 1999, pp. 42–43). Having individually designed each person means that God sees beauty in every individual as well as their potential and worth, regardless of ability or disability. Disability, even from birth, is not outside of God's sovereignty or foreknowledge, nor does having a disability preclude a person from living a meaningful life and furthering God's purpose.

## The Goodness of God

In addition to sovereignty, other major characteristics of God revealed in the Bible are omniscience, omnipotence, omnipresence, holiness, immutability (unchanging nature), and goodness, which is the essence of God's character (Sire, 1997). Each of these characteristics of God is significant for our understanding of exceptionalities. God is infinite, eternal, and unchangeable in all his attributes. God's sovereignty, wisdom, love, grace, and goodness are not threatened, even though a child is born with a disability or a person acquires a disability through an accident or as a result of a disease. Nor is his essential goodness challenged by his not miraculously intervening to prevent or correct a disabling condition. God's goodness to all people is shown in his common grace, wherein he "makes his sun rise on the evil and on the good, and sends rain on the just and on the unjust" (Matthew 5:45). And God's goodness is shown in his special (saving) grace on believers (Ephesians 2:8–10). Piper (2012) linked God's sovereignty and his goodness:

> Since God is sovereign and has promised *not to turn away from doing good to his covenant people,* we can know beyond all doubt, in tribulation and distress and persecution and famine and nakedness and peril and sword [and for our purposes, we can add "disabled"], that we are more than conquerors through him who loved us (Romans 8:35–37). (p. 172, emphasis in original)

A former colleague was informed that the unborn child she was carrying had Down Syndrome, a genetic disorder which can result in physical problems and cognitive impairment. She admits that upon learning this her faith was challenged, just as Job's theology was challenged through his suffering, but her belief in God remained. As she wrestled with the situation, in light of God's sovereignty and continuing love, she realized that asking God to reconstruct the chromosomal structure of each cell in her unborn child was inappropriate and may even demonstrate a lack of faith. She chose instead to pray that God would give her a heart of love for the child and the daily strength and patience needed. This led to growth in her assurance of God's ongoing love, goodness, and presence despite what lie ahead. Her son does indeed have Down Syndrome, and it would be misleading to say that raising him has not presented challenges from time to time (what child does not?), but he is a loving boy and a welcomed part of her family.

As a characteristic of God, goodness describes how he freely relates to us through his covenant of grace and his promise to remain loving, just, merciful, faithful, and forgiving. God's goodness is expressed in many ways through his holiness and love (Sire, 1997). We rejoice in the goodness of God, which endures forever (2 Chronicles 6:41, 7:3). God is good despite what befalls us, but his goodness, just like God himself, remains something which we, as created beings, cannot fully understand (cf. Isaiah 55:8–9). His goodness must not be confused with our subjective feeling of happiness or what we consider acts of kindness. God is good in the way he promises to be, not in every way we might wish him to be. He does not promise that he will be as beneficial or charitable as possible to as many people as possible. Nor has God promised to prevent suffering, or to relieve, remove, or prevent pain. God remains the *summum bonum*—the ultimate Good—"not only because he is by nature incorruptibly good, but also because he is the overflowing *source* of good" (Plantinga, 2002, p. 112). True happiness is found in relation to and in submission to the Lord (as Christ taught in the Sermon on the Mount in Matthew 5–7), leading us to say with David, "Surely goodness and mercy shall follow me all the days of my life and I shall dwell in the house of the Lord forever" (Psalm 23:6). With Paul, we must stress contentment over happiness (cf. Philippians 4:11–12). And we are reminded in Hebrews 13:5 of God's promise that he will never leave us or forsake us, even if we become disabled.

God's sovereignty, wisdom, love, and grace are *not threatened* by disability. God's goodness is *not challenged* if he does not intervene to prevent or to cure a disabling condition. God's nature is beyond our understanding, but his faithfulness is sure and everlasting. God is the source of hope in the midst of life's uncertainties.

Some believe that Christians ought to be immune from evil and suffering and, by extension, disability, based on a loose interpretation of Jeremiah 29:11. Those who hold to this position would conclude that for someone *not* to prosper is at least a sign of a lack of faith, if not proof of unconfessed sin. Actually, Jeremiah's words about God's plans to prosper and not to harm refer to peace (shalom), not necessarily physical and material health and wealth. Jeremiah's words—addressed to the nation, not to individuals—were designed to bring encouragement to the exiles in Babylon by assuring them that God had not forgotten them and that there would be deliverance for those who remain faithful: the promised return of the Jews from exile. Certainly God desires that we have shalom (peace) with him; this he has brought about through Jesus Christ (Romans 5:1–2). But this does not mean there will be no suffering, struggle, even disability. Paul continued (Romans 5:3–5) to speak about rejoicing in suffering and the blessings that suffering can produce, not to show that God's peace means an absence of suffering. The misconception of the health-and-prosperity teaching results in denial of the reality of suffering among God's people while at the same time denying the universality of moral and natural evil that can also lead to suffering and disability. Nowhere in the Bible does God promise believers that they will, or should, experience only health and material prosperity or that they will be free from disability or suffering, at least not in this life. Our human tendency is to focus on the present rather than the future. But God sees the end from the beginning. Our tendency is to expect blessing, health, and absence of suffering *now*, rather than acknowledging that this life/world is temporary. Believers, however, should possess a more future-oriented perspective, in anticipation of God's eternal blessing. A future orientation, which recognizes the temporariness of this world, is more appropriate to the Christian life. In anticipation of eternal blessing, the Bible urges contentment rather than *happiness* which, from a Western, materialistic mindset, is often centered of the accumulation of things which bring a temporary feeling of self-satisfaction, or is dependent on circumstances. The Bible instructs us to be content with what we have (Hebrews 13:5), and in whatever our circumstances (Philippians 4:11–12). This *spiritual* contentment draws from knowledge that it is God who works in us, "both to will and to work for his [God's] good pleasure" (Philippians 2:12).

## God and Human Weakness

Because God is righteous, all that he does is righteous (Deuteronomy 32:4; Psalm 7:11, 48:10, 145:7). He cannot fail to live up to who he is by nature. We sometimes attempt to shape God after our own image or liking rather than admit that because we are mere mortals God is beyond our capacity to fully understand. God's ways (purposes) are mysterious and far beyond our ability to comprehend (Isaiah 55:8–9).

Moreover, Paul reminds us that God is able to bring good out of what we perceive as bad (Romans 8:28). God is not limited by a person's disability; in fact, God is able to use our weakness or disability far more than any strength or ability we possess (characteristics which are also given to us by God, by the way). Joseph and Paul are two excellent Scriptural examples of God using something evil or undesirable to bring glory to himself (Genesis 50:20; 2 Corinthians 12:7–10). A modern-day example is Joni Eareckson Tada, whom God has used to bring a blessing to many persons around the world—both those born with disabilities and those who are only temporarily able-bodied—despite her becoming quadriplegic as a result of a diving accident at age 17.

God is able to teach much about himself to and through persons who are disabled; sacred things such as grace, patience, love, kindness, and gentleness. And Jesus teaches us not only about the need for a servant attitude, but provides opportunities for us to serve others through our interaction with people who are disabled. Such as by being a special education teacher. God provides opportunities for both able-bodied and disabled persons to become the hands and feet of Jesus reaching out in ministry to others.

## The Nature and Character of Humankind

### Created in the Image of God

The Bible teaches that humankind was created in the image of God. Genesis 1:26–28, 31; 2:7 and Psalm 139:13–16 describe people as creatures designed by a personal God, having a material nature ("from the dust of the ground") and a non-material nature (God "breathed … the breath of life, and the man became a living being"). The term *living being* or *living soul* in Genesis 2:7 describes the whole person with all the physical, intellectual, and moral characteristics we associate with being human. God has created each person as a reflection of himself, meaning that we mirror God, and in mirroring God, we represent (re-present) him on earth. Hoekema (1986) put it this way:

> As a mirror reflects, so man should reflect God ... only in man does God become visible. But in the creation of man God revealed himself in a unique way, by making someone who was a kind of mirror image of himself. This means that when man is what he ought to be, others should be able to look at him and see something of God in him: something of God's love, God's kindness, and God's goodness. ... If it is true that when one looks at man he should see something of God in man, it follows that man represents God on earth. (pp. 67–68)

Scholars have debated about what is meant by *image of God.* Four views have been suggested (Estep, 2010):

*Substantive view:* This is the more traditional view and focuses on characteristics of humankind which reflect in some way attributes of God. These "communicable attributes" include those things which we share with God, though to a lesser degree, such as rationality, communication, imagination, creativity, and so forth.

*Functional view:* This view, sometimes regarded as a subset of the substantive view, stresses dominion and stewardship. God placed humankind in the position of steward over all that God had created. As vice-regent under God, Adam (humankind) was to exercise responsible stewardship of all that God had created, caring for creation and discovering the possibilities hidden within God's creation.

*Relational view:* This third view stresses relationships, with God and with others. The primary element of relationship is love: Humankind was created to love God and to display that love in interactions with others (Mark 12:29–31). This also entails the spiritual elements that are part of a Christian's imaging God: mercy (Luke 6:36), holiness (1 Peter 1:15–16), love (1 John 4:8–11), and service (John 13:14–17).

*Teleological view:* The teleological view emphasizes the ultimate objective or purpose of human existence. It maintains that the image of God is a current reality—we are God's image-bearers today, but it will not be until eternity that this is fully realized (Estep, 2010). This more dynamic view acknowledges that human beings bear the image of God, but that image was fully embodied in Jesus Christ (John 1:14, 14:9; 2 Corinthians 4:4; Colossians 1:15; Hebrews 1:3), to whose likeness we are now being conformed (2 Corinthians 3:18).

These four understandings of the image of God are not mutually exclusive. A proper understanding of the image of God must include all four:

> God's image within humanity is what we are and, in turn, is reflected in the components of our existence, relationship capacity with one another and God, in our function to fulfill God's expressed purpose for humanity, and even in the eschatological reality that awaits us. (Estep, 2010, p.19)

Hoekema (1986) held that image of God describes both in the way human beings function and the kind of being we are. Being in God's image, therefore, refers to who we are in all our fullness. A more accurate conclusion is not that we are created *in* God's image, but *as* God's image. "The image of God isn't just something we *have* or *do*;

it's something we *are*. To be human is to be the image of God, the representative of the Creator" (Clark & Emmett, 1998, pp. 50–51). The image of God refers to mankind's overwhelming suitability to image Christ's glory.

All creation reveals or mirrors God's virtues and perfections; every creature is, in essence, an expression of God's imagination. The Bible teaches that God made fish, birds, and other animals according to their kind, in their own likeness (Genesis 1:21–25). But only humankind is created as "God's kind"—the image of God, the highest revelation of God, the crown of the entire creation.

Even after the fall that image is intact, though damaged (Genesis 5:1–3; 9:6). James 3:9 affirms that fallen humanity still carries the image of God, which is the basis for God's displeasure when human beings curse one another. Mankind is never "nothing" because the image of God is not something that can be lost, just as it is not something that is gained when a person accepts Christ as Lord and Savior, nor earned through human accomplishment. All human beings bear the image of God from conception.

## The Significance of Being God's Image

Being created as God's image and representative means that humankind was intended to serve as an ambassador of God. Hoekema (1986) suggested several ways in which humankind was to represent God: by expressing the authority of God, advancing God's program for the world, supporting and defending what God stands for, and promoting what God desires. It is through mankind, as God's representatives, that God "works out his purposes on this earth" (p. 68). This has particular significance for Christians, in whom "people should be able to encounter God, to hear his word, and to experience his love" (p. 68).

When God created Adam and Eve, they (and by extension, all humankind) were given the position of vice-regents or trustees of all that God had created. They were in that respect *under–rulers*. God was not absenting himself from final control and authority, but appointed Adam and Eve as administrators of God's "estate." As agents of the Creator as well as being responsible to him, good stewardship through exploring, developing, and using his world wisely as servant-managers is to be expected. The role of mankind as stewards has not diminished because of the fall. It has become more difficult, but it has also become more necessary for Christians, because we recognize that nothing is ours—everything belongs to God (including humankind). God expects us to exercise principles of good stewardship as we use the talents and abilities he built into us as individually designed and gifted persons, and as we use what he has made available to us in the world. God's desire is that our stewardship of creation (including ourselves) will bring honor and glory to him.

## God's Image and Human Worth

Our value as human beings lies in the fact that we *are* God's image. Shelly and Miller (1999) stated, "The Christian understanding of human beings as created in the image of God bestows dignity and honor on every person, regardless of social, mental, or physical status" (pp. 61–62). *All* persons have value before God, not because of having earned a certain degree of status based on ability, intelligence, appearance, or any other humanly valued characteristic, but simply because we are bearers of the image of God. Our fallen (sinful) human nature leads us to create hierarchies whereby some people are elevated above others (meaning that some are consciously placed lower on the scale), but God does not recognize these distinctions: we are all equally his by creation, equally created in his image, equally fashioned to glorify God, equally responsible to God, and equally in need of salvation.

Our value is not rooted in what we do, but in who we are as God's representatives. Status is derived from being a member of the human family, where each person—without regard to intellectual capacity, physical mobility, sensory ability, achievement, personal attractiveness, or familial or tribal lineage—*is* the image of God. Thus, there is never a time or a circumstance when the dignity of human beings and their right to proper respect disappears, not even when profound and multiple disabling conditions exist.

## God's Unique Design

The Book of Genesis indicates intentionality in God's creating humankind in his image (Genesis 1:26–31). There is no accident in our design: "Being human means being created in the image of God, by God, out of God's desire and decision to do so" (Bartel, 2001, p. 10). God has uniquely designed every person, including our personal strengths and weaknesses. To each person, including those with disabilities, God has given unique abilities, gifts, and talents, as well as certain limitations. Both the Old and the New Testaments speak of God as a potter and humankind as the clay (Isaiah 29:16, 41:25, 45:9, 64:8; Romans 9:21). This presents a strong image of God carefully handcrafting each individual, similar to David's observation in Psalm 139:13–16 that we have been woven in the womb by the hand of God. God personally fashioned each person, with deliberate intent in our design and careful attention to every detail. God sometimes includes disability in that design—not as punishment for someone's sin, but for reasons known only to him (cf. Exodus 4:11). Because God's ways and wisdom are beyond our comprehension (Isaiah 55:8–9), in these instances we must rest in the Bible's assurance that God's actions are always righteous: "The Lord our God is righteous in all the works that he has done" (Daniel 9:14; cf. Psalms 71:19, 116:5; Isaiah 45:21). As his creation, we have no reason to question the actions of our sovereign God. We are also assured in God's Word that he is able to bring good out of what we perceive as bad (Romans 8:28) and, as chapter three will bring out, God can, through individuals with disabilities, teach us many things. Yong's (2007a) conclusion is that "God uses disabilities to accomplish myriad purposes ... and ultimately, God's justice and glory will be revealed in the lives of people with disabilities" (p. 39).

## Stewardship and the Image of God

In addition to the innate talents, abilities, and interests that God has designed into each individual, God has also given Spiritual gifts to every believer (1 Corinthians 12:4–11). Paul indicates that these gifts have been given "for the common good" (1 Corinthians 12:7), which clearly implies that they are to be used, not buried for safekeeping, as was done by the "wicked and lazy" servant in Jesus's parable (Matthew 25:14–20). Scripture does not suggest that the distribution of spiritual gifts was only to persons of sound mind and body.

The principle of good stewardship also requires that we provide whatever assistance or instruction that is needed to enable others, including persons with disabilities, to develop to their full potential. It is imperative that God-given talents and spiritual gifts in all persons be identified and their use encouraged, including talents and gifts of those whom the world wrongly sees as of lesser value or as persons to be pitied.

## Image of God and the Meaning or Purpose of Life

Does our life have meaning and purpose? Shelly and Miller (1999) asserted, "To be created in the image of God means that we must look to God for our meaning, purpose, and direction"(p. 63). Scripture teaches clearly that God had a purpose for creating the world. Consequently, all human life has meaning or purpose. Humans often take an anthropocentric position and assume God's ultimate purpose is to make us happy by satisfying our desires, rather than taking a theocentric view which sees God's ultimate purpose to be bringing glory to himself. Hodge (1871), in his classic *Systematic Theology*, stated that the glory of God is the great end toward which all of creation is purposed; ultimately, every tongue will confess that Jesus Christ is Lord, to the glory of God the Father (Philippians 2:11). Drawing primarily from Psalm 104, Piper (2012) explained that God rejoices in his works of creation because they express his glory, bring praise to him, reveal his incomparable wisdom and power, and point beyond themselves to God (pp. 69–75). The heavens are faithful in declaring the glory of God (Psalm 19:1), and humankind, created as God's image and appointed to be his representative, was intended to serve this purpose as well. In our original state (before the Fall) humankind was particularly fashioned to bring glory to God and, following this final act of creation, God pronounced his work "very good" (Genesis 1:31). It is only as we fulfill that purpose that we experience a deep sense of meaning in our life.

Does having a disability mean the person has no purpose? Even though the image of God in humankind is tarnished, that some aspect associated with God's image either does not function properly or is absent altogether, does not mean the individual has no purpose or is condemned to living a meaningless life. The image of God is an essential part of our being, and cannot be lost, despite being born or becoming profoundly disabled.

It is a characteristic of human nature to seek coherence and purpose in life—to make things fit into a package we can understand.

This may be the reason behind David's question in Psalm 8, "What is man that you are mindful of him?" The tendency of many to view the disabled as inferior, leads them to question what purpose or meaning there could be especially in the life of someone with severe or multiple disability. To ask such a question reveals an assumption that disability prevents an individual from living a meaningful life. But does having a disability—especially a severe impairment—limit or prohibit "meaningful existence" (a concept that also needs definition)? It may be more the case that those who are temporarily able-bodied[†], out of ignorance or prejudice, limit those with disabilities by their attitudes. Parents and teachers of students who are disabled must take care that they are not also guilty of so limiting the students, even inadvertently, when designing individual education programs for the students.

For some, having a disability may actually be more empowering than limiting. Students who have a disability can teach others through their example about patience, courage, determination, and inner strength, while at the same time helping temporarily able-bodied classmates—and teachers—learn compassion, service and sacrifice, and community. Working with students who have disabilities can also help special education teachers to develop professionally, as they seek to learn or develop teaching methods that will be more effective with the students. And both teachers and students who do not have a disability can come to recognize their own shortcomings and fragility, as well as our mutual dependence upon God for daily life and breath.

This is not to suggest that students with disabilities are simply an object lesson. Care must be taken not to look at persons with a

---

†    Since all people are vulnerable to accidents and illnesses which can result in becoming disabled, and since all people age, which increases the possibility of becoming disabled, it has become common to refer to people who are presently non-disabled as *temporarily able-bodied.*

disability from a position of false superiority or power, but to see them as equals in the sight of God.

## Disability and the Image of God

God created man in a state of innocence, declaring his creation of humans "very good" (Genesis 1:31). Even if God's fashioning someone in the womb included a disability, this does not negate the individual's being in the image of God, or suggest that the person has no value. As was said previously, God is good by nature; nothing he does can be construed as being anything but good and in accord with his purpose and decree. Exodus 4:11, taken in concert with God's full revelation, is God's declaration that in his view and providence, all people are beautiful, accepted, and loved. Neither ability nor disability alters God's pleasure in what he has created—nor does disability interfere with our ability to find joy in the Lord. Humankind was created for God's pleasure—to celebrate God who is worthy to receive glory, honor, and power, for he created all things, and by his will they exist (Revelation 4:11). Piper (1998) commented that humankind is "made for the soul-satisfying glory of God in the gospel" (p. 39). For us to glorify God does not require a whole body or "whole" mind; our weakness, in fact, provides a means by which God can bring glory to himself (cf. 2 Corinthians 12:7–10). In reflecting on disability, Browne (1997) raised a provocative question:

> May not the presence of imperfection be a vibrant indication that something more, something radically transcendent to finite measures, lies just beyond? Can't we see that this apparent design aberration does not deflect God's beauty, God's ineffable perfection, but

simply evidences our lack of imagination, our limited finite capabilities? (p. 35)

Neither our present imperfect and sinful condition nor any disability is a result of poor workmanship on God's part. Ultimately, we must recognize that we live in a fallen world and that many disabilities are the result of this state. Reynolds's (2008) broad view of what it means to be created in the image of God is instructive for our consideration of disability:

[T]o be created in the image of God means to be created for contributing to the world, open toward the call to love others. Three dimensions are implied: creativity with others, relation to others, and availability to others. The point to be stressed is that all people can be contributors, representing a range of both gifts and limitations; disability is not an incomplete humanity in this regard. (p. 177)

Let me offer an example of someone with a disability who also had a gift for serving others. Mariamu, a young girl my wife and I encountered when we were serving in Cameroon, was born without arms (a congenital amputation). By the age of six, she had learned how to use her feet like hands and joyfully served her more disabled peers in her school, gently feeding those unable to feed themselves because of severe cerebral palsy. She also served them when the class was engaged in arts and crafts activities by drawing, coloring, and using scissors with her feet to cut paper for those who could not do this for themselves. Mariamu would even blow up and tie small balloons for her friends!

And she would push the wheelchair of her classmates from room to room by leaning against their wheelchairs.

## Implications for Special Educators

Estep (2010) drew several implications from our being created *as* God's image, three of which are particularly relevant in relation to disability: (a) humanity's existence and identity are dependent on God; (b) humanity was created unique and distinctive from the rest of creation; and (c) the image of God is the basis for human dignity and has significant ethical implications (pp. 15–16).

In sharing his experience caring for a young man (Adam) with very severe disabilities, Henri Nouwen (1997) encouraged his readers to consider what it means to be created in the image of God—to reflect on the uniqueness of each individual and the true meaning of humanity. He suggested that God reveals himself through and in even the most disabled of persons:

> Adam's humanity was not diminished by his disabilities. Adam's humanity was a full humanity, in which the fullness of love became visible for me, and for others who came to know him ... We were friends, brothers, bonded in our hearts. Adam's love was pure and true. It was the same as the love that was mysteriously visible in Jesus, which healed everyone who touched him. (pp. 50–51)

Nouwen's experience with Adam is a clear reminder that "bearing God's image establishes for every person a fundamental dignity which cannot be undermined by wrongdoing or neediness" (Pohl, 1999, p. 65).

Because humankind bears the image of God, Christians must have transformed attitudes toward people, characterized by great dignity and respect for all of human life and transformed behaviors, characterized by great appreciation for the diversity of people we encounter (Habermas, 1993). Special education teachers do not just help their students learn and develop compensatory skills, but serve as an advocate to promote these changes in attitude and behavior. They advocate, actively and by example, for the students they work with to the students' non-disabled peers, school administrators, other teachers, staff, the families of their students, and ultimately, the community.

Scripture suggests that God highly values those we tend to see of lesser importance (cf. Deuteronomy 14:28–29 and God's judgment on the nations as recorded in the prophets). We are told in Proverbs 14:31 that to oppress the poor is to show contempt for their Maker, but kindness to the needy brings honor to God. That what we do "unto the least of these" is in reality done unto the Lord is emphatic in Jesus's teaching in Matthew 25:34–40. Persons who have a disability must logically be included in the groups Jesus mentioned in that parable. Showing love and compassion to these individuals honors God because they, like us, are creatures of worth who bear the image and likeness of their Maker.

A strong understanding of humankind's being created as God's image is essential to a biblical worldview. It informs our understanding of God's purpose for us and what it means to be human. Dunavant (2009) pointed out that this is particularly important to understand today, as our culture continues to move toward devaluing man, thinking that man is little more than an animal produced through the random "chance" of evolution. A clear implication, then, of the Bible's presentation of humanity as the image of God is the affirmation of the dignity and worth of every individual, regardless of a disability.

A biblical understanding of disability underscores the sanctity of life, both in regard to abortion issues and more generally, requiring that we treat others (including those with disabilities) with respect and reverence. A theology of special education, which must take account of all persons being created in God's image, encourages compassion toward those in need. As Dunavant (2009) stated, "Clearly, the image of God in man condemns any type of bias toward, discrimination against, or exploitation of anyone on the basis of skin color (racism), gender (sexism), economic status (classism), ethnic origin (ethnocentrism), or age (ageism) as sin." To this we can add disability or *ableism*, which is to demean the inherent value of someone who has a disability, or to reject them outright.

For the special education teacher or others who serve students with special needs, this understanding of humankind gives direction to all of our professional activity, from the way assessment data is collected to creating an educational plan for the students—especially for students who are the age when transition issues are brought into the planning—to advocating for appropriate inclusion, to securing needed related services, to collaborating with other professionals, to communicating with parents and siblings, and to encouraging positive interpersonal relationships with the student's peers.

CHAPTER THREE

# Special Education
# as Practical Theology

When people think of theology, they probably imagine some scholarly endeavor undertaken by very religious people wherein large volumes of theological thought are produced. Their thoughts turn primarily to doctrine, neatly systematized into categories such as Christology, soteriology, pneumatology, eschatology, and so forth. Systematic theology, so conceived, provides a linear and somewhat theoretical analysis of God's revelation, which makes it easy to reflect on and discuss without necessarily considering how these concepts directly affect one's daily life. The result is often a false separation between Christian doctrine and daily life, between the sacred and the secular. While the intent of systematic theology may be practical (i.e., to be applied to living), it often remains in the realm of the cognitive, particularly for those not seminary-trained. Though theological reflections may be included in a sermon, those sitting in the pew may limit their response to simply agreeing (or disagreeing) with the concepts. The theological lesson, no matter how accurately and expertly presented, may stop short of being integrated into everyday life, and theology remains on the surface, having no effect on the way we live.

In a recent issue of *Christianity Today,* Perry Glanzer presented a thought-provoking essay regarding the moral dimension of education in Christian colleges and universities (Glanzer, 2012). He offered four suggestions as to how Christian colleges and universities can maintain their distinctive moral contributions to their students' education and resist the pressure to narrow their focus to simply building professional qualifications necessary to satisfy state licensure or certification requirements. Each of Glanzer's suggestions is of great importance as faculty in Christian colleges and universities seek to help students see their chosen profession as not merely a job, but a way of serving God and mankind (i.e., a ministry) by using the gifts, talents, and interests God has designed into them. Two of Glanzer's suggestions seem especially relevant to helping students reflect on the integration of Christian faith and special education:

- Teacher-educators need to help students understand "what loving God looks like when engaged in a particular discipline," including helping them understand and acquire "the virtues and practices necessary for loving God and gaining knowledge of God's creation" (p. 21).
- Teacher-educators need to introduce their students "to complex theological, ethical, and academic discussions about what it means to be fully human" (p. 22).

Glanzer's second point speaks to the Bible's teaching that God is the sovereign Creator (discussed at length above in chapter two), uniquely and individually fashioning each person, including strengths and weaknesses, interests and abilities, and sometimes including disabilities in that design. Whether disability is part of God's design or results from the general consequences of the Fall (illness, accidents, violence) or activity of Satan, because God is sovereign, disabilities fall within God's direct or permissive will (Yong, 2007a). But because, according to the Scriptures, God is righteous and full of wisdom, all that he does is good, perfectly fitting his eternal purposes, which are ultimately beyond our understanding. Yong's words are instructive: "While God's creative sovereignty is shrouded in mystery, God's providential activity is ultimately redemptive" (2007a, p. 169).

## The Place of Theology in Life

The Bible does not specifically address issues of special education. How, then, does theology relate to special education or being a special educator? We begin by examining the place of theology in our lives. Miller (2009) held that since God exists and is sovereign, everyone relates to him in one way or another: "We cannot avoid having a theology" (p. 72). Whether consciously or unconsciously formed, good or bad, theistic or humanistic, everyone has a theology or worldview which shapes their lives. Even an atheist or agnostic can be said to have a theology, or an attitude or perspective on God, even if it is to deny or question his existence. Because God is living, our theology must also be living and relatable to our situation in life (especially as significant changes occur, such as illness, job loss, or becoming disabled). Humans are *hermeneutical beings* (Osmer, 2008); we have an innate need to interpret, to make sense out of our experience, so as to feel some degree of control over our lives.

Developmental psychologist, Jean Piaget, also believed that humans have an propensity to organize their experiences and observations (Eggen & Kauchak, 2009). Piaget held that this organizational tendency made the thinking process more efficient, but saw it as having a biological basis. I believe it is more accurate to align this organizational tendency with the biblical view of humankind. Since God is a God of order, not chaos, our need to make sense out of our environment and experience is related to our being created as God's image. This meaning-seeking is our response to all new learning and experience, and it can be a particular struggle when a person first encounters disability in themselves or a family member, or when confronted with times of crisis or challenge throughout life. These encounters send us on a quest to understand what God is doing in our lives, to ask "Why" or "Where was God?"

Answers to the question "why?" may never come, just as God did not explain to Job why he underwent such suffering. But having one's life disrupted by disability—personal or familial—does not have to destroy faith. It does not indicate that God is either not loving or not all-powerful, or both. Nor does disability mean that a person cannot play an important role in God's kingdom movement, though understanding what God is doing or allowing, and why, may come slowly, or not at all. As educators who seek to understand how Christian faith (theology) integrates with special education, we engage in this hermeneutic activity so that we can see God in disability and in our work—even in the students with whom we work—and to understand how being a special educator fits into our calling as Christians.

Migliore (2004) described theology as an ongoing search for the fullness of the truth of God. For theology to become integrated into our lives requires deep reflection, an unrelenting search for the truth to which traditional doctrine points. The essence of theology, then, is "interrogative rather than doctrinaire" (Migliore, p. 2). Theology becomes relevant in the context of special education in several ways: (a) as we analyze and interpret disability from a biblical perspective (discussed in chapter two), (b) as we consider the meaning and integrity of the ministry of special education, (c) as we seek to interpret specific incidents in the classroom and the appropriateness of our response from a biblical perspective, and (d) as we seek to discern what God is teaching us through students who have a disability and our interactions with them.

## What Is Practical Theology?

The readiness to question is what makes theology *practical*. Much of the literature on practical theology focuses on the applied skills or disciplines of ministry, such as preaching, church education, pastoral counseling, and evangelism. I want to use this term outside the ministry of the church and consider the connections between the Christian faith and the social context—specifically, to the ministry of special education. My premise is that theology is embedded in human "life and practice" and, therefore, is legitimately something which applies to special education. I will explain this more in a later section. First, we must look more at the concept of practical theology and consider Jesus as a model "practical theologian."

Practical theology is theology in action. Rather than a theoretical or analytical approach to the Bible with the goal of categorizing biblical teaching to create a doctrinal statement, practical theology reads Scripture in the context of ministry. Practical theology "extends systematic theology into the life and praxis of the Christian community" (Anderson, 2001, p. 23). Its aim is to state and test the implications of Christian thought in the arenas of human activity (Browning, 1981), to provide a frame of reference that enables a theological interpretation of activities, or even of society itself (Kim, 2007). This takes us beyond the boundaries of the church and into the world, inviting us to read and interpret the "texts" of current experience in the light of God's revelation of himself and his purposes in Scripture. A slightly more technical explanation is that of Wolfteich (2000): Practical theology "takes as its primary object of study the contemporary situation as it relates to faith, ministry, and public religious leadership" (p. 8). This brings theology alive as we seek to apply it in our lives.

The full meaning of the various doctrines of the Christian faith (e.g., creation, incarnation, redemption, reconciliation) are not truly understood until their significance in the present life and experience of an individual is understood (cf. Rowland & Bennet, 2006). Thus, practical theology is context-related, beginning with the present life-experience rather than with academic reflection on Scripture. The focus on understanding the implications of faith to guide actions in contemporary circumstances is what makes practical theology *practical.*

Practical theology does not just ask "What is going on?" in a situation but, drawing on biblical revelation, goes on to ask "What *should* be going on?" "How are we to live?" "How should I respond to what is happening?" "Where is God in this experience or situation?" Questions such as these bring theological reflection to the events or situations faced by individuals, families, and even whole communities. They are intensely practical questions, but they are also deeply theological (Anderson, 2001). The kind of inquiry involved in practical theology opens us up "to the forming and transforming Spirit of God who remakes us as the image of Christ" (Osmer, 2008, p. 34). Hence, doing practical theology necessitates that basic Christian doctrine (theology) is known, at least at a surface level, in order to ascertain its application to understanding a situation and to respond *Christianly.* In simple terms, practical theology is expressed in faith-based action flowing from the questions "What would God have me do?" and "What would God have me learn?" in any particular instance.

## Jesus: Practical Theologian

The gospel writers portray Jesus as engaging in practical theology. His theology was revealed not only in his teaching, but by his life and actions as well. Anderson (2001) aptly concluded, "The *ministry* of Jesus ... is as authoritative and revealing of God as the *teaching* of Jesus" (p. 30, emphasis added). Jesus was not *a* word from God, but *the* Word of God (John 1:1, 14); a living embodiment of God's Word. Jesus was *living* practical theology; his life *was* the message, a demonstration of his theology.

From the gospel narratives, it is clear that Jesus did not restrict his preaching to the Sabbath; he preached and taught in the streets, on the shore, on the hills, every day as the opportunity afforded itself. The context of his preaching and teaching came from everyday situations and life experiences to which he applied biblical teaching, or from which spiritual significance and theological application was drawn, often expressed in the form of a parable. Rather than a formal exposition of doctrine, Jesus's preaching and teaching was a living application of theology to specific incidences of the human experience. He explained and showed the spiritual significance of various events, in the process correcting faulty interpretations, and he taught and modeled how we are to live.

Jesus's theology of God, humankind, sin and salvation, grace and restoration, the end times, etc., were the subject of his teaching and living. Jesus's interpretation of situations and the actions he took particularly (but not exclusively) revealed his theology of God. For example, his parable of the lost sons (Luke 15:11–32) was not so much a story of repentance as a depiction of the extravagant grace of God. His teaching about not being anxious (Matthew 6:25–34) spoke God's sovereignty and love into situations of debilitating worry. His interpretation of "the man born blind" (John 9:1–3) corrected the theology of the disciples and pointed to the sovereign purposes of God.

His teaching stretched people's understanding of biblical/theological ideas, as in the many times when Jesus's teaching followed the pattern "You have heard that it was said ... But I say to you" (e.g., Matthew 5:21, 27, 31, 33, 43). Similarly, Jesus's use of questions was sometimes designed to make people engage in their own theological reflection, such as his asking the disciples "Who do people say that the Son of Man is?" followed with the question "Who do you say that I am?" (Matthew 16:13–20), or his response to the rich young man in Matthew 19:17, "Why do you ask me about what is good? There is only one who is good." In both instances, people were challenged to think through their understanding and their theology. The Bible also records times when Jesus was amazed with the theological understanding shown by individuals who were Gentiles, the Syrophoenician woman (Mark 7:24–30) and the Centurion (Luke 7:1–10), for example.

Swinton (2000) claimed that "actions are themselves theological and as such are open to theological reflection" (p. 11). Consequently, we need to look deeply at Jesus's miracles, his display of compassion, his interactions with people considered outcasts by the Jewish leaders of his day, so that we can identify the theological significance of his actions. And we need to reflect deeply on our own interactions with the special needs students with whom we work to seek spiritual and theological meaning and significance.

That Jesus called us to be his disciples *here and now*, not once we get to heaven, has significant implications for our lives, regardless of our professional endeavor. Through Jesus's teaching and the example of his life we learn how we are to live. Jesus was the ultimate change agent, breaking down barriers between genders, ethnicities, social status, and disability/ability. Stearns (2010) explained that "being a Christian ... requires much more than just having a *personal* and transforming relationship with God. It also entails a *public* and transforming relationship with the world" (p. 2, emphasis in original). His point is that believers have not just been saved *from* something, in which case God could have simply taken us to be with him at the moment of conversion; God also saved us *for* something: Believers are commissioned to continue Jesus's mission of restoration and reconciliation as he explained it in the synagogue of Nazareth:

> The Spirit of the Lord is upon me, because he has anointed me to proclaim good news to the poor. He has sent me to proclaim liberty to the captives and recovering of sight to the blind, to set at liberty those who are oppressed, to proclaim the year of the Lord's favor. (Luke 4:18–19)

This passage is associated with the Day of Jubilee (cf. Leviticus 25:8–55), a time of restoration for the people of Israel. The Jubilee year would eliminate poverty and slavery among God's people and revert the land to its family of origin. Even the land itself would be restored, as it was to lie fallow during the Jubilee year. In claiming this passage as referring to himself, Jesus declared that with his coming, the true year of jubilee had begun or, in his words, the Kingdom of God had come.

Before returning to the Father, Jesus authorized his disciples to continue the work he began (Matthew 28:18–20). He charged his disciples, then and now, to teach all that he had commanded—meaning what he taught orally and what he taught by demonstration. In short, Jesus was telling his disciples (including us) to be practical theologians, applying theological principles to all areas of human interaction and in all situations of life. The basis for practical theology is that God has called us to be salt and light in the world (Matthew 5:13–14, 16; Romans 6:4), to re-present Jesus to the world through words and life (Acts 1:8; 1 Timothy 4:12, 16), to be a sign of the kingdom (John 13:36; Philippians 2:15–16). We know that the Kingdom of God will not be fully realized until the triumphal return of Christ, but as we saw in chapter one, Jesus taught that the kingdom had already come and is within those who follow him (Luke 17:21). The Christian's task is to further that kingdom, not just by sharing the gospel message and calling people to repent and believe, but also (and especially) by promoting biblical justice and reconciliation, speaking out on behalf of those who have no voice, defending the rights of the oppressed—and, as is the specific concern of this book, in doing special education.

Browning (1981) spoke of a practical theology of care by which lives, both in the church and in the larger society, are shaped. His assertion was that the church "should be interested in a Christian theological interpretation of the major milestones and phases of the human life cycle … A practical theology of care in this sense is interested in the theology of significant life issues" (p. 159). Since the "church" is people, not a building or an organization, as Christians following the Lord into special education, we need to bring theological reflection into our professional activity.

## Practical Theology and Special Education

Anderson (2001) claimed that "The litmus test of theology is not only what it says of God but what it does to persons when it is … practiced" (p. 202). This implies there should be some effect on us (beyond just an emotional reaction), an effect that will lead to our spiritual growth and to God's glory. There must be hermeneutical reflection on the context of special education teaching in light of Scriptural and theological teaching.

Through engaging in this reflection, theology becomes contextualized rather than remaining abstract and formal. Our focus is on the meaning and integrity of special education practices: how Christian theology informs and is revealed in the ministry of special education—what our activity as special educators teaches us about God, humankind, and the character of those who work with persons who have a disability. It involves meditating on our teaching and classroom experiences to grasp their spiritual significance, to understand what God is revealing of himself through these experiences.

## Why Is Practical Theology Necessary?

Practical theological reflection is not something in which special educators engage in order to have theological discussions with families affected by disability (although there may be times when this might be appropriate). Rather, such reflection helps us to understand both what *is* going on, and what *should be* going on in our lives and professional activity. As we reflect on issues of disability and special education biblically, we are better able to bring every thought into captivity to Christ (2 Corinthians 10:5) and to combat "operational secularism," wherein faith is separated from our daily work. We are also in a better position to speak truth in the situation.

Christians "face the world as a response to the call from God" (Seymore, 2004, p. 355). Being a follower of Jesus requires that our lives show evidence of the same attitudes, actions, character, and manner of Jesus. "As a fulfillment of our vocation as Christians, we are called to repair the world" (Seymore, p. 281). Rowland and Bennet (2006) concluded:

> [P]ractical discipleship becomes the dynamic within which theological understanding takes place. Understanding of God and the world comes about and is altered in a life of service to those who are the least of Christ's brothers and sisters. It means interpreting everyday life by means of the Bible rather than the study of the Bible being an end in itself cut off from involvement in everyday living and the exegetical insights which this offers to the theological task. (p. 9)

Thus, we must reflect on special education theologically, and assume the role of practical and public theologians of education. Browning (1981) wrote specifically about a practical theology of care (pastoral theology), but his ideas relate to special education as practical theology. He described practical theology as focusing on a theological interpretation of significant life issues and held that the task of practical theology is "to state and test the implications of the Christian themes for the norms of human action as they relate to a variety of practical spheres" (p. 162). Our exploration of biblical/theological themes in chapter two drew several implications for special education and disability studies, and the significant life issues that are associated with disability and special needs education.

I suggest that we think of the word "theology" as a verb, and speak of "doing theology" in special education. This corresponds to what I said earlier about theology being "living" in the sense that we "live out" our theology. Practical theology asks that we not simply react to a situation, either as an individual or as a teacher seeking to help students learn, develop skills, become more self-aware and self-understanding, change behaviors, etc. As special education teachers, we need to be theologically reflective practitioners.

# Reflective Special Educators

Schon (1987) described two aspects to being a reflective practitioner. The first involves critically assessing the teaching act, in terms of both our activity and the student's response to the lesson—*reflecting on action*. The second aspect involves *reflecting* in *action*, meaning reflection as the lesson is being taught. This in-process reflection in response to the student's processing of the lesson content allows the teacher to make spontaneous adjustments to the teaching plan or strategy in order to facilitate learning. This reflective activity focuses on the teaching event and allows teachers to gain deeper insight into the lesson content as well as to broaden their repertoire of methodologies in order to accommodate students' needs. Questions to guide reflection at this level might include: What happened? What worked or did not work? What could I do differently? How did the student respond to my teaching or intervention? What might be the student's goal or motivation for a behavior? Was my reaction appropriate? What was the inner motivation of my response? How did my action or words contribute to the student's reaction to the teaching or intervention?

To Schon's forms of reflection we can add *relational* and *spiritual reflection*. Relational reflection involves assessing the teacher's relationship with the student, which is often of greater importance than the methodology employed. The teacher's relationship with the student, especially students with special educational needs, must be supportive, patient, and encouraging, communicating both concern for the student and a confident expectation that the student can learn the lesson when appropriately presented. Students will often work harder and longer when *they believe* the teacher likes them (even if the teacher really does not) and has confidence in the student. Teachers need to reflect on what their nonverbal behavior may be communicating to the student and whether that could be interfering with the student's learning performance. A conscious effort must be made to keep "life stresses" from affecting the teacher's relationship with the students. Paul's teaching that "whatever you do, do all to the glory of God" (1 Corinthians 10:31) applies in the relational area, too. And with regard to working with students who are disabled, we need to remember Jesus's words in Matthew 25:40, "as you did it to one of the least of these my brothers, you did it to me." Jesus views acts of compassion toward those in need as being done for him.

Spiritual reflection is where practical theology more directly comes into play. Spiritual reflection may be directed at the teacher's actions and attitudes: Did I model Jesus in my response to something the student did or said, or did I display anger and impatience? Were Christian virtues evident in my actions or words?

Spiritual reflection also means asking questions about ethics and decision making practices in special education in areas such as assessment, identification, and placement—decisions which have immediate and long-term consequences (Colton & Sparks-Langer, 1993). We know that there are legal guidelines in each of these areas, but we also know that pragmatics often skew how—or how consistently—these guidelines are applied. The teams responsible for making these decisions include special educators who should be an advocate for the student, arguing for the best, most appropriate educational provision. But limitations in funding, staffing, and actual program options can lead to settling on less than optimal planning—for instance, in determining which and how many students qualify for special education services, and the amount and type of services provided. Federal laws linking school funding to students' scores on standardized tests may lead to writing goals and objectives designed more to accommodate school success than to provide an appropriate education for the students. Smith (2010) raised concern over the status of inclusion in America's schools and identified several disincentives to inclusive and effective education for students with intellectual disabilities. From his review of the literature, Smith concluded that the primary stakeholders—students and families, schools and teachers—are at the mercy of federal and state legal (not necessarily educational) authorities. Although teachers may feel they have little power to change this situation, I would hope that *Christian* special education teachers, looking at the situation from the perspective of practical theology, would be bothered by the resulting injustices and take a stand, at least verbally, for what they believe is necessary for the student.

Relational and spiritual reflection moves the teacher beyond just considering the surface structure of special education to addressing deep-structure elements. Reflective questions of this nature might include: How is God present in my teaching and in the specific situation? How has my theology of God and of humankind affected my teaching behavior? Were my actions based on a proper understanding of God and human beings? How has this incident affected my view of God and persons with disabilities? What can I learn about God, humanity, and Christian living through this interaction? Have I contributed (positively or negatively) to the spiritual development of the student? What is God showing me about myself, himself, grace, forgiveness, humility, relationship, etc.? Recognizing that things do not just "happen" in a world over which God is sovereign, what does God want me to learn from this about myself and about my students?

## Practical Theology and Teaching Methods

Part of doing practical theology involves giving thought to the methods used in special education. Methods are based on worldviews.

They reflect values and beliefs, such as how humankind is understood and what is life's goal. Cooling (2010) noted that "education is always based on a vision of what it means to flourish as a human being" (p. 40), which itself is derived from a worldview. The biblical concept of flourishing is often significantly different from secular views.

As a simple example, Ellsworth and Sindt (1992) argued that "the society that best develops the rational potentials of its people, along with their intuitive and aesthetic capabilities, will have the best chance of flourishing in the future" (p. 7). While the characteristics endorsed by these authors, perhaps especially rationality, which often seems lacking in individual or national behavior, are important, there is no thought given to the spiritual part of our being. But from the perspective of a biblical worldview, to truly flourish as a human being requires being in relationship with Christ. Ellsworth and Sindt's worldview does not go far enough.

Special education programs, to a large extent, have drawn from behavioral theory, both in teaching academics and for reducing undesired behaviors (behavior modification). Underlying this theoretical approach is a worldview that understands humankind as simply a biological animal, albeit a highly developed animal. From this perspective, behavior is determined and controlled through the use of external reinforcement, and the goal is conformity to that which society values. For relatively simple levels of learning, elements of behaviorism (e.g., repetitive drill and reinforcement) may be useful, but much of classroom learning involves more complex demands, such as classification, conceptualization, deductive reasoning, and problem solving (Galindo, 1998). Behavior modification has nothing to do with thinking or understanding (Ellsworth & Sindt, 1992, p. 77). The use of behavior modification techniques for behavioral change reflects a very limited (or limiting) view of humankind. Questions must be asked about who is controlling the reinforcement—what is their motivation, and what behaviors are they encouraging or discouraging? Conformity to society's values may sound good, but what, specifically, are those values? Do they correspond to God's values as revealed in Scripture? Behavioral shaping techniques often work, but what is the behavior that is desired?

Ultimately, there are two undesirable consequences to the behavioral approach: (a) it allows persons to deny responsibility for their own actions by shifting the blame to those who shaped their behavior, and (b) it can lead to a utilitarian point of view. The underlying assumption of utilitarianism is usefulness or benefit. Applied to those with severe disabilities, it would ask what is their "use" to society? What benefit do they provide? If they are unable to earn a living for themselves, pay taxes, and otherwise contribute to society, why should limited resources be spent on their education (or even their survival)? What benefit would they receive from an education? An extreme utilitarianism suggests that those with severe intellectual impairments are not really persons, because they are assumed not to have the same reasoning ability nor the same self-awareness as non-impaired persons. Chimpanzees, on the other hand, can learn and exhibit meaningful social relationships; therefore, by this same definition, they *are* persons. It is not difficult to see how these views significantly deviate from or deny the biblical understanding of human persons.

How do we know that someone with severe or profound intellectual impairment is completely unable to reason or has no self-awareness? How much reasoning ability or self-awareness does a newborn infant have? Shelly and Miller (1999) addressed this issue: "Western dualism tends toward utilitarianism. Human value is determined by whatever seems best for society and, on a personal level, whatever is more beneficial to me" (pp. 54–55). Such a view, they explained, discounts human personal relationships. In contrast, "in biblical theism we find human community and practical caring at the deepest level" (p. 55).

Practical theology asks that we consider the method that may be used and its underlying assumptions, and question whether it is compatible with God's view as revealed in the Bible. This would not necessarily mean that a particular method cannot be used, but it does ask that we reflect critically on what we are doing and why. This reflection may lead to new insights into our humanity and the awesomeness of our creation or to ways that Christian thought can add to the theory.

For example, the information-processing model is often used to help understand and explain learning disabilities and other cognitive impairments, and from this model come suggestions as to the student's needs and methods of intervention. The model "traces the flow of information during the learning process from the initial reception of information through a processing function and then to an action" (Lerner & Johns, 2009, p. 166). A key feature of this model is an hypothesized "executive control mechanism," which controls and directs mental activities such as planning and predicting, organizing, memory retrieval, problem-solving, monitoring and self-regulation, evaluation of outcomes, etc. These components of mental activity are part of *metacognition*, loosely understood as "thinking about thinking." A metacognitive approach seeks to help students become more aware of their own thought processes, and to teach them a more structured approach, thus becoming more active, strategic learners (Ariel, 1992; Lerner & Johns, 2009). A biblical understanding of humankind suggests that we include spiritual reflection as part of the metacognitive process. It recognizes that a person's theological understanding can significantly affect how events are interpreted, perhaps even being more formative of our understanding than sensory perception and enculturation.

# Learning from Students Who Have a Disability

Christians who are special education teachers and others who work with people with disabilities need to remember that those they work with (both their peers and the students) are people whom God created as his image, and who are individually loved and designed, including their gifts, talents, interests, abilities, strengths, and weaknesses. The same is true about themselves. Taking this one step further, special educators also must recognize that God has, in his providential wisdom, chosen them to be a part of the life of the student they are serving; that their own God-given talents, abilities, temperament, and weaknesses were built into them with the child they are working with in mind. We must be open to learning from our students, even as we expect them to learn from our teaching.

One common fallacy is to think that students who are disabled are not capable of doing anything for themselves. It is important to recognize the varieties of disabilities students may be dealing with, and the fact that disabilities can be mild, moderate, severe, or profound. Students may be severely limited in functioning in one area, but quite gifted in another; the label "disability" draws attention to the limitation or inability and overshadows the individuality and potential of the child. Disability labels—and in general, the whole focus of special education—is on what the student is *unable* to do. These labels tell us nothing about what the student *can* do. This makes it important for teachers to move past the label, or even statements on the student's individual education plan (IEP), and get to know the student as an individual. Teachers need to learn as much as possible about the individual and seek to build a positive, friendly relationship with the student.

We need to remember that two individuals with the same disabling conditions may be very different in terms of their needs and abilities. It is helpful to learn about the child's disability in general so that teaching approaches can be creatively adjusted as necessary, and in order to anticipate and avoid situations where the student may experience difficulty or frustration. "Simple acts of respect and appreciation, presence and friendship are indispensable parts of the affirmation of human personhood" (Pohl, 1999, p.84). The student must be accorded the same respect as non-disabled students, and generally should be held to similar expectations as others (with appropriate accommodations as necessitated by the disability).

We must also take care not to assume that the disabled student must always be the recipient of help. Teachers and non-disabled students must not presume that they are always the "better" person in the sense of ability or knowledge (or spirituality). Care must be taken not to define persons with disabilities by their needs, but to be open to receive the gift which they are or bring to the classroom through their presence. In chapter two, I noted that God has designed each person with certain abilities and interests; if the student is a believer, he or she will also have at least one Spiritual gift (1 Corinthians 12:4–11). As all humans are stewards of God's creation, including themselves, we must recognize that God expects that these gifts, talents, interests, and abilities will be used wisely and responsibly in service to him and to others. If God has included disability when forming an individual in the womb, we know that God has a reason for this, and a specific purpose for that individual. Hence, even a child who is severely limited by his or her disability may still be able to minister to other children and to us; having a disability does not prevent the individual from becoming "teacher" to those who are able-bodied.

It is imperative that teachers help non-disabled students in the classroom understand these things about students with disabilities, in order to create a welcoming, accepting classroom environment.

In chapters which follow, I will say more about creating hospitable classrooms and building interdependence among the students, two theologically sound principles applied to inclusion. For now, let me share a few simple examples of children with disabilities becoming teachers to others.

Emily Colson (2010) wrote a book about her son, Max, who has autism. In the epilogue to the book, Chuck Colson (Emily's father) commented, "Some people in Max's situation have uncanny musical or artistic abilities, or the ability to have joyous communion with God, undistracted by the world's temptations—abilities often limited by the fall. This characteristic gives the disabled an almost prophetic role" (p. 191). Colson shared how Max brought joy and love to others, even in his fascination with commonplace things like vacuum cleaners. Though at times disruptive, Max, like others on the autism spectrum, showed complete openness and honesty. "Max truly sees the world more as God intended—he's not judgmental or impressed by looks, status, or finances" (p. 190). Perhaps the manner in which some children who are disabled interact with the world—even those with intellectual impairments—is a model for people who are able-bodied but have lost the sense of wonder at all that God has created.

Wolf Wolfensberger (2001), formerly a professor at Syracuse University, also suggested that persons with cognitive disabilities play a prophetic role by challenging the idea that our importance or value is tied to intelligence, achievement, or technological advances. The biblical prophets sought to help people know God and his will for them, calling people to focus on God rather than self. In an analogous way, people with disabilities challenge the intellectual arrogance and the idolatry of our age. Wolfensberger held that the visibility of people with cognitive disabilities in today's society can cause us to rethink ourselves and our nature:

> The person, no matter how profoundly impaired, is another version of myself and asks me questions: who am I, what am I, what am I made of, what about me is important, what is the meaning of the differences among us, how do we all fit together in society?" (p. 18).

Wolfensberger held that the presence of people with significant disabilities can have a gentling effect on those who are temporarily able-bodied, and opined that it is through the presence of cognitively impaired persons that "the presence of God may be made powerfully manifest" (p. 23).

While admitting that Wolfensberger may have overstated his case, Yong (2007a) acknowledges that Wolfensberger "rightly calls attention to the prophetic quality of the lives of people with intellectual disabilities for those who have eyes to see, ears to hear, and hearts ready to be transformed" (p. 221). Yong connected this prophetic dimension of disability with Paul's teaching in 1 Corinthians 1:27–31 that God has chosen what the world regards as weak or foolish to confound the wisdom of the world. Yong claims that the lives of those with intellectual disabilities "embody the wisdom of God in ways that interrogate, critique, and undermine the status quo" (p. 221)

Jill Ruth Harshaw is one who would agree with Wolfensberger and Yong. Harshaw (2010) also spoke of "prophetic voices" of persons with disabilities. Working off the biblical principle that all humankind is created in the image of God, and that a significant aspect of that image involves relationship—a relationship of dependence upon God and interdependence with others, Harshaw shared what she has learned through her relationship with her daughter, Rebecca. She explained that Rebecca, who has a severe intellectual disability and is not able to speak words, has clearly spoken an embodied message to those who are open to receiving it.

> In her way of being, she speaks penetratingly of our self-seeking relationships, saying, "You choose whom to love on the basis of the love they might be willing to give to you. You spend time with those who will affirm the pleasure of your company. In disobedience to the words of Christ, you welcome into your homes people who will invite you back—all this in a search for the priceless jewel of being accepted, liked, loved—the jewel you rarely seem to recognize as the object of your search, a search you seem not to be conscious of taking part in. You perceive words as the key to communicating with one another when often they are simply bricks in the barriers you erect behind which to hide who you really are. How often do you say what you really mean or really mean what you say?" (pp. 320–321)

Virginia Breen described her autistic daughter, Elizabeth, as having become her teacher: "I am learning to think about life, faith, and relationship in a whole new way" (Bonker & Breen, 2011, p. 18). Though unable to speak, Elizabeth writes poetry that reveals deep spiritual insights many would not expect in a person with autism. Elizabeth's expressed desire, communicated in writing, is "to teach people how to improve their lives, make their space a better place, and be happy and healthy" (p. 27). Breen said:

> [T]hrough her perseverance and her poetry, Elizabeth …
> is teaching me to slow down, to appreciate the beauty
> in nature, and to be more patient. She is teaching me
> about love and the power of faith. She is teaching me to
> have compassion, because each of us is fighting a great
> battle. (Bonker & Breen, p. 216)

Her conclusion about autism is that it "makes a mind that is *different but not less"* (p. 206, emphasis in original).

Mike Cope (2011) wrote lovingly about the life secrets he learned from his daughter, Megan, a mentally impaired and medically fragile child who lived for only ten years. He wrote of how her life altered his world and what he thought was important. Despite what the world would call weaknesses, or perhaps through her weaknesses, Megan bore witness to Jesus through a life filled with love:

> She taught me that God will use my brokenness to
> his glory. She reminded me that the power is God's,
> not mine. She made me remember that we are often
> fascinated with things that are impressive from the
> outside but which may not be that important to God.
> She taught me that what really matters has to do with
> the heart: keeping promises, seeking justice in a brutal

world, learning to see those in greatest need, and living
with courage, joy, and unconditional love. (p. 29)

Perhaps disability, rather than being a limitation, gives a spiritual
advantage to the individual and the families affected by disability.
Perhaps they can more easily recognize their dependence upon God
and see the importance of being interdependent with others. Perhaps
they are more thankful for what they do have than persons who are
able-bodied.

People with developmental disabilities can bring us back
to focus on the really important issues of life—matters
of the heart. What purpose can be higher than to reward
others, to bring joy to others, to show others the value
of a smile? God has given this group a special gift. A
gift to teach others patience, the value of concentrating
on simple things, the value of just being together. A gift
to teach joy. (Brown, 1996, 2003, p. 221)

These words were written by the Reverend Doctor Cordell Brown,
a gentleman with whom I have had the privilege of teaching about
disability ministry to pastors, church leaders, and teachers in Ghana.
He is a delight to be around, partly because of the sincerity of his
message, and partly because of his great sense of humor. Now retired,
Cordell is the founder of Echoing Hills Village. Beginning with one
camp in 1967 with 32 campers who were disabled, Echoing Hills
Village now comprises 12 residential facilities and a camp for persons
with disabilities that have allowed thousands of disabled individuals
to live in less restrictive or unrestricted settings throughout Ohio.

Sharing time, teaching, and meals with Cordell, it is easy to forget that he was born with cerebral palsy. His awkward gait, shaky hands and arms, and sometimes difficult-to-understand speech disappear as I am caught up in his stories and infectious laughter. In the foreword to Cordell's autobiography, Joni Eareckson Tada said, "Our society doesn't naturally value people like Cordell, but should.... While not everyone who has a disability will accomplish everything that Cordell has, everyone with a disability has value and something unique to bring to life."

Elliot is a young boy my wife and I worked with in Cameroon. Elliot's cerebral palsy results in his inability to speak and has significantly limited his movement. While we were in Cameroon, Elliot graduated to using a walker instead of a wheelchair, but his academic progress remained slow despite his apparent intelligence. He became a model for my wife and me of enthusiasm and courage. A physical therapist who worked with Elliot and several other children, arranged hippotherapy sessions (a form of physical therapy using horseback riding to provide motor and sensory input and improve postural balance and body control). None of the children had ever been near a horse before, but at the first session, Elliot's excitement was uninhibited as he eagerly volunteered to be the first to ride. There was no sign of hesitation or fear on Elliot's part, which served to encourage his peers as they waited their turn to ride. Each time thereafter upon seeing a horse somewhere in the vicinity, Elliot beamed and reacted exuberantly, hoping that the horseman was coming for him. Despite his inability to speak, in worship and Bible study times, Elliot could lead all of us to deeper worship as he "sang" and "prayed" with words that only the Holy Spirit could understand.

Each of these examples illustrates the ability of persons with disabilities to teach and model behaviors for those without disability. Failure to get beyond the disability label or the list of needs and accommodations needed by a student, or to overcome our fear of difference, denies us the opportunity to experience the joy of relationship, and to learn what God may want us to know, thus stifling our own spiritual growth.

## Practical Theology and Special Education: A Correlation of Procedures

As practical theologians, Christian special educators bring particular contexts and issues of the special education classroom and students into critical and creative conversation with a theological framework. Questions often faced by special educators, whether dealing with students who have academic disabilities or behavioral disorders, are:

1.  How do we understand and interpret the specific situation in which we must act?
2.  What should be our approach, response, or action in this particular situation?
3.  How do we defend our interpretation and response in this situation? (Cf. Browning, 1991)

These questions deal with the praxis of special education. Our answer to the questions (i.e., our response to the immediate situation) requires theoretical reflection to understand the issue and determine whether to respond with a behavioral, developmental, or academic approach. But these questions also have practical theological significance. A proper response, therefore, also requires theological reflection. The situation confronting the special education teacher, of course, requires an immediate response; there is often no time for deep theological reflection (especially if the problem is emotional or behavioral). A more appropriate time for theological reflection is *before*—during teacher-training—and *after*—when doing an inquiry—sometimes referred to as an autopsy or post-mortem—on what occurred, the response made, and the outcome. This kind of practical theological reflection should become a lifestyle for the special education teacher.

At a more specific level, a connection can be observed between the core tasks of practical theology described by Osmer (2008) and assessment and program planning practices in special education. The following table compares practical theological interpretation and special education procedures.

**Comparison of Practical Theological Interpretation and Special Education Procedures**

| Core Tasks of Practical Theological Interpretation[1] | Typical Procedures of Special Education |
|---|---|
| *The Descriptive-Empirical Task*<br>Gathering information to discern patterns and dynamics in particular episodes, situations, or contexts | Comprehensive assessment of student; assessment of a particular behavioral situation; functional behavioral analysis |
| *The Interpretive Task*<br>Drawing on theories of the arts and sciences to better understand and explain why these patterns and dynamics are occurring | Consideration of the nature of the disability; cultural factors, including stigma and the psychological meaning attached to disability; family systems theory and sociological theories |
| *The Normative Task*<br>Using theological concepts to interpret particular episodes, situations, or contexts, constructing ethical norms to guide responses, learning from "good practice" | Comparing present level of functioning with the "norm"; curriculum-based assessment; evaluating response to intervention data |
| *The Pragmatic Task*<br>Determining strategies of action that will influence situations in ways that are desirable and entering into a reflective conversation | Creating an individual educational plan; selecting strategies and action steps for new skill development; changing classroom or school ecosystem |

[1]Drawn from Osmer, R. R. (2008). *Practical theology: An introduction.* Grand Rapids, MI: Eerdmans., page 4.

Osmer held that practical theological interpretation, following the these four steps shown in the table, "often circles back like a spiral as new insights emerge" (p. 11). Similarly, the assessment and program planning in special education circles back as new data becomes available, or as the student's academic progress is monitored and evaluation is made of the student's response to behavioral intervention.

## Final Thoughts

Special education generally locates "brokenness" in the individual and attempts to compensate for that brokenness through accommodations and appropriate educational services. Others disciplines (disability studies) see the problems faced by persons with disabilities as residing in sociocultural contexts and seek to end prejudicial attitudes and discrimination (Smith, 2010). I believe that special education teachers need to engage in both these approaches. A Christian worldview recognizes that students who have a disability are whole beings, despite the brokenness of mind or body that signals the need for special education. The biblical perspective is that we are all "jars of clay" (2 Corinthians 4:7)—we could even say "cracked pots"—because of the effect of sin. The brokenness of disability does not negate being human and does not mean the individual ceases to be God's image. The brokenness of disability cannot always be fixed (in this life), but it is only the shell that is broken; the humanity of the individual is intact. Thus, we endeavor to break down the oppression and prejudice towards people with disabilities, both in the school (through education, integration, and inclusion) and in society at large.

Special education teachers need to see their students not as the subjects of their employment but as potential messages from God. Practical theology asks that we analyze our students, our interactions with the students, our teaching activity, and ourselves in order to understand what God wants us to learn, what he is revealing about himself and his world. Breen's conclusion is to the point:

> I believe that in compassion for our frailty, God has surrounded us with signs of divine loving-kindness that are constant reminders of a holy presence strong enough to sustain us yet gentle enough not to overwhelm us. In a world of pressing demands and constant distractions, however, it is easy to overlook these quiet love notes from God. (Bonker & Breen, 2011, pp. 182–183)

Rephrasing a question raised by Smith and Carvill (2000), we can ask "What difference would it make to the way we teach if we thought of our students as primarily spiritual beings and if we viewed special education teaching as contributing to our students' spiritual development?" In this case, *spiritual development,* not meaning Christian, or even religious, is used to describe a universal human characteristic.

One further thought: Our bodies are the primary way we experience life and interact with the world of objects and people (cf. Shelly & Miller, 1999). Children with severe physical or sensory disabilities (especially if disabled from birth) and children with autism experience the world differently than children without such disabilities. What might this mean in terms of how they understand and experience God? What might we, as temporarily able-bodied persons, be missing in our experience and understanding of God *because* we are not disabled? How might we benefit from this reflection?

The concept of special education as practical theology can be summarized by the following thought borrowed and adapted from

Migliore (2004). I suggest that these three basic questions form the direction of special education as practical theology:

1.  Is our activity as special educators true to what is revealed in Scripture about God, humankind, and the redeemed life?
2.  Does our manner of interacting as a special education teacher with students their families, peers, etc., represent God as a living reality in these contexts?
3.  Do the truths of Scripture lead to transformed practices in our personal and professional life? How is our life an "embodiment of faith and discipleship" in our professional activities?

# CHAPTER FOUR

# Theology and the Character
# of Special Education Teachers

In chapter three, I referred to Glanzer's (2012) idea that teachers need to acquire "the virtues and practices necessary for loving God and gaining knowledge of God's creation" (p. 21). There, the discussion of special education as practical theology addressed the issue of gaining knowledge of God's creation as theological principles were applied to the practice of special education, and as special educators seek theological meaning in their work with children with special needs. This chapter will delve into another aspect of the "deep structure" of special education: the character of the special education teacher. The basic issue of concern is "Does being a Christian make a difference in how we teach?" The focus is not on the teacher's methodology, but the teacher's demeanor: What impact does the fact that we are Christians—representatives of Christ—have on how we go about the daily responsibilities of a special educator?

## Being Christlike

We might ask what people who came to Christ saw. What did they find him to be, or what did they *find* in him? They found acceptance (Luke 7:36–50), forgiveness (Luke 5:12–14), healing (Mark 1:29–34), deliverance (Mark 1:21–26), encouragement and hope (Luke 12:4–7, 22–31), restoration (Mark 1:40–45), friendship (Luke 5:17–20), blessing (Matthew 5:1–12), peace (John 14:27). Since we are being conformed to the image of Christ—since we are his hands and feet today—what do people find when they come to us? What do our students see us to be in (and out of) the classroom? Whose image do we reflect? Do our students (and colleagues and students' families) find in us any of these characteristics and blessings found in Jesus?

For the special educator to *be* Christ means that we model Christ to our students, faculty peers, school administration, parents, and other professionals we collaborate with to meet the educational and social-affective needs of our students. Watkins (1994) claimed that social ministry (which I maintain includes special education) "emphasizes the demonstration of Christlike concern because Jesus is our model for helping persons in need" (p. x).

In Romans 8:29, Paul declared that Christians are predestined to be conformed to the image of God's Son. Slightly different wording was used by Paul in 2 Corinthians 3:18, where he described believers as being transformed into the image of the Lord (cf. 1 Corinthians 15:49). The process of transformation has both future and present reference. The future element is that we will fully reflect Christ in heaven when the image of God mankind was originally created in will be completely restored. But its significance for the present is that we are continuously, throughout our lifetimes, being transfigured to reflect Christ *now*. We are to reflect Christ in our attitudes, behaviors, and words.

*Being Christ* requires becoming Christlike in our character and worldview. Paul gave this instruction to all believers:

> I appeal to you therefore, brothers, by the mercies of
> God, to present your bodies as a living sacrifice, holy

and acceptable to God, which is your spiritual worship. Do not be conformed to this world, but be transformed by the renewal of your mind, that by testing you may discern what is the will of God, what is good and acceptable and perfect. (Romans 12:1–2)

When Paul said "present your bodies as a living sacrifice," he was obviously drawing an analogy to the Old Testament sacrificial system wherein an animal was presented as a burnt offering (Exodus 29:19; Leviticus 1:1–17). Just as the animal was completely consumed on the altar, we are to present ourselves, as a living offering, dedicated or completely surrendered to God, to whom we belong by creation and redemption. We are no longer to fashion ourselves after the world (present age) but are to be entirely renovated (transformed) through renewal of our mind and the consequent outward change implied in the words "testing and discerning" (Romans 12:2), wherein we refuse the norms of conduct and thought employed by the world and adopt those of Christ. Paul taught that we are now "ambassadors for Christ, God making his appeal through us" (2 Corinthians 5:20). As an ambassador, our message (in life as well as words) is not our own, but that of the One we represent. This transformation (the Greek word Paul used, *metamorphoô*, translates as metamorphosis) is an ongoing process of renewal as we offer ourselves to God (also a continuous act) and are fashioned into the image of Christ. This transformation begins at the time of our redemption when, in Christ, we become a new creation (2 Corinthians 5:17).

Transformation is something that the Holy Spirit does, but not without our cooperation. Hence, Paul's command in Ephesians speaks of both active and passive activity. We are told to …

> Put off your old self, which belongs to your former manner of life and is corrupt through deceitful desires [active], and to be renewed [passive] in the spirit of your minds, and to put on the new self [active], created after the likeness of God in true righteousness and holiness. (Ephesians 4:22–24; see also Ephesians 5 and Colossians 3)

These verses make clear that there is a close link between our faithful obedience and our transformation. The "likeness of God" Paul refers to in this passage is Jesus Christ, who becomes "the measure and model of new humanity" (Anderson, 1985, p. 52).

Jesus called us to be light in the world (Matthew 5:14). Micah 6:8 helps us understand what it means to be that light: We are told that the Lord requires that we embody justice, mercy, and humility—the same characteristics that Jesus displayed in his earthly life. Walking humbly with God implies an intimacy with God and attention to what he desires and loves (Keller, 2010).

Paul declared that we are God's workmanship, created for good works (Ephesians 2:10), and asserted that the Bible was "breathed out" by God to teach us what is right or true and to correct what is false in our lives in order to be aligned with God's will and purpose, so that we are fully equipped to do every good work (2 Timothy 3:16–17). The meaning of "good work" must not be narrowly understood to mean church-related activity only. Paul is not referring only to our new creation (regeneration). His focus is on God's preparing and equipping *all* his people for *every* good work—those good works for which God has designed or predestined us (Ephesians 2:10). Without doubt, our new birth is accomplished by God, but his original design of each person in the womb (Psalm 139:13–16a) was also part of God's preparing us to do what he intended for us to engage in from the beginning, which will ultimately bring glory to God.

"All the days ordained for me were written in God's book" (Psalm 139:16b), said David, referring not just to the length of our life (number of days), but also to the good works that God has prepared beforehand for us to do. This includes God's leading some into special education and, in God's providential wisdom, even the specific individuals we work with as we live out our calling. Of course our work is also to be "good" in the sense that it is done wholeheartedly, as though working for the Lord (Colossians 3:23), striving for excellence out of a desire to bring glory to God rather than self-aggrandizement.

God's Word is not just a guide to lead us to future, eternal life. Its profitableness is for the whole of our life as a follower of Jesus. It is important, therefore, that we see our work in special education as a ministry, not just a "job." God has called us to join with him in bringing restoration, freedom, and release to others (Luke 4:18–20; Matthew 28:18–20) in this present life, not merely to join him in eternity. Seeing special education as a response to our call from God to bring reconciliation and hope affords greater dignity and purpose to our work. Migliore (2004) put it this way: "God freely elects creatures to be partners in the mending of creation. Election is a call not to a privilege, but to service ... as a Christian one is called to be a partner in God's mission in the world" (p. 246).

The life and works of Jesus serve as a model for us in performing the ministry of special education. To understand theology and the character of the special educator, I will stress several aspects of Christlikeness toward which our transformation is geared, but I want to begin with some general reflections. What we have been speaking about is what Glanzer (2012) called the "virtues and practices necessary for loving God." At the root of the matter is the understanding that special education is not simply an expression of our concern for students with disabilities, but is a way of responding to God's love for us, expressing God's love to others, and demonstrating our love for God. We begin by considering an ethic of love.

## The Ethic of Love

Jesus brought the power of love to bear on all situations and relationships, thereby loosening the grip of evil and setting people free (English, 1992, p. 118). The term for love used most often in the New Testament is *agape*. It connotes a self-giving, other-centered love, the kind of love displayed by God in sending Jesus (John 3:16; John 15:12–13). The New Testament confidently asserts that God is love (1 John 4:8, 16). Love, being an essential characteristic of God, means that God, in himself, defines love. Earlier in his epistle John said that "God is light" (1 John 1:5), light symbolizing goodness, truth, and holiness. We conclude, therefore, that God's love is a holy love or, stated differently, God's holiness is expressed in love. Agape love, then, is more than affection or simple benevolence (charity). God's love is not a love of passion but a love of intention (Womack, 1998), an all-encompassing characteristic of God by which he continually gives of himself to others, seeking their benefit. With this as our model, we understand our loving others to involve self-giving as well. The source of our love is God (1 John 4:7–8), through the Spirit's enablement (Romans 5:5; Galatians 5:22), and involves our thoughts, feelings (attitudes), and actions. Paul said that love must be genuine (Romans 12:9a) and that we must "walk" in love (Ephesians 5:2). Jesus said that we are to love as he loved (John 13:34–35).

Wiersbe (2001) stated, "What God is determines what we ought to be." Therefore, God-like love (agape) must characterize us as believers, and must be evident in our interactions with our students and others. Acting in love, we seek the best interest of the students with whom we work.

Agape love existed within the Trinity "before the foundation of the world" (John 17:23–24). In all God's actions from creation through redemption—and ultimately until the consummation of history—God has displayed his love and grace and has modeled for us the loving behavior he expects from his creation toward himself and toward others. The Bible repeatedly presents God as essentially loving by relating the many times God was motivated to act on behalf of his covenant people, Israel (Stewart, 2012). Jesus expressed this love in his life and teaching and, ultimately, in his death and resurrection.

Paul's description of love in 1 Corinthians 13:4–7 should be characteristic of special education teachers and the classroom atmosphere:

> Love is patient and kind; love does not envy or boast;
> it is not arrogant or rude. It does not insist on its own
> way; it is not irritable or resentful; it does not rejoice
> at wrongdoing, but rejoices with the truth. Love bears
> all things, believes all things, hopes all things, endures
> all things.

As agents of the kingdom of God, in our work as special education teachers we are to give witness to the characteristics and values of God's kingdom (Snyder, 2004). In working with students who have disabilities, this means displaying unconditional love and creating an environment where all students feel welcomed and accepted by the teacher and by one another. We must see students with disabilities as people who are valuable in themselves—regardless of the severity or type of disability—and help others in the school community see this as well. Our interactions with the students must communicate respect for them as people made in the image of God. In practice, this means that we allow for weaknesses, imperfections, or problems in our students, accepting them where they are (developmentally, academically, behaviorally), while not leaving them at that level but seeking their betterment.

## The Ethic of Care

Closely related to an ethic of love is an ethic of care, which stresses individual and community relationships (Murdick, Gartin, & Crabtree, 2002). Estep (2010) highlighted the idea that ethics involves more than a mental decision-making process, arguing that the scope of ethics includes both affect and behavior (p. 143). In a classroom that exhibits an ethic of care, fairness is not simply treating students equally, as if they are all the same. An ethic of care requires recognition that to be fair means giving due consideration to the differing needs of each student (perhaps in the spirit of Philippians 2:4). In such a classroom, benevolence assumes a greater role as the teacher seeks to give to each student what he or she requires in order to learn effectively.

If theology is the study of God and the truths of God, then ethics is the application of theology. For example, consider Luke 10:25–37. Jesus is asked a question related to theology: "What shall I do to inherit eternal life?" In response, Jesus refers to the great commandment, "You shall love the Lord thy God with all thy heart and with all your soul and with all your strength and with all your mind, and your neighbor as yourself." The follow-up question from the lawyer moves from theology to ethics: "And who is my neighbor?" The parable of the

Good Samaritan, given in answer to the question, deals with the ethical implications of the theology contained in the commandments.

Estep (2010) asserted, "ethics and morality are not simply a human or societal product; rather, they are *dependent* on God" (p. 143, emphasis in original). Similarly, Nuffer (2010) held that "Theological ethics begins not with man but with God" (p. 104). This means we must look to Christ as our example for ethical behavior, since Christ is "the radiance of the glory of God and the exact imprint of his nature" (Hebrews 1:3). The love principles of the Old Testament (Deuteronomy 6:5; Leviticus 19:18) were reinforced by Jesus (Matthew 22:37–40) and echoed by Paul (Romans 13:9–10; Galatians 5:14) and James (James 2:8). Jesus's command to love our neighbors (even our enemies: Matthew 5:43–44) distinguishes the biblical ethic of love from other ethical systems on love. Luke 6:27–36 captures the depth of Jesus's teaching on this principle of love:

> Love your enemies, do good to those who hate you, bless those who curse you, pray for those who abuse you. To one who strikes you on the cheek, offer the other also, and from one who takes away your cloak do not withhold your tunic either. Give to everyone who begs from you, and from one who takes away your goods, do not demand them back. And as you wish that others would do to you, do so to them ... But love your enemies, and do good, and lend, expecting nothing in return, and your reward will be great, and you will be sons of the Most High, for he is kind to the ungrateful and the evil. Be merciful, even as your Father is merciful.

The love that is required goes beyond simple obedience. It means patterning our love of others after God's love. In the case of special education, this both prohibits ignoring students who are disabled—or their needs—and necessitates being proactive in affirming them "constructively as well as compassionately"(Watkins, 1994, p. 64). This is not a debatable issue.

Peskett and Ramachandra (2003) concluded:

> Given Jesus's orientation of his ministry towards the "nobodies" and the "outsiders" (i.e., "the poor") of his society, our own relation to "the poor" of our contemporary societies, and indeed our global world, becomes not merely a question of "social ethics" but lies at the heart of our response to the gospel itself. (p. 166)

Jesus's parable of the Good Samaritan (Luke 10:30–37) exemplifies the attitude and actions of compassionate care. In the parable, Jesus rewords the lawyer's question from "Who is my neighbor?" to "Which of these three proved to be a neighbor to the man who fell among the robbers?" This change in emphasis shifts the focus from others (who is my neighbor?) to ourselves (to whom can I be neighbor?).

In so doing, any thought of how deserving the "other" is falls away. Applying this principle to special education, we are encouraged to be aware of the students around us, seeking, as did Jesus, to identify and meet their needs as God enables us, using the skills and methods of special education, and, if necessary, searching for or developing new strategies.

Our desire to help our students is consistent with God's desire, for the students and for ourselves, and reflects the love and servant's heart of Jesus. An ethic of care requires the teacher's compassionate presence—being available to the student—and active listening—meaning not just listening to the student in conversation, but being tuned in to the whole teaching-learning activity in order to determine the effectiveness of the teaching and identify what factors (physical, emotional, strategic, and environmental) may have helped or hindered the student in the learning experience. When a lesson does not go as planned, special education teachers must resist the temptation to blame the student for his or her failure or lack of effort; neither must they assume that the outcome was entirely due to the student's impairment (e.g., limited attention span, distractibility, etc.). Instead of "blaming the victim" the teacher needs to question what, in the lesson design, method, or presentation, may have prohibited or disrupted the learning. The care we have for the student's development causes us to ask what *we* may have overlooked in the lesson planning, missed in our assessment of the student's strengths and weaknesses, or to ask what mistake we may have made in carrying out the lesson.

The relationship the teacher establishes with the students is paramount in the ethic of care. That relationship must be based on a recognition of the worth and dignity of every individual, including those with severe and profound impairments. Morris (2001) wrote about constructing an ethic of care that promotes the human rights of persons with impairments. One of her points was that we must be careful in offering assistance to students who are disabled. This is especially important in inclusive classrooms where a non-disabled student may be paired with a student who has a disability to be a "buddy" or helper. We need to avoid reinforcing, in the special-needs student and in the helping student, a notion that disability means dependence.

An ethic of care will encourage students who have disabilities to do as much as possible for themselves, helping them to gain a sense of self-control. It will also necessitate taking time to effectively prepare the helping students to show good judgment in determining how much they should do and how much the disabled student should do. Fostering *interdependence* is the goal. Morris wrote from the perspective of a feminist ethics of care, which is based on "a recognition of interdependence, relationships, and responsibilities," and views unfavorably an overemphasis on autonomy and independence (p. 13). This is consistent with a biblically-based ethic of care.

In chapter seven, we will explore interdependence and inclusion in greater detail. An ethic of care is also built on the biblical concept of hospitality, which is the focus of chapter eight.

## Demonstrating Christ in the Classroom

Being Christlike in the classroom requires the teacher to create a classroom atmosphere where the ethic of love and the ethic of care are visible. The teacher will be concerned that he or she, and the classroom environment itself, display characteristics and concerns that were evident in Jesus's ministry.

### Reconciliation

Reconciliation builds on the ethic of love and the ethic of care discussed above. While reconciliation is something that could be directly taught to students, it is more important that it becomes visible through the teacher's actions and the classroom environment created—love and reconciliation should so permeate the learning environment that students learn them experientially (Steensma, 1971). Chapter six will address reconciliation more deeply in relation to special education. Here, I will just draw a few implications of reconciliation and community as related to the classroom environment and the teacher's actions.

Reconciliation has to do with restoring relationships. It is the principle behind Jesus's teaching in Matthew 5 where he speaks of being merciful (v. 7), being peacemakers (v.8), and dealing with anger (vv. 21–26). Being a peacemaker in the classroom entails respecting each student as a complete human being regardless of disability, creating space for students to grow and mature, openly communicating with the students, adapting expectations as necessary, celebrating differences among people, and giving careful attention to those with the greatest need. Paul's instructions to Titus echo these ideas: "Show yourself in all respects to be a model of good works, and in your teaching show integrity, dignity, and sound speech that cannot be condemned" (Titus 2:7–8).

Reconciliation involves forgiveness and active promotion of harmony. The classroom environment must be a place where the students can experience forgiveness, as for example, when teaching students with emotional or behavioral disorders whose misbehavior (intentional or impulsive) demands intervention. The teacher needs to exhibit self-control by not overreacting or displaying anger or frustration that could escalate the problem (the opposite of being a peacemaker!). Acceptance is also needed in this instance: it is the behavior that is unacceptable, not the student. This must be evident in our words and actions in responding to the student.

In my experience working with students with emotional and behavioral disorders, misbehavior was seldom intentional (except for when the student was seeking attention); rather, the misbehavior generally resulted from the student's frustration with an academic or relational challenge, resulting in an impulsive reaction and inability to think through the consequences of his or her action.

Forgiveness and reconciliation need to be possible in the classroom, and promoted in the behavior of the students, as well. Paul spoke of reconciliation in Galatians 3:28 when saying "there is neither Jew nor Greek, there is neither slave nor free, there is no male and female, for you are all one in Christ Jesus" (cf. Ephesians 2:11–22). Obviously, asserting that the various groups mentioned are "one in Christ" does not erase ethnic, gender, or other distinctions, but it does unite the groups into a new living spiritual community. A similar principle applies in creating a classroom community that features reconciliation and relational healing. In the Beatitudes (Matthew 5:2–12), Jesus conferred honor on people who are meek, in mourning, poor, and others who are often "invisible" (Cope, 2011). By extension, people with disabilities are included in Jesus's teaching. In his actions, Jesus's loving concern for disabled individuals was clear (e.g., Mark 2:1–12; Mark 5:1–20; Luke 18:35–43; John 9:1–34), and this was reinforced in his direct teaching (e.g., Luke 14:12–24).

## Authenticity

Another part of loving and establishing a reconciled and reconciling community is the teacher's authenticity. For teachers to "be real" requires knowing one's strengths and acknowledging one's weaknesses. Authenticity includes being willing to admit mistakes or misjudgments and take responsibility for them, and being willing to attempt something new despite the risk entailed in leaving one's comfort zone. Modeling this authenticity confirms to the students that both teacher and students are unique human beings, individually designed and loved by the God who created them both, whether disabled or able-bodied. Teachers who show themselves to be authentic persons become a "source of life" (Steensma, 1971), a motivating force for students with disabilities, through their encouraging attitude and confident expectation that the students can become successful coupled with an unwillingness to give up on the student and a desire to search for or create new ways of teaching and enabling their students to demonstrate their learning and growth. Authentic, special education teachers will in no way appear condescending to their students; they will keep their expectations high but realistic, accommodating to the student's needs but not settling for minimal gains. This will impact goals and objectives established for the students as well as the determination of appropriate services and placement alternatives.

In chapter two, I spoke of two essential theological themes that inform special education: the character of God and the character of humankind. These also provide a basis for understanding how the special educator presents herself or himself to the students. Jesus provided a model for us to emulate. He was authentic—genuine and unpretentious in his life. Much of his time was spent with people who were cast aside by the civil and religious leaders of the community, such as people with disabilities or diseases, widows, children, and non-Jews. Special education teachers can relate to this, as in many schools, students with disabilities may be pushed aside by their peers, either openly or by being made the source of ridicule, and may still be unwanted or unappreciated by general education teachers. Estep, Anthony, and Allison (2008) said of Jesus, "His authentic and simple lifestyle lived out in the open for all to see became a most powerful weapon" (chapter 6, "The Character of Jesus the Teacher," para. 8). In the same way, the authentic lifestyle of the teacher can be a powerful tool in working with special education students, their non-disabled peers, their parents, and other professionals.

## Vulnerability

Vulnerability is closely linked to authenticity. It could be argued that God made himself vulnerable in creating a world that included human creatures who could freely choose to reject him and his love. In laying aside the privileges of Godhood to take on human form, Jesus made himself a model of vulnerability. Knowing the purpose for which he came and that his earthly ministry would culminate in crucifixion did not deter him from carrying out his God-given mission. Jesus's prayer in Gethsemane (Matthew 26:39, 32) acknowledges his vulnerability as well as his complete submission to the Father (cf. Jesus's anguish and need for angelic strengthening in Luke 22:43–44).

For special education teachers to *be Christ* calls us to recognize our own vulnerability—to being misunderstood, rejected, or challenged by students, their families, faculty peers, or school administrators. But it also is a reminder of our dependence upon God and drives us to acknowledge that whatever is accomplished through our ministry is really God working through our weaknesses—something that God wants more than our strengths, which can become an obstacle to ministry. Paul came to understand this and gloried in his weakness so that the power of Christ could be displayed through him (2 Corinthians 12:9–10).

Understanding that vulnerability is not necessarily a negative trait allowed Browne (1997) to speak of the gift and the power of vulnerability made visible in persons with disabilities. He described vulnerability as helping to build relationships and interdependence, reversing the false notion of total personal independence. Interdependence is something essential to successfully including students with special needs in the regular classroom (more will be said on this in chapter seven). The biblical concept of interdependence is what allowed Browne (1997) to conclude, "In shifting the paradigm of inclusivity from disability to vulnerability, we come to see how the disabled have a particular gift to contribute precisely because they are limited" (p. 103).

Authenticity, as was said earlier, involves a willingness to leave our comfort zone. According to Billings (2004), leaving our comfort zone promotes the establishment of relationships and puts us into a better position to advocate for others. The principles of authenticity and vulnerability are also characteristics of agape love. "This is all part of the responsibility humbly to come close to persons in relationships of love" (Billings, p. 197).

Being Christlike calls for vulnerability and humility on the part of teachers who work with students with disabilities. A prime illustration of Jesus's humility and vulnerability is his washing of the feet of his disciples as an example for them to follow (John 13:1–16). The timeless principle behind Jesus's example and teaching is not foot-washing; it is the attitude of humility and servanthood. For us to represent Christ in the classroom and world demands that we be of the same mind as Jesus (Philippians 2:3–8). Recognition that all humankind *is* the image of God results in transformed attitudes toward people, characterized by greater dignity and respect for all, and transformed behaviors, characterized by greater appreciation for the diversity of the people we encounter (cf. Habermas, 1993), coupled with authentic love and humble vulnerability.

## Hospitality

The ethic of love, as expressed in reconciliation, acceptance, and a recognition of the value of interdependence promotes inclusive education through community building. Noted apologist R. C. Sproul (1999) stated, "The Gospel calls us to live as obedient servants of Christ and as his emissaries in the world, doing justice, having mercy, and helping all in need, thus seeking to bear witness to the kingdom of Christ" (p.103). Creating and maintaining hospitable classrooms is one way that Christian teachers, regardless of where they are teaching or the level at which they teach, can demonstrate this kind of obedient servanthood. Chapter eight will have more to say about biblical hospitality in relation to inclusive education.

## Justice and Peace

Jesus taught that we are to seek first the kingdom of God and his righteousness (Matthew 6:33). In the context of Matthew 6, Jesus was specifically contrasting a focus on wealth and material things with concern for the "spiritual." But as we saw in chapter one, the kingdom of God is not just a future "place." Jesus inaugurated the kingdom and called us to life in that kingdom, a life lived under his Lordship and committed to kingdom ethics being exercised in our daily life. Justice and peace are key elements of God's kingdom. Jesus's announcement of the kingdom embraced the total well-being of people and led him to "challenge the religious formalism, legalism, misuse of power, and unjust economic structures that oppressed and marginalized people" (Longchar. 2011, p. 6). Similarly, we need to challenge policies and practices in schools that oppress and marginalize students with disabilities. And we need to reflect on whether the classroom we create displays or furthers the kingdom of God.

"Injustice is a violation of God's own being" (Peskett & Ramachandra, 2003, p. 42). Anything or anyone that limits a student who is disabled from participating as fully as they are able in social, educational, or economic activities where non-disabled students engage falls under the heading of *injustice.* This includes prejudging the student's ability to be integrated into a regular classroom, or overestimating the student's need for assistance simply because he or she has a disability. Jesus's concern for the diseased, the disabled, and the outcasts of Jewish society was evident in his ministry.

Jesus taught and demonstrated God's intention to break down barriers of religion, gender, ethnicity, and (dis)ability. The Jewish leaders seemed dismayed by Jesus's concern for these outcasts and often focused not on a person's having been cured of disability but on the fact that Jesus had done this on the Sabbath, thereby, in their opinion, breaking the Sabbath laws (e.g., Matthew 12:9–14; Mark 2:1–12; John 5:1–7). The leaders even judged (condemned?) those whom Jesus cured of their disability or disease (cf. John 9). To Jesus, illness and disability were things to be struggled against. Our struggle is against the limiting effects of a student's impairment and the disabling attitudes of others that prohibits the full integration of people with disabilities into the school and in society.

Jesus's concern for justice must be our concern also. The history of special education discloses that individuals with disabilities have experienced significant discrimination and prejudice, which federal laws (civil and educational) have tried to eliminate. Special education teachers, of necessity, are involved in programs of change; even more so, *Christian* special educators.

A Christian's career is secondary and supportive of our call and centers on a commitment to seeking first the kingdom of God (Matthew 6:33). Our focus must be on the kingdom, and our efforts to promote that kingdom must be seen within the sphere of stewardship. "The emphasis must be on giving, not taking, on furthering the kingdom through service to others, not advancing oneself by furthering one's career" (Farnsworth, 1985, p. 101). In living out the gospel in our daily lives, we are to work for reconciliation between persons with disabilities and those who are temporarily able-bodied, seek justice and equality for those affected by disability, and promote optimal cognitive, physical, emotional/social, and spiritual development of persons with disabilities.

Chapter nine goes into greater detail in relating biblical justice to inclusive education.

## Servant-Leadership

Just as Christ came as a servant (Matthew 29:28; Mark 10:45), our ministry as teachers involves service to others, seeking their welfare by embodying justice and loving kindness, through helping in their education, development, and inclusion in the educational community and beyond, all in faithfulness to God (Micah 6:8). Paul taught that we are to have the same attitude of humility and servanthood as Jesus (Philippians 2:5–7). Peter likewise taught that we are to "live as servants of God" (1 Peter 2:16), using the gifts received from God to serve others (1 Peter 4:10).

While I was director of graduate programs in special education at Bethel University (St Paul, MN), the Education Department developed a new model for all the programs in education: *The Teacher as Servant-Leader* (Anderson, 1997). The model emphasized teaching as a ministry or helping profession in response to God's call to serve others. It was our belief that teachers who are servant-leaders have an orientation toward others that motivates them to assist students to grow as persons—developmentally, intellectually, affectively, and spiritually. Particularly in reference to special education, teachers as servant-leaders focus on individual learners and helping them learn or discover methods that capitalize on their strengths. There is a parallel in this approach to the way Jesus tended to zero-in on the specific needs of those he ministered to (for example, the paralytic in Mark 2 and the Samaritan woman in John 4).

Christian stewardship means first that Christian teachers exercise their teaching gifts in service to God out of obedience to his call to be a part of his grand mission. They also serve society at large in helping to develop an educated and responsible citizenry. But Christian special education teachers most directly serve the children they teach, helping them to grow and develop to their potential. As servant-leaders,

Christian teachers are servants first, and in serving, they lead, out of concern for the needs and welfare of the students (Anderson, 1997).

The Bible is unambiguous in its emphasis that Christians are called to serve others. Mulholland (2000) defined spiritual formation as "the process of being conformed to the image of Christ *for the sake of others*" (p. 25, emphasis added). This succinctly captures the idea of servant-leadership. To have the mind of Christ (1 Corinthians 2:16b) is to share his concern for people who are in some way disenfranchised, such as those with disabilities for whom there has been a history of exclusion from education and community life.

Instead of servant-leaders, Page (2008) used the term *missional* to describe a Christianity that integrates concern for both evangelism and social ministries. He proposed that missional incorporates what most Christians have in mind when speaking of "living out the Christ life" (p. 19). Page traced characteristics of Nehemiah to describe missional leaders, identifying several that seem relevant and necessary for special education teachers: godly character, Christlike concern, spiritual fruitfulness, integrity, conflict management skill, vision, courage, commitment, communication, accountability, and celebration of victory.

"The constant message of the Scriptures buttressed by the stunning example of Jesus is that *God's Kingdom people are to use their authority, power, and prestige to help and serve, never to hurt, those without authority, power, and prestige*" (Kraft, 1996, p. 313; emphasis in the original). That certainly applies to working with students with disabilities.

## Incarnational Teaching

Most believers, if asked about the Great Commission, think of Matthew 28:18–20. This verse is the fullest statement by Jesus regarding our participation in his mission. Some form of the great commission is found in each of the gospel accounts and in the Book of Acts (Mark 16:14; Luke 24:26–28; John 20:12; Acts 1:8). Each is worded differently; each adds a different tone to Jesus's command. Here, I focus on Jesus's words to his disciples in John 20:21—"As the Father has sent me, I am sending you." I suggest that the word *as* in this verse is crucial in understanding Jesus's commissioning of his disciples. The emphasis is not simply on the idea that because Jesus was sent, we are sent. I believe the important point is that we are sent *in the same manner* in which Jesus was sent. This leads us to examine how Jesus was sent. What has already been discussed about "being" Christ in the world is part of this. Here, my thoughts are more analogical than strictly theological, but I suggest that "incarnation" is a critical concept in understanding what it means to be Christlike.

The concept of incarnational ministry is implied in these words from Plantinga (2002):

> Jesus invited all of his followers, including any of us today who believe in him, to participate in the kingdom as its agents, witnesses, and models ... to be a "Christ person" is to be a "kingdom person." Working in that kingdom is our way of life. (p. 107)

The primary passage of Scripture that forms the basis for incarnational ministry is John 1:14a: "the Word became flesh and dwelt among us." When we speak of Jesus and the incarnation, what immediately comes to mind is his taking on bodily form (incarnate technically means *enfleshment* or embodiment). While not losing his deity-state, Jesus became fully human, totally identifying with humankind, yet without sin. We already have a body, so that is not a concern in incarnational teaching. But Christians are described as the "Body of Christ" (1 Corinthians 12:27; Ephesians 4:12). I take that to mean not just that we are united with him in a spiritual sense, but that we are the "location" of Christ's ongoing ministry in the world today.

All ministry requires embodiment and action (Watkins, 1994, p. 85). *Incarnational teaching*, then, refers to entering into the world of those we serve—in our case, students with disabilities and their families. We serve them by walking alongside them, as it were, just as Christ served and walked alongside his disciples and others in his earthly ministry. In a sense, we model the principle behind the Apostle Paul's statement, "I have made myself a servant to all, that I might win more of them" (1 Corinthians 9:19). The modern proverb that "to know someone you have to walk a mile in their shoes" captures the same idea.

A second passage of Scripture that relates to incarnation is Philippians 2:5–8:

> Have this mind among yourselves, which is yours in Christ Jesus [*or*, which was also in Christ Jesus], who, though he was in the form of God, did not count equality with God a thing to be grasped, but emptied himself, by taking the form of a servant, being born in the likeness of men. And being found in human form, he humbled himself by becoming obedient to the point of death, even death on a cross.

These verses help us to understand that incarnation involves adopting the same attitude that Jesus displayed in his teaching and ministry—servanthood and humility being stressed by Paul. Having the same mind as Jesus lies behind Paul's instructions in Romans

12:1–2, where he says that we must not be conformed to the world but be transformed by the renewing of our mind—a renewal accomplished by the Holy Spirit as we are "metamorphosed" into the likeness of Christ.

Paul focused on the example of Christ's humility. The principle of humility involves not placing ourselves above others (in our instance, students who are disabled, some of who may often be looked down upon by their peers or adults). Humility as a characteristic of incarnational teaching also means acknowledging our dependence on God and our need for regular communion with God. Jesus frequently sought times to be alone with God in prayer (Luke 5:16, 6:12, 9:28, 11:1; Matthew 14:23; Mark 14:23). In the same way, we need to remain close with God, praying for ourselves, our students, and their families, and committing ourselves to serving the Lord and the students he has entrusted to our care and teaching. Said Watkins (1994), "The nature and activity of God is revealed in Jesus Christ as an expression of love, compassion, and sacrificial service" (p. 85). Incarnational teachers will similarly express these attributes of God, and recognizing the principle of humility and their own vulnerability, will also express the forgiving nature of God.

As Jesus, in his incarnation, reached out to and served others, so incarnational teachers will seek opportunities to serve, which ought to be a major reason for entering the field of special education in the first place. We must not be passive in our relationship with the students, nor should we force our help on them, but as God took the initiative in sending Jesus into the world, so we need to be aware of our students' needs and frustrations so that we can step in before a student melts down or blows up—yes, it happens, as I know from having worked with students who had emotional and behavioral disorders. And that is why I quote Watkins (1994) from experience: "It is our Christian responsibility to make our helping presence available in such a way that the person can receive it and use it" (p. 100).

According to John 3:16, Jesus is the embodiment of God's love. For us to become like Jesus means that love for others must be an identifying characteristic of our lives. This is clear from Jesus's example of loving others (even to the point of personal sacrifice) and from his teaching (John 13:34–35; Luke 10:25–37, as well as the teaching of other New Testament writers (Galatians 6:1–2; James 1:27; Hebrews 13:6; 1 John 3:14–17). As Christians involved in special education our focus is obviously on people who are disabled. To be "incarnate" with them does not require that we become disabled (though simulations of disability in our ongoing training can help us gain at least a modicum of understanding of how persons with disabilities experience life). But we do have to come alongside them, accept them, love them, and serve them rather than remaining distant and fearful. Just as Jesus was sent to be with and live among the people, spending much of his time interacting with those oppressed or discriminated against by the Jewish society, so we reach out to and interact with students whose disabilities have often resulted in being pushed aside by the educational system. As Jesus broke down barriers through his ministry, we must be willing to dismantle barriers that prevent individuals who are disabled from experiencing God's love, receiving an appropriate education, and being accorded the same respect and valuation as students without disabilities, and to challenge schools and even whole societies to recognize the humanity and the needs of *all* peoples. And we must encourage others to do the same. As Christians, we have not been called to leave the world but sent to the world—to be among the people to whom God calls us to minister.

Jesus's life and works become a model for us in our own ministry (Browne, 1997). Being Christ is not role-playing; it is not a face we put on, or a facade like the cathedrals we build. Being Christ is a reality to which we have been called and commissioned, so that we may continue his ministry of bringing release and liberation, in this case from bondage or discriminatory attitudes and actions that prevent students with disabilities from receiving an appropriate education and reaching their God-given potential. Just as God's prophets did in the past, we must address social, institutionalized sin that keeps people—disabled and non-disabled—in bondage: poverty, prostitution, disease, prejudice, and all forms of injustice. Like the prophets and like Christ himself, we speak for those who cannot speak for themselves (cf. Proverbs 31:8–9).

We have already spoken of how Jesus used Luke 4:18–19 to characterize his mission as one of bringing hope to those without hope and freedom to those in bondage; a time of restoration, renewal, and reconciliation with God and one's fellow man. Before returning to the Father, Jesus authorized his disciples to engage in that same mission (Matthew 28:1–20), a mission in which we are charged with doing our part in creating a God-centered community that offers salvation, health, physical care, nurturing, economic support, reconciliation, restoration—in short, biblical *shalom*.

Understanding special education as incarnational ministry allows us to be Christ in a very practical way as we bring these things to students who are affected by disability. Living incarnationally is to live in a consciously Christian manner, "manifesting the living spirit and teachings of Christ in [our] lives, in [our] communities, and in [our] workplace" (Miller, 2009, p. 72). Through Jesus, God's love was not distant, but was brought close in a personal way. In the same way, approaching special education as incarnational ministry brings tangible expression of God's love to the students we serve. Incarnational teaching means practicing righteousness, justice, mercy, and love as reflections of God's nature and in obedience to His call (Watkins, 1993). In other words, special education as incarnational ministry embodies (incarnates) God's love: "As long as the social minister is in the world, he or she is the incarnation of God's character, which is best described as unselfish, self-giving, enduring, and aggressive love" (Watkins, p. 58).

Benner (1988) asserted that Christian spirituality has its roots in a commitment to Jesus and a transformational approach to life that is demonstrated by "sharing of the goodness of God's love with others and in care for his creation" (p. 105). This moves us out of our comfort zone and into the world where suffering and injustice are the experience of many. It motivates us to *incarnate* the message of hope, acceptance, reconciliation, and justice in our work with the poor, the marginalized, and the disabled, and to seek to ameliorate physical and attitudinal conditions within the school and society at large that restrict the development and integration of students with disabilities.

## Redemptive Teaching

Nouwen (2003) believed that ministry and spirituality cannot be separated. He suggested that too much attention has been given to the *content* of teaching while neglecting the teaching *relationship*, which he saw as most important in the ministry of teaching. In the world of special education, we might similarly ask whether the mechanical and legal aspects of special education (e.g., meetings and paperwork) have taken priority over the teacher-student relationship and perhaps the relationship *between* students, especially in inclusive classrooms.

Nouwen spoke of a redemptive form of teaching that centers more directly on the teacher-student relationship (2003, pp. 18–20). "Redemptive form of teaching" means that each partner in the teacher-student relationship learns from the other, thus enabling both to grow as *persons*, not just grow in knowledge. This is particularly important in teaching students with special educational needs who may have developed a negative self-image because of academic or relational difficulties and frustrations, or from the adverse response of other students, their teachers, or even their parents. Some students with disabilities may see themselves as a disappointment to their parents, or as creating a burden or an embarrassment to their family.

A redemptive teacher-student relationship requires that teachers believe in the potential of their students, be available to them, and cultivate mutual trust and confidence between the students and themselves. As part of this redemptive process, special education teachers actively seek to promote in the classroom a community of acceptance, respect, and caring (see the discussion of hospitable classrooms in chapter eight). There must be an openness on the part of the teacher to learning from their interactions with the students—learning about the students, their needs, their responsiveness to the intervention or instruction; and through theological reflection, learning about oneself, humanity, and God.

## For Continued Reflection

In line with what we have said about servant-leadership, Dahlstrom (2011) pointed out that "living outwardly" has always been a critical element of Jesus's vision of following him. Being a disciple means trusting in God's active involvement in our daily lives, in submission and dependence. From this place of security, "we're invited to live outwardly, finding creative ways to spill hope into the world" (Dahlstrom, p. 15).

What does it mean for a special education teacher to *embody hope?* How do we "spill hope" in the lives of our students? How do reconciliation, authenticity, vulnerability, and service play out in our lives and in our teaching? In Matthew 25, Jesus taught about the final judgment and told of God's separating the "sheep" from the "goats." To the sheep, the king will say,

> Come, you who are blessed by my Father, inherit the kingdom prepared for you from the foundation of the world. For I was hungry and you gave me food, I was thirsty and you gave me drink, I was a stranger and you welcomed me, I was naked and you clothed me, I was sick and you visited me, I was in prison and you came to me. (Matthew 25:34–36)

When questioned by the sheep about when they had done these things, the king answered "Truly, I say to you, as you did it to one of the least of these my brothers, you did it to me" (Matthew 25:40). How does being a special educator tie in with these words of Jesus? What does our career in special education do for "the least of these"?

Christian teachers, as a form of caregiver, become advocates of God's presence as they create a "healing" community in the classroom by extending grace in practical ways to their students. This is possible because the Spirit of God indwells believers, who are the temple of the living God (Anderson, 2001; cf. John 14:18–23; 1 Corinthians 3:16, 6:19; 2 Corinthians 6:16; Colossians 1:27).

Nouwen (1974) suggested that the persons who have meant the most to us—those who have had the greatest influence on who we have become—are not those noted for giving advice or solutions to our problems, but those who chose to share our pain or bind up our wounds like the Samaritan in Jesus's parable (Luke 10:25–37). The friend who cares is the one who is not ashamed or afraid of our weakness, nor of his or her own powerlessness. Caring as Jesus cared involved reaching out to people at their level, coming alongside, being present to them and entering into their experience as best we are able. The legal, mechanical aspects of special education often seem overwhelming and time-demanding. This can be dangerous to the life of the special education teacher and can have a negative impact on the students themselves (it is not uncommon for special education teachers to complain that more of their time is spent on paperwork than in teaching the children). To counter this, Nouwen suggested that we look at teaching as a form of hospitality. Doing so "might free it from some of its unreal heaviness and bring some of its exhilarating moments back into perspective" (Nouwen, 1975, p. 89). We will return to the biblical concept of hospitality as an informant of special education, especially in inclusive classrooms, in chapter eight.

# CHAPTER FIVE

# Special Education as Spiritual Warfare

This chapter reflects on a theology of exceptionalities and the hermeneutics of special education, and develops the notion that there is an aspect of special education that can be understood as spiritual warfare. The main thesis is that providing access to an appropriate and the least restrictive education possible for people with disabilities involves "demolishing strongholds" (2 Corinthians 10:4)—that is, removing barriers of ignorance, prejudice, stereotype, cultural mythology, and misconceptions about disability and the personal worth of individuals who have disabilities. The discussion is situated within the context of Nicholas Wolterstorff's work on teaching for shalom (2002, 2004). After briefly defining the biblical concept of shalom and its relationship to education, we will examine the Christian's involvement in spiritual warfare. I will then address special education as an aspect of spiritual warfare and draw implications for inclusive programs and practices that

"Special Education as Spiritual Warfare," originally published in the *International Christian Community for Teacher Education Journal*, 2(1), 2006. http://icctejournal.org/issues/v2i1/v2i1 anderson/ Reprinted by permission. The article is based on a paper presented at The Stapleford Conference, The Hayes Christian Conference Centre, Swanick, Derbyshire, England; January 6–8, 2006.

promote reconciliation and recognition of interdependence, thereby encouraging shalom in the educational community.

## Background: Teaching for Shalom

The Stapleford Centre's 2006 Annual Theory of Education Conference in the United Kingdom had as its theme "Teaching for Shalom," in response to the writings of Nicholas Wolterstorff (2002, 2004) who posited shalom as the goal of Christian education. The Hebrew word *shalom*, often narrowly understood to mean "peace" in the sense of absence of conflict, is a very rich biblical concept descriptive of completeness or wholeness—a well-being characterized by right—or harmonious—relationships with God, oneself, others, and all of creation (cf. Conn & Ortiz, 2001; Schaefer, 1996; Wolterstorff, 2002, 2004). Shalom reflects the wholeness and togetherness that God intended (Graham, 2003). The significance of the biblical term is heightened in the psalms and prophetic writings of the Old Testament, where shalom expresses "the fulfillment that comes to human beings when they experience God's presence" (Richards, 1991, p. 479). The New Testament equivalent of shalom is the Greek word *eirene,* which carries a similar richness of meaning, especially connoting restoration and relationship as barriers that separate us from God and from each other and that are replaced with unity in and through Christ (cf. Ephesians 2:14–17; 1 Corinthians 14:33; Colossians 3:12–15).

Whether or not we agree that shalom provides an adequate foundation or goal of education that is Christian, we can probably all agree with Harro Van Brummelen's (2002) assertion that schools ought to be about nurturing shalom: "the biblical peace, justice, and righteousness that heals and restores broken relations with God, with other humans, with self, with other creatures, and with nature" (p. 62). He continued:

> To experience shalom, schools seek to replace abuse, racism, sexism, and bullying with love and justice. They honor all students and teachers for their gifts and roles. They replace selfishness and faith in the autonomy of the individual with self-sacrifice, humility, and servanthood. (p. 62)

To Van Brummelen's list of what needs to be replaced, we need to add handicapism—"the assumptions and practices that promote the unequal treatment of people because of apparent or assumed physical, mental, or behavioral differences" (Smart, 2001, pp. 144–145). This has led to disabled persons being devalued and segregated, and often to an attitude of social benevolence in which those who are temporarily able-bodied view the disabled as objects of pity rather than individuals to be respected.

We live in times when shalom is missing from our lives, families, nations, the world as a whole—even from many churches. Many look to education for the answer to the problems of living in the 21st century. Christians, however, are quick to say that answers—and shalom—can only come through Christ, making Christ-centered education crucial, and making it essential that educators who are Christian act as peacemakers (Matthew 5:9) to promote shalom in the individual classroom and throughout the school community—in the lives of the administrators, board members, teachers, staff, students, and their collective families.

## Spiritual Warfare

Understanding spiritual warfare is necessary before we can explore its connection with special education. Although Christians acknowledge that sin is the reason for the absence of shalom, many evangelical Christians, especially in Western culture, focus more prominently on the individual, and the need for each person to "get right with God" through confession and repentance. Without denying the need for accepting Christ into one's life, to focus solely on an individual's personal salvation causes us to lose sight of the spiritual conflict that continues to exist in the world. While we may recognize that some problems in our individual lives may be attributable to Satan ("the devil made me do it"), many do not understand the reality of spiritual conflict nor appreciate the Christian's role in that battle.

To speak of spiritual warfare conjures up for many Western Christians ideas of demonization and exorcism. In fact, these are but a small part of the cosmic conflict between God and satanic forces that has filled history since Satan was cast out of heaven (Isaiah 14:12–15). Tony Evans (1998) defined spiritual warfare as "that conflict being waged in the invisible, spiritual realm that is being manifest in the visible, physical realm" (p. 18). He explained that although spiritual warfare is the battle between angelic and demonic forces, that battle affects all of us. Evans described the impact of spiritual warfare as something seen and felt in individual lives, families, culture, and even churches. While it is important that we avoid "spiritualistic reductionism" (Chan, 1998), which would suggest a demonic explanation behind every problem, it is equally important that Christians maintain an awareness that, as followers of Jesus, we are caught up in this spiritual battle.

Satan's basic warfare strategy is deception. This is seen in his interaction with Eve in the Garden of Eden: "Did God say ...? Did

God *really* say …?" Through his deception, Satan is able to confuse our thinking and lead us to question—in the case of Eve, to question God's motivation: "'You will not surely die,' the serpent said to the woman. 'For God knows that when you eat of it your eyes will be opened, and you will be like God, knowing good and evil'" (Genesis 3:4–5, NIV). Then Eve "saw that the fruit of the tree was good for food and pleasing to the eye, and also desirable for gaining wisdom" (Genesis 3:6, NIV).

In Ephesians 6:11, Paul said that the devil uses "schemes" to deceive us. The Greek word is *methodeia,* literally meaning "traveling over"—one gets the image of trampling upon something with the intent to damage or destroy. The word connotes travesty or treachery; purpose behind the devil's actions. Paul warns that we must not allow Satan to outwit us, since "we are not unaware of his schemes" (2 Corinthians 2:11, NIV). Here Paul uses a different Greek word, *noema,* variously translated as schemes, devices, or thoughts, clearly conveying motivation or intentionality in Satan's actions.

Satan operates today in essentially the same fashion as he did with Eve: twisting God's words to confuse or delude, questioning the meaning of, or motivation behind God's words, getting us to focus on what we do not have or to ask the often unanswerable question "why?" Satan does not hold to the truth, we are told, for there is no truth in him: "When he lies, he speaks his native language, for he is a liar and the father of lies" (John 8:44, NIV). We learn from the Bible that Satan is a master of deception, out to deceive the entire world (Revelation 12:9). Indeed, we are told that "the whole world lies in the power of the evil one" (1 John 5:19). The counterfeit views of truth that Satan encourages include atheism, relativism, materialism, pantheism, animism, scientific-rationalism, humanism, and individualism. Following the lie, people determine their own self-image, their own meaning, their own value—often at the expense of others, leading to racism, ethnocentrism, "superior-ism," and handicapism wherein they also assign meaning and value (or the lack thereof) to others.

Jesus asserted that the thief comes to steal, kill, and destroy (John 10:10). Satan, the consummate thief, seeks to destroy the perfection that God created—to keep things in a chaotic state, like the "without form and void" of Genesis 1:2, words that refer to a wasteland, worthless confusion, emptiness, or indistinguishable ruin. Satan seeks to destroy God's image by "stealing" our mind and body, to kill our spirit and soul, to hold us captive unto himself as part of a rival kingdom he seeks to establish. Satan seeks to kill or destroy our spirit, our hope, or any semblance of shalom (spiritual or otherwise) we enjoy.

It is in this light that Jesus announced the purpose of his ministry in Luke 4: "The Spirit of the Lord is on me, because he has anointed me to preach good news to the poor. He has sent me to proclaim freedom for the prisoners and recovery of sight for the blind, to release the oppressed, to proclaim the year of the Lord's favor" (vv. 18–19, NIV).

Writing extensively about the cosmic warfare motif found in the Bible, Greg Boyd (1997) pointed out that nearly everything that we read in the New Testament about Jesus and the early church revolves around "the central conviction that the world is caught in the crossfire of a cosmic battle between the Lord and his angelic army and Satan and his demonic army" (p. 72). Ephesians 6:10–20, perhaps the most well-known passage regarding our struggle against the devil's schemes, is understood by many as primarily defensive: donning God's armor in order to stand against Satan's attacks.

But I believe our commission also involves offensive action: Spiritual warfare is something we are to be actively engaged in, reclaiming in the name of Jesus territory that Satan has occupied, though in a uniquely Christian way. Paul said, "For though we live in the world, we do not wage war as the world does. The weapons we fight with are not the weapons of the world. On the contrary, they have divine power to demolish strongholds. We demolish arguments and every pretension that sets itself up against the knowledge of God, and we take captive every thought to make it obedient to Christ" (2 Corinthians 10:3–5, NIV).

The weapons we fight with are God's weapons: truth, righteousness, peace, faith, salvation, the Word of God, and prayer (Ephesians 6:14–18), all wielded with love and compassion in the name of Jesus Christ. These weapons, brandished through right doctrine and right living, have divine might; literally, they are "mighty through God." The power by which we wage this military conflict is not our own, but God's. And through it, we pull down—we destroy or extinguish—"strongholds" which the spiritual forces of evil have helped people to erect: castles or fortresses in which people have become entrenched, mindsets that hold people hostage believing that they are "hopelessly locked in a situation," powerless to change (Evans, 1998, p. 71). The strongholds to be demolished include thought patterns or ideas that cloud people's reasoning, leading some to believe themselves to be above God, or to lead a self-centered lifestyle, or to become entrenched in feelings of hopelessness. The most dangerous strongholds are "those which are so hidden in our thinking patterns that we do not recognize them nor identify them as evil" (Frangipane, 1989, p. 32). Many of these develop as a result of information and experiences of everyday life, the conclusions we draw from them, or the interpretation that we and others assign to them. Ephesians 2:1–3 describes unregenerate life as "following the ways of this world and of the ruler of the kingdom of the air" and "gratifying the cravings of our sinful nature and following its desires and thoughts" (NIV)—or in the words of Chan (1998), the world (sin around us), the devil (sin beyond us), and the flesh (sin within us). Francis Frangipane (1989) simply identified the strongholds that keep people captive as "the lies the devil has sown into our thought processes which, as we accepted and believed them, became reality to us" (p. 100), leading people to define reality from their own perspective and their own "truth," rather than God's. Demolishing and removing these old ways of thinking amounts to pulling down strongholds.

## Special Education as Spiritual Warfare

How does this relate to special education? Satan's greatest lie is that God does not care. He attacks God's love, justice, caring, compassion, and integrity—just as he did when speaking with Eve. He encourages the mythological and superstitious thinking about disability and disabled persons that is common among people in developing nations, and often lies beneath the surface in the thinking of people in more advanced nations. He convinces people that weakness is just "the way things are" or that disability must be the result of a curse or one's sin or the sin of one's parents. Or he causes people to view those with disabilities as insignificant, less than human, people who can be discarded, thrown away. He even convinces disabled persons to see themselves this way, especially in cultures that overly emphasize strength, ability, achievement, beauty, and youth.

Satan would rather our focus remain on the *dis*-ability, the limitations caused by the handicapping condition, or that which the individual cannot do or do well. This keeps individuals with the disability bound in negativity, both in their own self-understanding and in society's view of them as individuals in need of pity. Satan stands against Christ; he is "anti-love, anti-forgiveness, anti-reconciliation" (Frangipane, 1989). He is anti-shalom. His desire is that humankind wallows in individualism, competitiveness, and separation; trapped in feelings of insignificance, weakness, envy, or depression. Satan wants us to remain captive in his lies and deception. But in Jesus there is light and truth, life and freedom. His focus is on what God desires: community, interdependence, relationship, and connectedness—shalom, with God, ourselves, and others.

Efforts to promote disability awareness and ministry in churches and to provide access to an appropriate education for people with disabilities is engaging in spiritual warfare, with the goal of freeing the captives and releasing the oppressed. Jesus said in Mark 3:27, "no one can enter a strong man's house and carry off his possessions unless he first ties up the strong man" (NIV). With even greater emphasis, Jesus stated in Luke 11:21–22, "When a strong man, fully armed, guards his own house, his possessions are safe. But when someone stronger attacks and overpowers him, he takes away the armor in which the man trusted and divides up the spoils" (NIV). Jesus has entered the strong man's (Satan's) house and has overpowered and bound him. Christian special educators are now among those commissioned by the Lord to plunder the strong man's possessions. Ours is a rescue mission authorized by Jesus (Matthew 28:18–20). But to see that rescue mission as simply "saving souls" reflects a limited view of Jesus's mission and the task with which his followers are charged: to do our part to create a God-centered community that offers salvation, health, physical care, nurturing, economic support, reconciliation, restoration—in short, shalom.

Redemption and reconciliation are among Satan's worst fears. He seeks to frustrate God's work, to prevent salvation from occurring, to make believers ineffective—all with the goal of keeping people in bondage. Jesus came to destroy the work of the devil (1 John 3:8). Those who seek to bring about redemption and reconciliation, who play a role in God's restoration of all things to that which he originally intended, are Satan's enemies. As God has sent Jesus, so he sends us (John 20:21): with the same purpose as stated in the Luke 4 passage referred to above. Our mission, as individual Christians and as a body of believers, is to further the work of restoration that Jesus began and has authorized and empowered us to do (Matthew 28:18–20; Acts 1:8). As Christian special educators, we break down the walls that separate people from Christ, from one another, from society, from becoming "whole" through Christ. We seek to restore people whom society and even families have cast aside. We seek to bring shalom—wholeness and well-being, healing in the biblical sense that brings reconciliation with God, with others, and with one's self. We work with people who have been dispossessed of the truth as to who they are, and may have become convinced that they are worthless or that God is either powerless to help or does not care about them. In our work with disabled children and youth, with their families, with their peers in the classroom, and with our colleagues in education our goal is to promote shalom.

Even if done only for humanitarian reasons, special education still has elements of spiritual warfare in that it challenges the "darkness" of societal ignorance and prejudice that keeps disabled individuals in bondage to the limited views—of others and of themselves—as to who they are and what they may become. But as Christian special educators, we do not work solely from a humanistic or social agenda. Rather, we do what we do because of the conviction that people with disabilities are full human beings created in the image of God and loved by God just as are those who are temporarily able-bodied. Our calling to be special educators is based on biblical teaching regarding the image of God, sin, love, reconciliation, and relationships. These teachings help us to understand human needs and behavior, and guide us in structuring classrooms that can promote among students—disabled and non-disabled—a feeling of being valued, safe, connected, and cared for (Anderson, 2005).

## Implications for Practice

Understanding special education as spiritual warfare does not imply that our approach to children and youth who have disabilities should be characterized by prayer for divine healing or casting out demons. Nor does this view necessarily open doors to new approaches or strategies for teaching. But viewing the work of the special educator within the framework of spiritual warfare contributes to a hermeneutic of special education and a theology of exceptionality. It places special education firmly within the realm of Christian ministry, even if done in a secular school where direct presentation of the gospel message is prohibited. The integration of faith and practice, and a biblical rationale for certain practices—inclusion, for example—become clearer. The classroom is recognized as a battlefield where we seek to demolish "strongholds" of ignorance, intolerance, and inaccurate and demeaning stereotypes related to disability and disabled persons. These attitudinal barriers can be more difficult to eliminate than architectural impediments to independence and access for people with disabilities. Such strongholds can hold a person who is disabled in deeper bondage than the crippling effect of severe cerebral palsy or spinal cord injury, and necessitate efforts on the part of the Christian special educator to help the individual reconfigure his or her self-understanding as fully human and as having infinite worth as one who is the image of the Creator, loved and redeemed by Jesus, regardless of being disabled. I will briefly highlight three implications of this view of special education: peacemaking, reconciliation, and interdependence. The interrelatedness of the three should be readily apparent.

## Peacemaking

Jillian Lederhouse (1999) posited that the opposite of peace is not war, but fear. To become a peacemaker, therefore, teachers must create a classroom and school community in which the child's experience is one of safety and security. Children and youth with disabilities may face many fears: Will I be accepted or teased? How will I be viewed by the teacher and my peers? Will I be able to succeed, academically and socially? Will I be able to maintain some degree of control in this situation? Will I be embarrassed or humiliated by my teacher, my peers, or my disability? Can I keep my disability hidden, thus protecting what little self-worth I feel?

To some extent, we all—disabled or temporarily able-bodied—have experienced similar feelings in our own schooling; perhaps still, every time we enter a new situation. But for students with a clearly visible disabling condition, how they are seen and treated by their non-disabled peers and teachers, and how they perceive themselves in the classroom, can lead to fear-filled days. To promote shalom, the teachers must structure the classroom in a way that it neither reflects nor endorses a culture of individualism and thus fostering a competitive spirit that can disrupt shalom. Instead, they must promote a culture of community, which fosters a sense of belonging, a major part of which is shalom.

## Reconciliation

Clifford DeYoung (1997), speaking within the context of racial relationships, suggested three elements to the meaning of reconciliation: (a) being put into friendship with God and each other, (b) radical change and transformation of a relationship, and (c) restoration of harmony. This clearly relates to shalom as defined in this paper. Elsewhere, I have explored the theme of special education as reconciliation (Anderson, 2003, included as chapter six in this book). I will not reproduce that discussion here, but only repeat the point that reconciliation is needed between the person with the disability and his or her family, peers, and society in general if the classroom (and the world) is to promote true inclusivity. Roadblocks that lead to marginalization of persons with disabilities in school and society (including churches) must be removed. "Through reconciliation and acceptance of all people within the classroom, comes restoration of right relationships. From this comes resurrection of the spirit, leading to hope in place of exclusion, and a feeling of being valued rather than rejected" (Anderson, 2003, p. 33).

## Interdependence

A theology of special education must include an emphasis on interdependence, which is necessary to the inclusive culture that we wish to establish in the classroom (Anderson, 2006a). A school culture based on a theology of interdependence builds on the concept of reconciliation in which disabled and non-disabled persons are brought together in true community. The basic idea is that we need one another, that we can learn from one another regardless of ability or disability, and that what each person does will have an affect on the lives of others, particularly within more close-knit communities such as families and classrooms.

> Interdependence honors the value of all individuals, not by what they do, but by who they are, recognizing that each and every person contributes to the community by being, not by doing. Interdependence acknowledges not only our dependence on God and one another, but also God's dependence on us to be agents of God's healing compassion in the world. (Black, 1996, p. 42)

Creating a classroom that models a theology of interdependence requires rethinking what it means to be a human being and the

119

concepts of normalcy, community, and belonging. Seeing students with disabilities as "outsiders" who need to be brought in underscores difference and raises thoughts of dependency, inadequacy, and unworthiness. A theology of interdependence helps us see difference as an ordinary ingredient of our world and allows us to abandon the idea that students must become "normal," or earn their way into the regular classroom.

When we speak of inclusion, we mean more than simply creating a space for the student who has a disability. Rather, we mean creating a community in which all the students feel valued, safe, connected, and cared for; in other words, a community of shalom.

## Conclusion

The logical implications of the biblical view espoused in this chapter lend strength to what we currently accept as best practice in special education. Such approaches as collaborative teaching, cooperative learning, differentiated instruction, and focusing on strengths and needs of all students take on new meaning within the context of spiritual warfare and shalom.

The thief comes only to steal and kill and destroy, but Jesus came that we may have life "to the full" (John 10:10, NIV). Christian special educators are Jesus's hands and feet and voice in bringing hope to the students they serve. Spiritual warfare is a lifestyle. The battles will be many, but the ultimate victory is assured. We go with confidence that the strong man has been bound as we plunder his house, demolish strongholds, and set the captives free in the power of Christ. Stanley Hauerwas and William Willimon (1989) held that Christians are to be "examples of God's determination to bring the world back into a right relation to its Creator—which finally is what peace is all about" (p. 66). This seems particularly applicable to Christian special educators.

Donovan Graham (2003) suggested several ways our behavior as redeemed image-bearers should make a difference in our world:

- *healing*—physical illness, psychological suffering, social isolation, etc.;
- *reconciliation*—seeking to remove enmity and promote harmony; renewal;
- *deliverance*—from things which hold power over people such as drugs, poverty, and various forms of oppression;
- *justice*—in the way people deal with one another; and
- *peace*—dwelling in harmony with God, others, self, and the world; the wholeness and togetherness which God intended.

"Our calling," he concluded, "is to demonstrate our citizenship in the kingdom of God while existing in a place where Satan is still at work, even though his defeat has already been assured" (Graham, 2003, p. 114).

Special education is spiritual warfare, the essence of which deals with the question "who will define reality?" (Frangipane, 1989). To make shalom present in the classroom—to bring shalom into the lives of the disabled students we teach—means challenging the world's concept of reality, in this case, the reality of disability and the ability of those who are disabled.

# CHAPTER SIX

# Special Education
# as Reconciliation

## Introduction

Reconciliation, restoration, resurrection, and hope are terms
that have familiar theological significance. Their use here relates to
that spiritual meaning, but they are applied in a specific manner to
working with persons with disabilities. This chapter seeks to show
their application to working with persons with disabilities and to frame
special education as a ministry of reconciliation. The immediate focus is
on issues related to special education services within a North American
context, particularly the United States, but the principles discussed have
broader application. The views expressed were originally presented at
a conference of Christian teacher educators, thus the emphasis is on
higher education. Nevertheless, the inclusive worldview encouraged
applies at all levels of education and in every arena of Christianity.

Let me restate my belief that special education is a ministry of
healing. We may not be able to bring physical healing to the disabled
as did Jesus, but we can help these individuals to grow within the

"Special education as reconciliation," Anderson, D. W., was originally published
in the *Journal of Education and Christian Belief,* 7(1), 23–35, 2003. Reprinted by
permission.

limitations of their bodily or intellectual capacity (perhaps even going beyond the world's perception of those limitations), and to accept their handicapping condition as another aspect of their personhood. Biblical teaching on living and loving; on relationships with God and with our fellow man; on sin, grace, and forgiveness, all have direct relevance to the special education profession (cf. Anderson, 1998; Anderson & Pudlas, 2000).

## Reconciliation and Special Education

We are familiar with the theological use of the term *reconciliation* as describing that which God has accomplished through the redemptive work of Christ—removal of the sin and enmity that separated humankind from God. As a result of God's work of reconciliation, those who are in Christ are a new creation—"the old has passed away; behold the new has come" (2 Corinthians 5:17). The term is commonly used in a context of conflict resolution, as when the animosity is removed and friendship restored between an estranged husband and wife or parent and child. Hill suggested three ways in which the ministry of reconciliation applies to the teaching process for the Christian:

(a) reconciliation of the student to society in the sense of helping students learn to challenge the culture with biblical truth, acknowledging the effects of sin on humankind and the need for all creation to be redeemed and set right with God;

(b) reconciling the "agents" of education, such as administration and staff, parents and teachers with one another; and

(c) reconciling the education of thought and feeling so that the student's "head and heart" are held in balance, each rightly attuned to God (Hill, 1976).

This aspect also relates to interpersonal relationships and their being characterized by acceptance and sensitivity. This latter understanding of reconciliation approaches the sense in which it is being used in this chapter.

In his analysis of reconciliation, DeYoung (1997) emphasized that reconciliation is relational—with God first and then with others. The element of personal relationship is evident in what DeYoung maintained are three main ideas that make up the meaning of reconciliation:

(a) being put into friendship with God and each other,

(b) radical change and transformation of a relationship, and

(c) restoration of harmony (p. 45).

There follow from this several ways in which the idea of reconciliation applies to special education. Persons with disabilities need, as do we all, to be reconciled to God. The message of reconciliation must be shared with all people, everywhere. DeYoung stressed how "the gospel of reconciliation reached out to the powerless in society by transforming lives among Samaritans, beggars, and others marginalized by society" (p. 56). An examination of the gospel record of Jesus's ministry clearly shows that persons with disability were frequently among those he ministered to (e.g., Matthew 9:1–8, 17:14–16; Mark 3:1–6, 7:32–35, 10:46–50; Luke 14:21, 17:11–17; John 5:1–18, 9:1–41). Christians today can do no less.

There may also be a need for the person with the disability to be reconciled with his or her family or peers, or with society in general, particularly in the case of persons with emotional or behavioral disorders. And there is a sense that persons with disabilities need to be reconciled to the fact that, though they have some disabling or handicapping condition, they are still whole as human beings, made in the image of God. Furthermore, some disabled individuals and/or their families may need to be reconciled with God, toward whom they may have much anger.

Focusing on the relational element brings to light another aspect of reconciliation: Reconciliation is needed also between the non-disabled and those with disabilities. This is not to imply that there is, necessarily, overt animosity between these two groups. I mean only to emphasize the separation—the dividing wall that has been erected by society (and even by some efforts at special education). If inclusion is to work, if the classroom is to become a microcosm of an inclusive community, this type of reconciliation is needed. It is this facet of reconciliation that is the specific focus of this chapter.

Although many things have changed since the mid-1970s when, by federal mandate, public schools in the United States were required to provide a free and appropriate public education to students with special needs, pre-service training programs may still do less than an adequate job of preparing general education teachers to serve in inclusive classrooms. This may be the case because faculty in elementary and secondary education training programs may have gained their classroom experience before the integration of students with disabilities in regular classes became as commonplace as it is today. Thus, these faculty may have neither a knowledge base nor experience related to students with disabilities to draw from in teaching methodology courses. The result is a concern among general education teachers regarding the adequacy of their training to meet the needs of exceptional students, despite their being in general agreement with the concept of inclusion (Pudlas, 1999). Some state departments of education, Minnesota for example, have given grants to institutions of higher education to promote collaborative efforts between their regular education and special education faculty in the preparation of all teachers as a means of addressing this problem. During my years of preparing graduate students (already licensed teachers in regular education) to become special education teachers, many anecdotes have been shared with the author regarding the attitude of some long-time general education teachers, who still voice, albeit more quietly, some hesitance regarding the integration of students with special needs in their classrooms, and show reticence towards collaborating with their colleagues in special education. The reasons for this situation are varied, including legitimate matters such as lack of money for training or for classroom assistants, limited or non-existent administrative support, pressure to meet state-mandated standards, and lack of time for the requisite meetings and joint planning. Pudlas (1997) provides an informative discussion of these and other barriers, real or perceived, to inclusion.

But there may also be other, unvoiced reasons for the difficulties in providing an effective and truly inclusive education. Mirroring conditions that remain prominent in society, despite changes in the laws (e.g., Public Law 101–336, *The Americans with Disabilities Act,* a Civil Rights Law enacted in 1990), some classroom teachers continue to question inclusion of students with special needs. Some may still question the validity of public education for students with severe disabilities, suggesting that such individuals might be better served through medical or social-welfare agencies. Such questions may reflect limited knowledge about disabling conditions and/or non-exposure to individuals with disabilities. Legal challenges continue to be brought by schools or parents concerning specific needs of individual students with disabilities.

These court battles frequently have an issue of expense as the "bottom line." Several school districts in my state have faced difficultly passing school-bond referendums to increase their budget. Though the issues involved are many and complex, concerns are still sometimes heard about the added expense of special education in these funding debates. Sometimes these concerns are raised by the school community; other times, members of the school board cite these costs as a rationale for the increased spending needs, thereby casting a negative shadow on disabilities; and sometimes, members of the press focus on these costs in a way that may raise negativity toward special education, and potentially toward the disabled.

Many teachers, administrators, and school boards operate from "the scarcity paradigm" (Webb-Mitchell, 1994). When applied to persons with disabilities, the scarcity paradigm causes one to question the wisdom of spending time and money on people with severe disabilities when the effort and resources might better be used in trying to solve "real" problems faced by society. The assumption is that valued resources are neither renewable nor expendable; they are limited, or scarce, and need to be used cautiously and in a way that will bring wide benefit. Such a view frames persons with disabilities negatively, suggesting that they create a drain on already limited time, money, staff, and resources, thereby inhibiting the advancement of the more able students. Though not always verbalized, questions are asked as to the value in serving those with disabilities, particularly those with severe impairments. Such questions may reveal underlying doubts as to the value, not only of working with the disabled, but the worth of those individuals themselves: 'Why spend scarce resources on persons who will never bring benefit to society in return?' Thus, a Darwinian-like attitude is fostered in which the "fittest" are favored to receive the benefit.

Mandates such as the *Individuals with Disabilities Education Act* (IDEA) in the United States and the view that inclusion is a way of serving students within the least restrictive environment are based on concerns of social justice and humanitarianism. These arguments take on greater significance when viewed from a biblical perspective. Including the excluded—reaching out to those ignored or pushed away by society—was a characteristic of Jesus's ministry and ought to be a hallmark of Christian educators and churches. Christian churches and Christian teacher training programs must seek to encourage and model an inclusive worldview in which individuals with disabilities are recognized as having equal value as bearers of God's image. Hopefully, graduates of these programs will carry the inclusive worldview into the schools where they teach as part of their ministry of reconciliation.

While helping persons with disabilities develop physical, social-emotional, behavioral, and academic skills is an obvious goal of special education, these are, in the words of Henri Nouwen, "secondary to a life lived together in a community of love" (1988, p. 62). Instead of emphasizing in a negative way the differences of those who require special education, the uniqueness of all students must be respected. Creating an inclusive classroom necessitates recognition of the *abilities* and *gifts* all students bring to the classroom community.

## Reconciliation and Restoration

DeYoung (1997) described reconciliation as our greatest challenge and greatest hope. His focus was specifically on racial reconciliation and harmony, but his discussion is equally applicable to the relationship between persons with disabilities and the non-disabled. Three of the roadblocks to reconciliation that DeYoung identified are particularly relevant in the present discussion—isolation, injustice, and denial. These roadblocks create barriers that "negatively influence our ways of thinking and perceiving" and "affect our ability and willingness to engage in efforts that might lead to reconciliation" (p. 15).

DeYoung suggested that these roadblocks stem from an attitude of superiority. Traditional special education has, perhaps unintentionally, fostered such an attitude because it has been built on a deficit model. Emphasis has been negative, focusing on the differences of those with disabilities, usually described as weakness, limitation, abnormality, dysfunction, handicap, or by some other pejorative term. The 1997 amendments to IDEA encouraged a strength-based, rather than deficit-based, approach to assessment and program planning. Nonetheless, even among those who advocate for these students, an aura of weakness or limitation clouds how they are viewed. Despite the paradigm shift from charity and exclusion to entitlements and inclusion (Pudlas, 1995), persons with handicapping conditions are often seen as deviant, problematic, and in competition for the limited resources available in the schools and society. The implication that these individuals are inferior and less worthy results in their continued marginalization.

## Isolation

Early efforts toward special education tended to segregate those with disabilities from the "normal" population, placing them in residential programs, special day schools, or special self-contained classes. Although the purpose was, ostensibly, to provide care for and otherwise meet the needs of these individuals, the isolation also served to "protect" society. But segregating those with disabilities also isolates the non-disabled population, limiting or constricting their own development and perspective on humanity by their not being exposed to the full range of human ability. This creates that false sense of superiority described by DeYoung, which he appropriately perceived to be "a direct challenge to the position of God in the world and a form of self-idolatry In truth, only God is superior. The rest of us are neither inferior nor superior. We are equally created in the image of God" (1997, p. 18).

## Injustice

Social and legal movements to promote normalization—inclusion and providing services in the least restrictive environment—were critical of the isolation of persons with disabling conditions that resulted from early efforts at special education. Questions can still be raised as to the equity of educational programs and outcomes between non-disabled and disabled students. Litigation and legislation in the United States since the 1950s have strongly emphasized the injustice of certain practices, and the rights of individuals with disabilities to an appropriate education and reasonable accommodations in the workplace.

Sadly, we must acknowledge that efforts to promote social justice on behalf of persons with disabilities were not championed by the Christian church, despite the clear Scriptural declaration of God's concerns in this regard, and the extent to which Jesus's ministry embraced social "outcasts," including those with disabilities (e.g., Luke 14:15–24 in the Parable of the Great Banquet, 2 Samuel 9 in the story of David and Mephibosheth, Matthew 9:36 regarding Jesus's compassion for the harassed, helpless, and scattered; i.e., those marginalized by society, and Matthew 25:31–46, "the least of these my brothers"). Webb-Mitchell (1994) held that not only have few churches welcomed persons with disabilities to fellowship with them, but such persons have even been "disinvited." Few have acknowledged including persons with disabilities in the social and political community as a matter of justice essential to the gospel (Senior, 1995).

## Denial

In terms of attitudes toward persons with disabling conditions, denial takes different forms and becomes a significant barrier to reconciliation and inclusion. Perhaps the most blatant form of denial is the head-in-the-sand or look–the-other-way approaches where those with disabilities are simply ignored. The isolation of disabled individuals into special schools or classes, while promoted as a humanitarian effort, actually allowed the general population to disavow themselves of any connectedness or responsibility toward these individuals or their families. This tended to reinforce that false sense of superiority among temporarily able-bodied persons, leading to denial of the full humanity of those who are disabled. Focusing on the limitations of those with disabilities—on what they cannot do—is one-dimensional and tends to further their isolation and marginalization (Senior, 1995). There is often a presumption that people with disabilities need pity and charity, "creating a hierarchical relationship where it is the role of people without disabilities to 'help' those people. This denies mutuality and the human giftedness in all of us" (Mades, 2001, p. 12).

Henri Nouwen (1997) described his work at L'Arche Daybreak Community in Toronto with a young man named Adam. Although Adam had severe disabilities, Nouwen passionately portrayed him as a whole person but acknowledged that, to most people, Adam was seen simply as a person with a disability with little to give, a burden to his family, the community, and society at large. Nouwen lamented, "as long as he was seen that way, his truth was hidden" (p. 31).

Nouwen's account described his own reconciliation with Adam. He detailed how his initial fearfulness in working with Adam dissipated as he grew to know this young man, to the point where he recognized Adam as a human being, rather than as a disability:

> Adam's humanity was not diminished by his disabilities. Adam's humanity was a full humanity, in which the fullness of love became visible for me, and for others who came to know him.... We were friends, brothers, bonded in our hearts. Adam's love was pure and true. It was the same as the love that was mysteriously visible in Jesus, which healed everyone who touched him. (1997, pp. 50–51)

## Reconciliation, Re-Envisioning, and Community

The message of the gospel is meaningless without reconciliation. As Sanders asserted, "The ministry of reconciliation is our collective commitment to overcome the barriers that divide and alienate people from each other by the healing power of love and unity that flows from the Spirit of God" (1997, p. 92). Much has been done in our society to eliminate *architectural* barriers that hindered people with disabilities from participating in normal life activities. But *attitudinal* barriers are harder to remove. Said Grant: "As long as our primary perception of ourselves is as persons who can see, or hear, or walk, or think rationally over against those who cannot do these things, our sin of stereotyping and exclusion remains" (1998, p. 85).

For the classroom to be truly an inclusive community, any negative attitude toward disabilities and persons with disabilities needs to be removed, whether that attitude is the result of ignorance, stereotype, prejudice, or the unintended outcome of past efforts at special education. For this to occur, a biblical attitude toward disabilities and those with disabilities is needed, one which involves a re-envisioning of people with handicapping conditions. We must be clear on what it means to be human from a biblical perspective. We need to acknowledge that every human being is created in the image of God, irrespective of the ability or achievement of the individual.

> A human being is not a disabling condition. Instead one has a disabling condition, along with other God-given abilities, gifts, and talents that are vital for the common good of the community he or she is part of and has meaning in. All persons, regardless of what they can or cannot do, are reminded [in Scripture] that their worth is not based upon their actions but is found in being created by God. (Webb-Mitchell, 1993, p. 31)

Moltmann saw no difference between the non-disabled and those with disabilities: "Every human life has its limitations, vulnerabilities, and weaknesses. We are born needy, and we die helpless. So in truth there is no such thing as a life without disabilities" (1998, p. 110).

Reconciliation is at the core of community, but community does not mean uniformity. Each person is an individual, having been made in the image of God, but each uniquely designed, and gifted, and purposed. Jean Vanier (1992, p. 44), founder of L'Arche communities, concluded, "That is what community is all about—each person is seen as unique and has a gift to offer ... *we must learn to love difference to see it as a treasure and not a threat*" (emphasis mine).

Without reconciled attitudes, persons with disabilities are easily stripped of their humanity. But as Moltmann (1998) observed, those who "disable" (i.e., who label and separate those with handicapping conditions) also lose their humanity because they themselves act inhumanely. Thus, they need reconciliation; "to become a humane people, persons without disabilities must be liberated from their assumption that they are healthy and from their fear of persons with disabilities" (p. 112). In Moltmann's words, "the more persons with disabilities are pushed from public life, the less we know about them. And the less one knows about the lives of those with disabilities, the greater becomes the fear of them" (p. 113). Great strides have been made in the United States and Canada following the passage of disability-friendly laws, but there is still room for positive change. Promoting an inclusive classroom and society can help to resolve this situation.

With the breakdown of fear through increased knowledge and living in community with persons with disabilities, people will come to appreciate the gifts that disabled individuals have and are. Scripture tells us that God has given to everyone at least one spiritual gift, as well as innate talents (cf. Romans 12:6–8; 1 Corinthians 7:7; 1 Corinthians 12:7–11; Ephesians 4:8–13). There is no indication in Scripture that having a disability—even severe and multiple disabilities—precludes one from such giftedness. Most evangelical Christians in the United States are aware of the ministry that Joni Eareckson Tada has despite, or perhaps because of her physical disability, and most are aware of the creative and artistic talents she is able to use to the glory of the Lord. Many students with emotional or learning disabilities demonstrate artistic giftedness. Other individuals with severely disabling physical, sensory, or mental conditions have produced artistic products that have been featured in art galleries in North America and Europe.

But there is also the gift of the individual himself or herself, which may be given in quietude and powerlessness. Nouwen helped us to envision this as he detailed his relationship with Adam:

> My daily two hours with Adam were transforming me. In being present to him I was hearing an inner voice of love beyond all the activities of care. Those two hours were pure gift, a time of contemplation, during which we, together, were touching something of God. With Adam, I knew a sacred presence and I "saw" the face of God.
>
> While I tended to worry about what I did and how much I could produce, Adam was announcing to me that "being is more important than doing." While I was preoccupied with the way I was talked about or written about, Adam was quietly telling me that "God's love is more important than the praise of people." While I was concerned about my individual accomplishments, Adam was reminding me that "doing things together is more important that doing things alone." (1997, pp. 53, 56)

Moltmann asserted that persons with disabilities help the "supposedly not disabled" toward a more accurate understanding of humanness by forcing us "no longer to base our self-confidence on health and ability, but to seek it in trust in God" (1998, p. 114). In suggesting that we seek to discover positive aspects of disability, Moltmann offered what he called a "provocative and annoying thesis," that every disability is also a gift:

It is a gift that we do not discover only because we are so focused on what a person is missing, what he has been deprived of. But if we were to free ourselves for a moment from the value standards of our own lives, then we would be able to understand the peculiar worth of the other life and its importance to us. Everyone affected might ask herself: What importance does the person with disabilities have for me and my life? In so doing, she would quickly discover the giftedness of that person with disabilities. (1998, p. 120)

Simply in receiving our help, even people with the most severe disabilities are simultaneously "giving grace to the giver" (Betenbaugh & Procter-Smith, 1998, p. 285), a realization that came to Nouwen through his living and working with Adam. Browne (1997) quoted from the *Pastoral Statement of U.S. Catholic Bishops on People with Disabilities*, written in 1978:

> When we think of persons with disabilities in relation to ministry, we tend automatically to think of doing something for them. We do not reflect that they can do something for us and with us.... Persons with disabilities can ... teach the able-bodied much about strength and Christian acceptance. (Browne, 1997, p. 98)

## Resurrection and Hope

Through reconciliation and acceptance of all people within the classroom comes restoration of right relationships. From this comes resurrection of the spirit, leading to hope in place of exclusion, and a feeling of being valued rather than rejected. Vanier said: "When we welcome people from this world of anguish, brokenness, and depression, and when they gradually discover that they are wanted and loved *as they are* and that they have a place, then we witness a transformation—I would even say 'resurrection'" (1992, p.15; emphasis added).

Accepting people as they are, with their disabilities but also with their gifts and their beauty, seeing them as human persons with great value, recognizing their potential for growth rather than seeing them as a conglomeration of limitations, joining with them in relationships of mutual teaching and learning—all can lead to true community. "To love someone is not first of all to do things for them, but to reveal to them their beauty and value, to say to them through our attitude: 'You are beautiful. You are important, I trust you, you can trust me'" (Vanier, p. 16).

People are more than things. Macquarrie asserted:

> [A]s long as there is life, there is possibility; we still cannot say what that person may become. Even when all natural possibilities have been reduced to the lowest conceivable level, when sight and thought and movement and decision are all in abeyance, for the Christian one has still not come to the point when that person can be written off as nothing. (Macquarrie, 1995, p. 39)

Resurrection can still occur; God can still "bring forth something new." I often remind my students as they work with children and youth with learning or emotional disorders that they are a continuation of the incarnation of Christ, and I suggest that meeting them might be the only time their students *see* Jesus. In his discussion of reconciliation, DeYoung (1997) reverses this thought by stating, "If we are honest with ourselves, we must admit that we sometimes fail to see Jesus in the person *asking* us for help" (p. 73; emphasis added). This is an attitude that needs to be cultivated in all Christian teachers as we promote reconciliation, restoration, resurrection, and hope.

## Conclusion

Washington and Kehrein (1996) affirmed reconciliation as the theological foundation for our faith, but cautioned that "the ministry of reconciliation can never be mere passive acceptance of a theological truth, but must include active participation" (p. 385). The ministry of reconciliation to which Christians have been called is not limited to evangelism (which emphasizes the reconciling work that God has already accomplished in Christ), but also challenges us to actively seek reconciliation of people across all barriers—racial, class, gender, and *ability*.

As Webb-Mitchell said, "God's healing presence, acceptance of what the person can and cannot do, acceptance of who 'I am,' because of whose we are, brings forth hope in the life of those who believe in God" (1994, p. 58). Christian educational programs must foster reconciliation between non-disabled and disabled persons as described herein in order to promote an inclusive worldview. Pudlas (1995) pointed to two risk areas related to inclusion: (a) the potential ineffectiveness of the general education teacher, and (b) the potential for disabled students to be rejected by their peers. Teacher-training programs can do much to directly address the first issue by stressing and modeling collaboration between regular and special education, and by helping their students develop the knowledge, skills, and disposition that supports inclusivity.

It is particularly important that programs that train teachers address the similarities, not just the differences, between non-disabled and disabled persons and design experiences for pre-service teachers that allow them to gain knowledge and facility in working with—including in their classroom communities—students with disabilities. Hopefully, these teachers will then be in a better position to influence the children and youth they teach so that the problem of peer rejection can be avoided.

There is an equal need for Christian colleges and universities to promote inclusive, reconciling attitudes among all their graduates. Those who prepare students for careers in business, communication, community development, medicine, psychology, social work, sociology, anthropology, and biblical and religious studies all need to model an inclusive worldview. Curricula and experiences in these areas should also be examined for how issues of disability are presented (if at all) and efforts made to acknowledge the personhood of those with disabilities, as well as the potential and real contributions of these persons to society. Jesus's focus on including the excluded must be that of all Christians.

CHAPTER SEVEN

# Inclusion and Interdependence: Students with Special Needs in the Regular Classroom

## Introduction

Hines and DeYoung (2000) described the human inclination to divide people into categories in a way that one's own group comes out on top as ghetto tendencies. This "ghettoizing" reveals a socially constructed stigma assigned to individuals who differ from those holding positions of power. I believe the term aptly depicts how schools and society have tended to view, and therefore treat, persons with disabilities. The result is a devaluing or discrediting of disabled individuals that has often led to limited opportunities for social interaction. Fear, ignorance, superstition, arrogance, and pride on the part of able-bodied persons have led to placing people with disabling conditions into a "ghetto"—if not by physically segregating those with disabilities, at least by mentally constructing an us-and-them distinction that discourages interaction. The creation of special schools

"Inclusion and Interdependence: Students with Special Needs in the Regular Classroom." Anderson, D. W., was originally published in the *Journal of Education and Christian Belief*, 10(1), 43–59, 2006. Reprinted by permission.

and classes for persons with disabilities, though promoted as an act of humanitarianism intended to serve and protect, may have reinforced this "ghetto" inadvertently by enabling general education teachers to disavow responsibility toward these individuals or their families.

Terminology used with regard to educating students with special educational needs has changed over time, from *mainstreaming* through *integration* to *inclusion.* Though each term slightly altered and broadened the concept, each retains an unintended bias. To speak of inclusion, for example, draws attention to the differences of those persons that led to their exclusion. Thus, an element of negativity may continue to influence how people with disabilities are perceived by others: they are not "one of us," but we must make efforts to include "them." To speak of inclusion may actually *devalue* the student—it may be just another way of emphasizing differences rather than truly bringing people together. Simply placing an individual with a disability in a regular classroom does not necessarily counter the ghettoization, especially if the inclusion is only surface-level; that is, though present *in* the classroom, the student may not be an integral part *of* the classroom.

Inclusive programming often seems to fall short of establishing "belongingness" in many classrooms. Saliers's (1998) observation regarding the presence of persons with disabilities in churches is applicable in the school context as well: the move from adopting an inclusive attitude to actually *becoming* a place of belonging necessitates a "theological and moral maturation" on the part of teachers and school leaders (p. 29). The moral side of this maturation has been the basis of arguments for providing a free, appropriate, public education for students with disabling conditions and for much of the related litigation that has occurred over the last several decades.

This chapter explores the theological basis for such arguments, emphasizing ideas of interdependence and community. Although I will allude to practices that are appropriate to creating and maintaining an inclusive classroom community, my concern here is not the how-to of inclusion. Rather, the focus is on the why-be-inclusive side of the discussion, as well as what is needed to establish an atmosphere of inclusivity.

Inclusion is currently regarded as a best practice and is supported by legal arguments. Arguments supporting inclusive schools and classrooms in the United States are generally based on the Fourteenth Amendment to the U.S. Constitution, which asserts that states cannot deprive citizens of life, liberty, or property without following proper legal procedures, or in any way deny them equal protection of the law. The U.S. Supreme Court, in *Goss v. Lopez* (419 U.S. 565 [19751), held that students have a constitutionally protected property interest in education.

Discussions regarding inclusion are usually cast within the framework of social justice and equal rights (cf. Schaffner & Buswell, 1996), using the same logic as prevailed in the Civil Rights movement that led to desegregation. My goal in this chapter is to move beyond these best-practice arguments and to provide a biblical and theological foundation for educational practices that promote inclusion and belongingness in the general education classroom. My thesis is that it may be the case that students with disabling conditions—particularly those that are more visible and significant—though *included* (present) in the classroom too often remain outsiders. Merely reaching out to include "them" is insufficient, as McCollum's analogy illustrates: "The fly caught in the spider web is included, but victimized" (1998, p. 184). Instead, the goal must be to incorporate the disabled fully into the body of the classroom.

*David W. Anderson, Ed.D.*

# Deconstructing Inclusion

Most reports from schools where some degree of inclusion has been implemented speak of academically oriented benefits to both students and teachers. Nevertheless, many general and special educators and administrators remain hesitant to adopt inclusion. A survey of 408 elementary school principals, for example, found only 1 in 5 to have positive attitudes toward inclusion; most were uncertain about the practice (Praisner, 2003). Agreement with inclusion came when the idea was presented in a generic manner, rather than in specific terms, and as a voluntary rather than a mandatory program.

Bruneau-Balderrama's (1997) brief review of the research highlighted several key problems: Many teachers felt that they had little input into placement decisions and that inclusion was forced upon them. Some expressed concerns having to do with class size, workload, and grading. General education teachers questioned whether they were adequately trained to work with students who had a disability. Some questioned their ability to attend equally to all students in the classroom (suggesting belief that the student with a disability will require too much attention, thereby causing non-disabled students to "suffer"). Moore and Keefe (2001) reported that elementary and secondary teachers who co-taught with special educators had concerns related to adequacy of planning time, degree of administrative support, availability of resources, and teacher willingness.

Pivik, McComas, and LaFlamme (2002) detailed the attitudinal barriers to inclusive education noted by students with disabilities and by their parents. Intentional attitudinal barriers included occurrences of isolation, physical bullying, and emotional bullying, which included name-calling and ridicule. Most disturbing to the students and their families were "condescending attitudes by teaching staff, and generally being treated differently from other students" (p. 102). Unintentional attitudinal barriers reported by the students and their families related to limited knowledge, understanding, and effort on the part of the teachers. Specific grievances included being given inappropriate work when teachers had failed to adapt the curriculum, being excluded from some classes without reason, and a lack of appreciation for either the limitations or the capabilities of the students. The study focused on students with physical impairments, but it is not unreasonable to assume similar concerns from students with other disabilities.

Though teachers' feelings may not be voiced publicly, it appears that some continue to harbor the idea that school, rather than being an entitlement, is a privilege to be earned by showing adequate achievement and by conforming to the "norm." Even special education programs in the past held to the idea that the development of skills was a prerequisite to inclusion (cf. Kunc, 1992). Any barrier that causes exclusion sends a subtle message of being unaccepted (or unacceptable), devalued. When faced with such a barrier once, initial resentment or disappointment can easily be set aside. When faced with these barriers on a daily basis, the message is more likely to be internalized.

Problems such as those described above suggest that attempts to create inclusive classrooms can result in the individual needs of the student with a disability being overlooked either intentionally, in the desire to treat everyone the same, or unintentionally, out of ignorance of disabilities and their impact on the student's functioning. Many teachers hold to an understanding of fairness based on the notion that "everyone gets the same thing," which can result in denial or disregard of diversity in order to promote uniformity. A more mature understanding of fairness is the idea that everyone gets what he or she needs (Hersch, Paolitto, & Reimer, 2005). This definition of fairness implies a shift from a principle-based ethic that stresses an abstract ideal of justice, to a value-based ethic of care, which stresses individual and community relationships (Murdick, Gartin, & Crabtree, 2002). At the lower level, fairness is simply equality (equalness or sameness); at the higher level, benevolence assumes a greater role, and consideration is given to the needs of others (perhaps in the spirit of Philippians 2:4).

The problem, as I see it, is this: Attempts to promote inclusion have brought physical access to a free and more appropriate education by opening doors to the regular classroom for many students with disabilities. But in some cases, this has merely removed a physical wall—the special education program has simply migrated from a separate classroom into the general education classroom where the special-needs teacher or a paraprofessional provides instruction to the student with a disability. This does not guarantee, however, that the "special" student is welcomed by the teacher or the other students as an equal—let alone valued—member of the classroom community. Acceptance into the room does not necessarily translate into solidarity with the community. To achieve that goal, re-envisioning the classroom is necessary. A theology of interdependence can lead to that end.

## Reconstructing Inclusion Around a Theology of Interdependence

Kathy Black (1996) spoke of a *theology of interdependence* when discussing the apparent conflict between our belief in a loving, compassionate God and the existence of disabilities. This idea provides useful insight into the culture or ethos Christian educators seek to establish, whether or not persons with disabilities are a part of their classroom. A school culture based on a theology of interdependence builds on concepts of reconciliation in which disabled and non-disabled persons are brought together in true community (cf. Anderson, 2003);

it is a school culture that actively seeks removal of the alienation created by *handicapism*.

Black (1996) reminded her readers that "we are all interdependent upon one another so that what we do affects the lives of others and the earth itself" (p. 34). This concept of interdependence runs counter to the ideas of independence and self-reliance that Western culture encourages. But the desire to "be our own person" must be tempered with scripturally based teaching regarding the interdependence of humankind. The Apostle Paul recounted our interdependence as members of the body of Christ in Romans 12 and 1 Corinthians 12, describing persons as having different functions but all belonging to one another. While Paul spoke of relationships within the church, the principle he espoused seems to capture the ideal desired in the inclusive classroom (indeed, *any* classroom), especially in Christian schools:

> [A]nd the parts that we think are less honorable we treat with special honor. And the parts that are unpresentable are treated with special modesty, while our presentable parts need no special treatment. But God has combined the members of the body and has given greater honor to the parts that lacked it, so that there should be no division in the body, but that its parts should have equal concern for each other. If one part suffers, every part suffers with it; if one part is honored, every part rejoices with it. (1 Corinthians 12:23–26, NIV)

My reference to this passage is not to be construed as assigning lesser honor or an unpresentable status to persons with disabilities. With Paul, I wish to emphasize mutual dependence and concern so that the needs of each part are met. The implied honor or respect due to each part applies to each individual, regardless of ability or disability. In Kathy Black's words,

> A theology of interdependence honors the value of all individuals, not by what they do, but by who they are, recognizing that each and every person contributes to the community by being, not by doing. Interdependence acknowledges not only our dependence on God and one another, but also God's dependence on us to be agents of God's healing compassion in the world. (1996, p. 42)

Interdependence as part of God's design is evident from the creation story. In Genesis 2:18 God says, "It is not good for the man to be alone. I will make a helper suitable for him" (NIV). That it was not good for man to be alone, and that God provided a companion perfectly suited to Adam, strongly suggests that the man and the woman each needed the other—not out of a dependency in which one is superior to the other, but as equals who are interdependent in a way that the two become one. According to Sailhamer (1994, p. 8) the word in Genesis 2:18 translated in the New International Version as "suitable helper" carries the idea of partnership. Interdependence, in this instance, brings completion, or wholeness.

Unity in diversity is seen in the New Testament description of the church: a community of believers from different national, ethnic, and socioeconomic backgrounds, yet one family through Jesus Christ. Paul's teaching about the variety of gifts within the church, which is yet still one interconnected and interdependent body, completes the image of unity in diversity. Paul teaches that each member of the body has received different gifts, but they are to be exercised within the oneness of the body: "So in Christ we who are many form one body, and each member belongs to all the others" (Romans 12:5, NIV); "to each one the manifestation of the Spirit is given for the common good" (1 Corinthians 12:7, NIV); "to prepare God's people for works of service, so that the body of Christ may be built up" (Ephesians 4:12, NIV). Our dependence upon one another is part of God's design, or as Petersen (1993) asserted, interdependence is "the core of the very definition of God's people" (p. 34).

## Humanness and Normalcy

Inclusion in the classroom built around a theology of interdependence challenges several aspects of our thinking, particularly our vision of humanness and normalcy, and of community and belonging. Saliers (1998), describing a spirituality of belonging, stated, "If 'inclusiveness' is to be more than a slogan, *our practice must lead to acknowledgment of* common *humanity in the image of God* and to the discovery of what it means to be 'present' to one another" (p. 29, emphasis added). Jean Vanier, founder of L'Arche communities, which serve persons with severe disabilities, echoed this thought:

> Until we realize that we belong to a common humanity,
> that we all need each other, that we can help each other,
> we will continue to hide behind feelings of elitism and
> superiority and behind the walls of prejudice, judgment,
> and disdain that those feelings engender. (1998, p. 82)

In the case of persons with obvious disabilities, the tendency is to focus first on the limitation rather than the giftedness of the person. Rarely, if ever, does one wonder what gifts may lie hidden beneath the exterior shell of limitation. For example, for someone unfamiliar with Joni Eareckson Tada, founder of Joni and Friends International Disability Center, the eyes would focus first on the wheelchair and the implied difficulties with mobility and independence. There is often an element of surprise upon discovering not only Joni's artistic talent and achievement but also her acceptance of her disability.

For classrooms and schools to be inclusive communities, negative attitudes toward disabilities and disabled persons must be removed, whether those attitudes are based on ignorance, stereotype, prejudice, or are an unintended result of special education practices. The term *special education* connotes teachers who have *special* training and skills enabling them to work with *special* students who differ from the majority in behavior or in cognitive, academic, or physical ability—all of which may reinforce negative feelings or even fear toward persons with disabilities. What is required is a re-envisioning of all persons, including those with disabilities, based on a scriptural understanding of what it means to be human and to be God's image-bearer; that is, recognition that bearing the image of God has nothing to do with whether one is able-bodied or disabled. And it requires a re-envisioning of the classroom based on a theology of interdependence.

Teachers must re-cognize (rethink) what normalcy means. Although the term *normal* is used in educational circles, what is often meant in reality is "average." For example, in identifying students with academic or cognitive disabilities, standardized assessment uses the concept of the normal curve. Identification is made based on the discrepancy between the student's measured performance or intellectual ability and the hypothetical average or norm (arbitrarily set at 100). Emphasis is on those students whose score differs significantly from the approximately 50% of the population who score in the average range (90 to 110), *average* being a mathematical term to describe the group in which a large proportion of people will score.

But to conceive of this group of average performers as the norm of society is quite different from saying their scores represent the average of the total population. To refer to this group as "normal" leads many to infer that anything outside this range is "abnormal." But the real world in which we live includes persons whose scores on these standardized instruments fall at either extreme. It can be argued, then, that a classroom containing only those scoring in the average range (90 to 110) is not "normal," because it does not reflect the real world where there are persons with profound intellectual disabilities and persons who are gifted. Dudley-Marling, professor of special education at Boston College, issued this caution:

> The naturalness of the normal distribution is open to question, however. Many (perhaps most) human behaviors do not distribute normally.... Most often, the normal distributions we have come to take as natural are a product of the tools we use to measure human behavior. Norm-referenced, standardized tests used to measure achievement and intelligence, for example, produce normal distributions because the developers insist that they must. (2001, p. 12)

As Dudley-Marling concluded, this concept of normality results in "the tendency to equate *normal* with *natural* and *abnormal* with *unnatural*" (p. 13, emphasis in original), thereby justifying discrimination (ghettoization).

My point is that the presence of diversity and difference in our world is typical (normal). Restricting a classroom to those who are of average ability, therefore, creates an artificial environment, though one that may facilitate ease of teaching. God did not create everyone the same: "Each of us is unrepeatable, a unique bearer and reflector of the glory of God" (Plantinga, 2002), with inherent strengths and weaknesses. Harrison (1995) said that, as we are all unique creatures of God, normality becomes a meaningless concept: "To talk of people being "normal" or deviating from the normal is not consistent with Christian teaching. It is to undermine the essential uniqueness of every individual" (p. 26.

Human pride causes us to elevate ourselves above people who display a significant weakness that society labels a disability. Focus then falls on the impairment rather than the potential. To help us see the person behind the disability, we need an "expanded vision of exemplars [that] would require serious reconsideration of people" (Patterson, 1998, p. 135). As quoted at some length in chapter six, Henri Nouwen's (1997) example in *Adam: God's Beloved* describes the beauty of the severely disabled young man with whom he worked and from whom he learned much about God and love and humanness.

For many, to speak of "students with special needs" signals dependency, inadequacy, and unworthiness and negates the reality that we all have individual needs. Rather than thinking of persons who have a disability as outsiders who need to be brought in, a theology of interdependence helps us to understand the different as ordinary. As Kunc (1992) aptly noted:

> When inclusive education is fully embraced, we abandon
> the idea that children will have to become "normal" in
> order to contribute to the world. Instead, we search for
> and nourish the gifts that are inherent in all people. We
> begin to look beyond typical ways of becoming valued

members of the community, and in doing so, begin to realize the achievable goal of providing all children with an authentic sense of belonging. (pp. 38-39)

## Community and Belonging

As was noted previously, the emphasis on inclusive education has brought access to the classroom but has not necessarily guaranteed that the student with a disability is welcomed as an equal member of the classroom family. Merely placing disabled students in a regular classroom environment is not the point: it is a means to an end. "*Inclusion* does not refer to a physical space; it refers to a condition or state of being. The concept of inclusion implies a sense of belonging and acceptance" (Volz, Brazil, & Ford, 2001, p. 24). Mittler (2000) agreed:

> Inclusion … is about changing schools to make them more responsive to the needs of all children. It is about helping all teachers to accept responsibility for the learning of all children in their school and preparing them to teach children who are currently excluded from their school, for whatever reason. (p. vii)

One contribution to the problem is the tendency to view disabled persons through the eyes of charity or pity. The inclination is to see the limitations caused by the disability and attribute that to the persons themselves. Rather than seeing *a person* who has a disability, many see a person who has (or is) *a need*. Indeed, many assume the disabled person's primary need is for our assistance, with no thought to the possibility that the disabled individual has something to offer those who are not disabled. Thus, even though that individual is included in the class, a psychological (spiritual) separation continues as non-disabled persons, perhaps unconsciously, see themselves as superior in some way to those with a disability. The non-disabled are the haves, the cans, the advantaged. Those with disabilities are the have-nots, the can'ts, the disadvantaged. We need to acknowledge with Sapon-Shevin (1999) that "all people need help. No one is really independent, although the myth of "making it alone" keeps many people from asking for and getting the help they need and deserve" (p. 87).

A theology of interdependence provides a foundation for reinventing education through its emphasis on community. Inclusive communities should be characterized by a recognition that differences in ability are natural, and by an encouragement of the gifts and talents of each individual, including those considered to have severely disabling conditions or disruptive behaviors. The idea of interdependence, though not specifically stated, is implied in the following assertion by noted proponents of inclusion:

> In supportive communities, everyone has responsibilities and plays a role in supporting others. Each individual is an important and worthwhile member of the community and contributes to the group. This involvement helps foster self-esteem, pride in accomplishments, mutual respect, and a sense of belonging among community members. *Such a community cannot occur if certain students are always the receivers of, and never the givers of, support.* (Stainback & Stainback, 1996, p. 195; emphasis added.)

What is typically considered an inclusive classroom may actually promote a sense of isolation, distress, or powerlessness (or at least distance, discomfort, and weakness) among disabled students, especially if these students are the recipients of "services" or "help" that, though well-meant, emphasize the limitations caused by the disability. Use of a buddy system or other mode of peer assistance, for example, may have the unwanted effect of underscoring the disability and creating a one-way relationship in which the student with a disability is seen only as one in need of assistance and the non-disabled student is seen as the helper (cf. Bishop, 1996).

Focusing on the needs of disabled students and the accommodations necessary for them to participate in ongoing instruction or classroom activity is a significant element of special education. Yet it still may carry the message that these students are defined by their disability. Certainly, it fails to acknowledge the gifts that these students have, bring to the classroom, and are. The thought that we might learn from them or gain from their presence in our classroom and our lives is overshadowed by the desire to take care of them, to protect them. Thus the inclusion that was intended to bring people together may instead highlight the separation or difference. As Black (1996) lamented, "All the basic institutions of our society often view persons with disabilities as *objects* to be dealt with rather than as *subjects* that have something to contribute" (p. 19; emphasis added).

"An overemphasis on the 'helper-helpee' relationship can easily skew the delicate balance of giving and receiving that is the precursor of true friendship" (Van der Klift & Kunc, 1994, p. 392). Recognizing the reciprocity implied in a theology of interdependence will help to counter this outcome and result in a new (or renewed) appreciation for the abilities and gifts of disabled persons. A classroom structured around a theology of interdependence would welcome and celebrate diversity and the contributions of each member of the community. A spirit of reciprocity would then surface where there is a mutual sense of both responsibility to and need of one another.

Promoting physical, social-emotional, behavioral, and academic development of students should be a concern of both special and general educators. But these goals remain, in the words of Nouwen (1998), "secondary to a life lived together in a community of love" (p. 62). Creating an inclusive classroom community requires acknowledgment of and proper regard for the abilities and gifts that every student brings to the classroom as well as recognizing that each individual, including those without disabilities, also has areas of weakness and need—more evident, perhaps, at certain times during the lifespan or in specific situations, but nonetheless real weaknesses and needs.

The ghettoizing referred to above has two sides: overly emphasizing perceived limitations of others and blindness about or disregard of one's own shortcomings. Community does not mean uniformity. Each member of the community is an individual—uniquely designed, gifted, and purposed by God, in whose image they are fashioned, but also possessing areas of vulnerability and relative deficiency. A caring community is one that "fosters mutual respect and support among staff, parents, and students," a community "in which we honestly believe that disabled children can benefit from friendships with non-disabled children" (Rogers, 1993, p. 5).

This definition has much that is commendable, but there is still an unintended negativity. The definition is unidirectional: The disabled student is assumed to benefit from friendships with non-disabled children, but nothing is said about mutuality of benefit. Though they do not always make their way into the professional literature, numerous anecdotes can be shared about the benefits received by non-disabled persons from friendship with persons having disabling conditions (cf. Smith, 2003).

Relationships and belonging thus become hallmarks of the type of community we seek to establish in our classrooms (and model in teacher-training through collaborative efforts of general and special educators). A theology of interdependence recognizes that we are not individually in charge of our own destinies, but each part of the community is important to the other (cf. 1 Corinthians 12:23–26). We could say that "community" refers not to a group but to a way of life—a situation in which interconnections are pervasive.

The need for schools to become communities in which all students feel valued, safe, connected, and cared for is described by Schaffner and Buswell (1996), who maintained that if "the element of community is overlooked or if its importance is underestimated, then students who present various kinds of diversity will continue to be disenfranchised and the school's desired outcomes for all students will continue to miss the mark" (p. 53). Students who feel disconnected from the classroom community (a lack of belonging) are less likely to reach their potential (cf. Kunc, 1992).

A culture of community runs counter to individualism, so prominent in Western society and schools, where competition is encouraged. Friendships tend to be linear—being friends with one person after another in a somewhat serial, disconnected fashion. In contrast, members of a true community not only occupy a common place (the classroom) but also share a common purpose. True community is one where there is a natural, emotional, and interdependent association among people. A contrived community, on the other hand, is characterized by associations that can be described as impersonal and alienated (Frazee, 2001, p. 200), associations in which change occurs frequently in order for the individual to secure what is perceived to be his or her immediate need. The first is what we would hope to find in our own family. The second is more characteristic of professional associations or even of the relationship between faculty from unrelated disciplines within the same university.

Imagine a classroom or school community where the need for a sense of belonging is met in the first way described above. Imagine the boost to one's self-esteem and personal identity as a kinship is felt with the others in that community. Imagine a classroom or school where relationships among disabled and non-disabled students develop into friendships as each comes to know and appreciate the other more fully, in contrast to the high level of reported loneliness among students with disabilities in inclusive settings (Pavri & Luftig, 2000).

An advocate for inclusive education, and a person with a disability, is quoted by Miles (2000) as asserting that "inclusion is about the intentional building of relationships where difference is welcomed and all benefit." Miles argued that diversity must be welcomed and relationships between disabled and non-disabled students consciously nurtured if there is to be meaningful change in the educational experience of marginalized students. "Belonging is … facilitated by valuing the unique contributions that each person makes to the community's well-being. Although each person's contribution may be somewhat different from those of the other members, all contributions are recognized, appreciated, and celebrated" (Walther-Thomas, 2000, p.7).

Sands, Kozleski, and French (2000) used the motto "Each Belongs" to describe schools where all students, disabled and non-disabled, belong, and to insist that everyone involved shares responsibility for meeting student needs. As part of this philosophy, they stressed every learner's right to be involved in school activities, acceptance and welcoming of all students, supporting student weaknesses while building upon strengths, and a spirit of togetherness "to meet the challenges of learning and living with one another" (p. 25). As Voltz,

Sims, Nelson, and Bivens (2005) pointed out, "Students should learn to value individual difference as a way for them to learn from one another and a way to make the world a more interesting place" (p. 17).

Recent educational legislation in the United States has made the phrase "No Child Left Behind" popular—or infamous, depending on one's response to it (US Department of Education, 2003). The phrase may be more appropriately used to mean that no child is excluded from the educational environment because of something external to his or her personhood, whether a matter of disability, gender, race or ethnicity, socioeconomic status, or other marginalizing factor. None of these makes that individual less than a human being, made in the image and likeness of the Creator. A theology of interdependence recognizes that each individual has both strengths and weaknesses and seeks to avoid the negativity that results from focusing attention only on limitations or differences. Strully and Strully (1996) asserted that "Inclusion means the process of making whole," and added, "Embracing differences rather than avoiding differences is what community is all about" (p. 149). In the biblical context, wholeness is integral to shalom, which Plantinga (2002) defined as "universal flourishing, wholeness, and delight—a rich state of affairs in which natural needs are satisfied and natural gifts fruitfully employed, all under the arch of God's love … in other words … the way things are supposed to be" (p. 15). This, coupled with Jesus's call for his disciples to be peacemakers, seems to have direct relevance to the type of community we wish to establish in our schools and classrooms.

## Implications of a Theology of Interdependence

What are the implications of a theology of interdependence for structuring classroom communities? How does this biblical principle inform educational practice? I believe there are several logical implications—not necessarily new ideas, but practices that can be supported by a theology of interdependence:

- collaborative teaching;
- cooperative learning activities and service-learning projects;
- teaming and peer tutoring (in both directions, not just assuming the student with a disability will always be the one in need of tutoring);
- differentiated instruction;
- classroom "bodyness" (here I am using an analogy similar to Paul's image of the Church as the body of Christ, made up of many parts in 1 Corinthians 12) with teachers and other adults as part of the body, but not always the "head," giving instruction or handing out tasks (the adults are part of the classroom community as well);
- focusing on the strengths and needs of all students in the classroom: helping them to identify develop, and exercise their unique gifts and talents as well as to receive the gifts of others; and
- recognition of mutuality of responsibility and interconnectedness of each member of the classroom community.

## Professional Relationships

Can merging of general and special education be accomplished effectively without a theology of interdependence that recognizes the interdependence of each professional and that communicates to the students that we all need and can learn from one another? Winn and Blanton (1997) argued that there must be shared beliefs among general and special educators related to students and the tasks of teaching and learning, including skills in collaboration and "a rich knowledge base about curriculum and instruction" (p. 11). A theology of interdependence provides one starting point for these shared beliefs.

An important element of successful collaborative teaching is a respectful attitude toward each professional. There is often a perceived lack of parity between general and special education teachers that creates a significant barrier to successful co-teaching (Keefe, Moore, & Duff, 2004). Marilyn Friend, an outspoken champion of collaboration, bemoaned educators' discomfort with a culture of sharing expertise:

> If in schools we would act in the understanding that some professionals should be experts in instructional strategies, some in the use of cooperative learning approaches, some in responding to troubling student behavior, some in assessment practices, and some in building students' self-esteem and social skills, we could draw on each others' knowledge and skills and collectively create more effective schools for our students. (Quoted in Brownell & Walther-Thomas, 2000, p. 224)

Instead, many special educators feel that their counterparts in the regular class do not recognize their expertise in modifying curriculum and adapting instruction, and treat them as teacher assistants. Often, co-teaching situations leave special education teachers feeling like they are filling the role of a paraprofessional rather than being part of a true collaborative unit (cf. Walsh & Jones, 2004). Recognizing the interdependence between professionals may also help diminish the perception of many special education teachers that general education teachers are not sensitive to or concerned with meeting the needs of individuals.

Ferguson (1995) commented:

> Neither general nor special education alone has either the capacity or the vision to challenge and change the deep-rooted assumptions that separate and track children.... *Meaningful change will require nothing less than a joint effort to reinvent schools to be more accommodating to all dimensions of human diversity* (p. 285; emphasis added)

A theology of interdependence provides a foundation for reinventing schools and accommodating all students in the classroom.

# Chapter Eight

# Biblical Hospitality
# and Inclusive Education

## Introduction

"Individual rights provide an important framework for concerns about justice, equality, protection, and provision. *The cost of our emphasis on rights, however, includes a devaluation of personal care and social connection*" (Pohl, 1999, p.78, emphasis added). The devaluation of personal care and social connection to which Pohl refers is reflected in the *im*personal atmosphere and lack of relationship that may characterize many programs or classrooms where inclusion of students with disabilities, though something to which they are entitled, is approached with skepticism or resistance.

The last three decades have seen a wider acceptance of the public school's role in providing special education, and some Christian schools have moved in that direction, at least for students with learning disabilities. This can be attributed largely to changes in society from professional and parental advocacy leading to legal and legislative action. However, an element of resistance to including students with

---

"Hospitable Classrooms: Biblical Hospitality and Inclusive Education," Anderson, D. W., was originally published in the *Journal of Education and Christian Belief*, 15(1), 13–17, 2011. Reprinted by permission.

exceptional needs in general education classrooms remains. Many teachers still hold to a "your kids/my kids" mentality that sees children having special needs solely as the responsibility of special education. Many assume that extra effort will be required when including students who have a disability in the mainstream classroom. Sometimes that extra effort is real, but often it exists only in the preconceptions of people who became teachers because of a desire to help students academically but then grow frustrated when children (disabled or non-disabled) do not make the progress envisioned, or even seem resistant to learning. In addition, the current emphasis in American schools on demonstrating adequate yearly progress through test scores may increase some teachers' resistance to the integration of disabled students, as well as encourage teaching to the test in order to be certain that schools show the progress required to maintain federal funding.

This presents a dilemma for those who are truly concerned about the development and welfare of students with disabilities. They recognize the value of these students being included with non-disabled children to the greatest extent appropriate, but they also fear that the students might not receive an appropriate education in that setting because of a teacher's unwillingness or inability to provide the necessary accommodations or modifications. The dilemma is further complicated both by advocates who promote inclusion as a one-size-fits-all approach and also by teachers who hold to a one-method-fits-all instructional design. Both may deny the student an appropriate education. Still missing from many teacher-preparation programs is adequate training for general education teachers in adapting or modifying instruction to accommodate learners who have a disabling condition or who demonstrate learning-style differences. Current interest in universal design (cf. Council for Exceptional Children, 2005; Gargiulo & Metcalf,

2009; Rose & Meyer, 2006) and on in differentiated instruction (cf. Tomlinson, 1999, 2005) hold promise in this regard.

## Present Focus

In my writing, I have sought to describe a Christian hermeneutic of special education by presenting special education as reconciliation, addressing special education as involvement in spiritual warfare, and by casting inclusion within a theology of interdependence (Anderson, 2003, 2006a, 2006b). I have discussed "reinventing" education around community and belonging, and argued that attempts to promote inclusion of students with disabilities have often resulted merely in *physical* access to general education classrooms. But this does not guarantee that these students are welcomed as an equal part of the classroom community. Some implications of a theology of interdependence I identified were developing classroom "bodyness," with teachers and other adults being part of the body; focusing on the strengths and needs of *all* students in the classroom, helping all to identify, develop, and exercise their unique gifts and talents as well as to receive the "gifts" of others; and recognizing the mutuality of responsibility and the interconnectedness of each member of the classroom community (Anderson, 2006a, p. 56).

Keep in mind the intent of this chapter is not to propose new methods for inclusion, but to further the development of a biblical framework—or hermeneutic—for educating students with disabilities within an inclusive setting. My suggestion is that the biblical concept of hospitality helps us understand the classroom environment in which persons with disabilities and other marginalized students can be effectively incorporated into the body of the class. Block (2002) reminded her readers that accessibility and hospitality are not the same; accessibility merely opens doors. The question was raised as to the value of being able to access public buildings or programs if you continue to feel like an outsider, an alien in a strange world (cf. Steele, 1994). I submit that the Christian virtue of hospitality, besides being a distinctive feature of individual Christians and the church, is also a necessary quality for classrooms to be truly inclusive. Hospitality, seen in the teacher's approach to students, and as characteristic of the classroom milieu, conveys welcome, acceptance, and belonging to all students.

Pohl (1999) stresses that "inclusion mandated by law ... cannot guarantee that people will experience the kinds of human connections and rootedness that give us a safe and meaning-filled place in the world" (p. 78). I believe her comments uncover a potential flaw in the practice of inclusion in educational settings. She asserts that "hospitality can easily reflect contemporary distinctions so that some guests are seen as deserving hospitality and that other guests are not seen at all" (p. 79). Perceptive readers will recognize that substituting the word *students* for "guests" in this quote describes what may still be happening in inclusive classrooms: students with disabilities— particularly disabilities that are more visible and significant—though physically included in the classroom may remain outsiders to the classroom community, or essentially unseen. Changes in school policy in the United States and other Western countries have successfully created space for students with disabilities in regular schools and classrooms. This is a positive move, but it is not simply space in the *classroom* that is necessary. My thesis is that biblical hospitality should characterize the classroom and the demeanor of any Christian educator, whether in Sunday school, public or Christian day schools, or higher education.

## Biblical Hospitality

Today, the word *hospitality* is seldom used outside of the *hospitality industry* (hotels and resorts, tourism and travel agencies), which provides a service for a fee. Business persons may think of hospitality as something that is part of an effective sales approach, offered with the expectation of gaining something in return (e.g., commission or promotion). For some, hospitality means simply "generic friendliness" (Newman, 2007, p. 11), while for others, offers of hospitality are restricted to family members or close friends and associates. But biblical hospitality is a concept rich with meaning, a concept that holds particular theological and practical significance for inclusive education. Old Testament narratives demonstrating the practice of hospitality include Genesis 18 and 19, where strangers are entertained by Abraham and Lot, respectively; 1 Kings 17, where the widow of Zarephath hosts Elijah; and 2 Kings 4, the story of Elisha and the Shunammite woman. The actual forms of hospitality in these instances included housing and shelter, washing the guests' feet, preparing a meal, and providing safety. Certainly, not all of these forms of hospitality will always apply to a classroom setting in a literal sense, but the provision of a safe environment should be a constant. Present interest, however, is not the *form* but the *posture* of hospitality.

Two of Jesus's well-known parables emphasize hospitality. In Matthew 25:31–46, the parable of the sheep and goats, Jesus explained the "kingdom mandate of ministry, which is to serve human needs without respect of persons" (Sanders, 1997, p. 27). Jesus described everyday acts of mercy that all Christians can perform regardless of their economic condition, intellectual level, or able-bodiedness. He spoke of acts of hospitality toward people who are strangers, hungry, in prison, poor, diseased, or disabled. Jesus said that as we practice hospitality, it should be done as if Jesus himself were the recipient. Luke 14:16–23 records Jesus's parable about a great banquet to which the invited guests have refused to come; their place is finally given to the poor, crippled, blind, and lame living in the streets and alleys of the city and in the country lanes. Pohl (2003) concludes that the Matthew 25 and Luke 14 passages shape what distinguishes Christian hospitality: the possibility that in welcoming *the least* we may actually be welcoming Jesus, and an orientation toward those who have little to offer by means of direct reciprocity. She noted that these passages "tie human responsibility to God's welcome, and God's presence and reward to simple acts of care" (p. 8).

Scripture shows clearly God's hospitality in the many passages that declare his concern for justice, particularly in the case of those who tend to be marginalized: aliens and strangers, people in poverty, widows, orphans, the diseased, and the disabled. Jesus continually crossed barriers of religion, ethnicity, gender, ability level, and other walls of separation erected by the culture. The parable of the good Samaritan helps us understand that when we see someone in need, that individual is not to be avoided; rather, we are to make ourselves neighbor to that man or woman. The parable is an illustration of how hospitality should be evidenced in the life of a Christian, and demonstrates the crossing of artificial barriers that are often erected.

Pohl (1995, 1999, 2002, 2003, 2003–2004; Pohl & Buck, 2004) and Reynolds (2006, 2008) have written extensively on the Christian tradition of hospitality. They concluded that hospitality was an important witness to the authenticity of the gospel during the early centuries of the Christian era. The Greek word translated as "hospitality" or "hospitable" in the New Testament is *philoxenia*, literally meaning fond of strangers or guests. The apostle Paul instructed Christians to "practice hospitality" (Romans 12:13) and listed being hospitable among the qualifications for church leaders (1 Timothy 3:2, 5:10; Titus 1:8). The author of Hebrews directed his readers not to neglect showing hospitality (*philoxenias*) to strangers, reminding them that "by so doing, some have entertained angels without knowing it" (Hebrews 13:2; cf. Abraham's and Lot's experiences in Gen. 18 and 19). Peter speaks of hospitality within the context of loving and serving others, with the ultimate motivation for such acts as bringing glory and praise to God (1 Peter 4:8–11).

Theologically, the significance of hospitality is that it recognizes and images *God's* acts of hospitality. In the Old Testament, the descendants of Abraham, living as aliens in bondage to Egypt, were a people whom God graciously redeemed and constituted as a nation. During their wanderings in the wilderness, God's hospitality to Israel was shown in his provision of food and water and protection from their enemies. God's covenant with Israel included a code of hospitality (Exodus 22:21; Leviticus 19:9–10, 33–34) based on God's holiness and graciousness (Leviticus 19:1–2). The code was to remind the Israelites of their wanderings and of God's faithfulness to them in providing safety and sustenance (McKinley, 2003; Pohl, 2003).

Christ's atoning work, through which our alienation from God is removed, is the extreme example of God's offer of hospitality to all people. "Christian hospitality is grounded in the hospitable God who through the Incarnation has received creation in himself and through Pentecost has given himself to creation" (Yong, 2007b, p. 62). Volf (1996) uses *embrace* as a metaphor picturing hospitality. Volf describes the embrace as "the will to give ourselves to others and 'welcome' them" (p. 29). Hospitality means making space for others, just as "on the cross, God made space in God's very self for others ... and opened arms to invite them in" (p. 214).

Rather than a series of tasks to be performed, or simply receiving strangers into one's home, hospitality "is a way of life central to the gospel" (Pohl & Buck, 2004, p. 11). It is "the creation of a free and friendly space where we can reach out to strangers and invite them to become our friends" (Nouwen, 1975, p. 79). But as Reinders (2008) states, "Space is a *necessary* but not a *sufficient* condition for inclusion" (p. 161). The hospitality envisioned, especially as applied to a classroom setting, is an intentional practice that reflects a process and perspective rather than specific tasks teachers must add to their already overtaxed schedules.

## Hospitable Classrooms

Mittler (2000) identified change in school culture as the deeper intent of the movement toward inclusion, a change that involves "helping all teachers to accept responsibility for the learning of all children in their school and preparing them to teach children who are currently excluded from their school" (p. vii). This is in concert with Kunc's (1992) assertion that fully embracing the concept of inclusion removes any insistance that students must become *normal* to make a contribution to the classroom. Instead, we value their presence in the classroom and school community, which engenders a sense of belonging.

This ideal can best be realized in hospitable classrooms where diversity, rather than being seen as a threat to community, is welcomed, and where relationships between disabled and non-disabled students are consciously nurtured. A sense of *belonging* to the classroom community is made possible when the unique contribution of each person to the community's well-being is valued. "Although each person's contribution may be somewhat different from those of the other members, all contributions are recognized, appreciated, and celebrated" (Walther-Thomas, Korinek, McLaughlin, & Williams, 2000, p. 7).

Hospitable classrooms will manifest an ambiance that conveys acceptance and community. But this does not suggest that no effort is required on the part of the teacher, or "host." Some students with disabilities may be more accustomed to being marginalized or invisible, necessitating the teacher's intentional communication of welcome through words and thoughtful acts of hospitality. This may be especially needed when the student, either because of the type and degree of exceptionality or because of prior experience in inhospitable settings, becomes a difficult "guest." In such circumstances, the Christian teacher will want to remember Peter's admonition to practice hospitality without grumbling, but out of love, with open-hearted sincerity (1 Peter 4:9).

A shift in orientation is required in which the *student* is the foreground and the *disability* becomes the background. It requires a re-envisioning of people with disabilities—of the whole concept of disability—recognizing, as Moltmann (1998) did, that "every human life has its limitations, vulnerabilities, and weaknesses" (p. 110).

The move from a strictly medical model of disability to a social model (cf. Albert, 2004; Reinders, 2008) has helped people understand that impairment refers to defects or dysfunctions of the body resulting from accidents, genetic abnormalities, diseases, etc., whereas disability, or handicap, is often created by society and imposed atop the impairment. Because they are based on negative stereotyping, inaccurate information, or fear caused by the recognition that these conditions could happen to anyone, people's perceptions of disability (and of persons who are disabled) often lead to devaluation of the individual, resulting in exclusion or isolation. Even the well-intentioned acts of special educators in the past, intended to help individuals with disabilities, may have inadvertently built a wall of separation between temporarily able-bodied and persons who are disabled. While the impairment, and the functional limitations it may cause, must not be ignored, hospitality demands that each child be seen in his or her wholeness, as an individual created in God's image. The cognitive, affective, or physical/sensory impairment obviously presents some limitation, but this is only one aspect of the person, not the totality of his or her being.

If the classroom community is to be truly inclusive, any negativity toward students with disabilities must be replaced with accurate information about disability and by getting to know people who are disabled. Hospitality is not charity but a concern and empathy focused on common humanity (cf. Pohl, 1995). To be good "hosts," teachers must recognize that the "stranger" (i.e., the student with a disability) is more like the other students than different; that is, students with a disability share with those who are not disabled many common needs, interests, desires, expectations, *and* vulnerabilities. Pohl's (1995) comment about biblical hospitality is directly applicable to inclusive classroom settings:

> Hospitality practices that offer a transforming social network to detached strangers require a heterogeneous community with multiple intersecting relationships and intersecting roles ... Without reciprocal relations and commitments, without hosts and guests aware of their need and dependence on one another[,] relations are flattened and commitments are too thin to give people a place in the world. (pp. 134–135)

Moltmann proposed that every disability is a gift that remains untouched because our focus is on what the person cannot do. Says Moltmann (1998),

> If we were to free ourselves for a moment from the value standards of our own lives, then we would be able to understand the peculiar worth of the other life and its importance to us. Everyone affected might ask herself: What importance does the person with disabilities have for me and my life? In so doing, she would quickly discover the giftedness of that person with disabilities. (p. 120)

## Operationalizing the Concept

Swinton (2001) explained that "praxis is action saturated with meaning ... the reflective movement between theoretical premises and human action" (p. 176). In our present focus, praxis represents the interface between human rights-based arguments related to inclusive education, a biblical view of hospitality, and the classroom reality. Applying biblical teaching on hospitality to inclusion requires that the concept of a hospitable classroom be operationalized: what would a classroom structured around Christian hospitality look like? Though the literature often speaks of the "classroom community," this is a reality not yet experienced by many students who have a label of a disability attached to them. Typical classrooms have often failed to generate a sense of belonging for students with disabilities or those considered at-risk (cf. Beck & Malley, 2003; Pivik, McComas, &LaFlamme, 2002). Beck and Malley held that teaching practices in today's schools often stress economy, efficiency, and technology over human relationships.

They point out that the emphasis on control and orderliness, grades and competition in large, impersonal schools is more likely to promote alienation and isolation for students marginalized for any reason than to encourage community and interdependence. We must ask, then, how might an atmosphere of hospitality lessen feelings of rejection and alienation among students who are marginalized because of disability or any other reason? How could it encourage a sense of belonging? How would a classroom in which Christian hospitality pervades contribute to dismantling barriers that often exist between individuals who are disabled and those who are temporarily able-bodied?

Nouwen (1975, p. 67) described hospitality as "a fundamental attitude" toward others that finds its expression in a variety of ways. Its specific articulation in individual classrooms will be colored by the personality and teaching style of the teacher. But using broad strokes, we can paint a picture of the ambience of hospitable classrooms and identify several essential characteristics.

## Breaking Barriers and Building Bridges

Biblical accounts of hospitality often focused on entertaining strangers or foreigners, people who were vulnerable because of being from the outside. People who, because of their difference, their alien status, or their obvious need were potential victims of abuse, either overtly (as in the case of the man who fell among thieves in Jesus's parable of the good Samaritan) or covertly (as in the intentional disregard of that unfortunate man by the priest and Levite who passed him by). In the same way, persons with disabilities may be seen as outsiders, lacking membership in the general education classroom or school community, and thus being vulnerable to isolation, even while in the classroom. Attitudinal barriers built from fear or ignorance often result in the person with a disability not being acknowledged as a true peer by those who are temporarily able-bodied.

The teacher can be regarded as the primary host who, by her words and actions, sets the tone for a hospitable classroom. In hospitable classrooms, Christian teachers demonstrate and promote healing and reconciliation (essential elements of the "good news" of the gospel) and help build bridges between students of varying ability levels, or who differ in socioeconomic status or ethnic and racial background. The teacher, by demonstrating acceptance and welcoming of everyone in the classroom, helps all her students to develop transformed attitudes and behaviors toward individuals whose diversity might set them apart.

However, hospitality must not be viewed simply as a means to an end, but as "a way of life infused by the gospel" (Pohl, 2003, p. 11). The hospitable teacher will make a conscious effort to dispel fear and ignorance related to disability in general and toward the specific students with disabilities who are a part of the classroom. It is incumbent upon teacher-training programs to provide accurate information and experience related to disability so as to prepare their graduates for working in inclusive classrooms and living in an inclusive society. The teacher will want to find out about the specific disabilities faced by her students and develop a more collaborative relationship with the special education teacher, related service providers, and the family. As well, the host-teacher will show intolerance for any unkind language or behavior that would tend to isolate or create a barrier between students (e.g., teasing, name-calling, or other forms of ridicule).

## Welcoming

The hospitable classroom will present a welcoming environment in which the person with a disability feels valued and safe within the "shelter of relationship" (Pohl, 2002a, p. 39) as students interact freely and respectfully with one another. It will be characterized by an affirmation of dignity and equality among all students in the classroom, both disabled or temporarily able-bodied, as well as an acknowledgment of the interdependence of all members of the classroom community. Respect for each student that recognizes the worth of each as an individual created in God's image, and that acknowledges the common interests, desires, and needs of all the students, will be evident. The teacher-host will communicate the expectation that mutual academic and social learning will occur as students who are disabled and those who are temporarily able-bodied interact, and will design opportunities to encourage both academic and social interaction. She will promote a "comfortableness" to the classroom, recognizing that learning occurs more readily when students are relaxed, engaged, and having fun in the learning process.

## Accommodations and Modifications

In a hospitable classroom, positive attention is given to all students, both those who have a disability and those who are temporarily able-bodied. The nature of the student's disability is taken into account, and necessary accommodations are made so that the student is appropriately included in all activities. Employing principles drawn from universal design of learning, differentiated learning strategies, and multiple intelligence theory can make classroom learning more available to students with differing learning needs and abilities, and make the classroom more hospitable.

Christian teachers should approach hospitality in the classroom following the same principle that was pertinent to Israel and the early Christians: God is our host; we are in his land. Therefore, the practice of hospitality is done out of gratitude and obedience to God who, as in Jesus's parable in Matthew 25, is the great Host as well as the potential guest. The teacher-host will not, then, make hospitality contingent on the student living up to certain expectations. To do so would dishonor the student, treating him or her "like everyone else," without acknowledging the accommodations or modifications necessitated by the disability (cf. Yong, 2007a). The words of Reynolds (2008) apply: "Hospitality embodies divine love, it neither condescends out of pity nor forces the other to conform … but rather lets the other be, yielding space for the others' freedom and difference" (p. 241). Hospitality is offered freely and openly to all the students in the classroom and takes into account that even students who are temporarily able-bodied are not all the same in learning style or in their ability to grasp the concepts being presented. This does not, of course, mean that academic and behavioral standards do not apply and that discipline, when needed, will not be forthcoming, but it will be done graciously and appropriately.

## Friendships and Reciprocity

The hospitable teacher will not simply assure physical space in the classroom for students who are "different" but will encourage the development of commitments and relationships among the students. Reinders (2008) expresses the importance of relationships to community and belonging by pointing out that "the practice and politics of inclusion will not create a lasting change for persons with disabilities unless there will be people willing to invest in friendships with them." He holds that participation is more an issue of friendships than of citizenship (i.e., rights), concluding that "without true friendships, disabled persons will enjoy the new opportunities created by their equal rights most likely as 'strangers in a strange land'" (p. 187).

To promote true friendships among the students, the hospitable teacher, in addition to promoting social and academic interaction, will encourage reciprocity in these relationships (Bishop, Jumbala, Stainback, & Stainback, 1996). It is important that partnering of temporarily able-bodied students with disabled students not be perceived solely along lines of helper/helpee, which, if overly emphasized, "can easily skew the delicate balance of giving and receiving that is the precursor of true friendship" (Van der Klift & Kunc, 1994, p. 392). The helper/helpee concept maintains the sense of difference: one "has" and the other "has a need." Obviously, the student with a disability will receive some benefit from this "help." But the helper/helpee relationship may inadvertently reinforce feelings of superiority on the part of the student who is temporarily able-bodied, thereby negating the intent of hospitality. Rather than helper/helpee, the concept of host and guest more accurately captures the dynamics of the intended relationship. The host/guest paradigm still recognizes that one has something to offer the other, but lacks an underlying notion of condescension. True hospitality is not pity or charity but the recognition of openness and sharing with one another. Oden's (2001) words are instructive:

> Hospitality does not entail feeling sorry for someone and trying to help.... The feeling of pity and the desire to better the lives of others is a good thing, often inspired by God in one's heart. But it is seductive, even dangerous, for the host to view herself as the helper. The would-be act of hospitality becomes an act of condescension and failure to see either one's own need or the true identity of the stranger in Christ ... Ego, self-satisfaction, a need to feel off the hook, demonstrating competence and righteousness, all too

easily enter the equation, with the host as hero and the guest as victim. (p. 7)

Christian hospitality builds more on mutuality and mutual respect, acknowledging what the "guest" brings to the relationship, thereby promoting friendships and solidarity in the classroom community by enabling temporarily able-bodied persons and those with disabilities to think of themselves as equals despite the obvious differences that exist. The biblical principle of loving others as you love yourself suggests an appreciation for this equality. "The hospitable teacher has to reveal to [all] the students that they have something to offer" (Nouwen 1975, p. 86).

The primary focus of this chapter thus far has been on the teacher-host creating a hospitable, inclusive classroom environment into which all students, especially those with disabilities, are welcomed and accepted. By extension, some would rightly assume that students who are not disabled would also be "hosts" to the marginalized student. The host/guest paradigm, however, recognizes that these roles can be reversed, making the student who has a disability "host" to the student who is temporarily able-bodied. It must be realized that persons with a disability may appear to have little to offer, but in fact might take the lead in the teaching–learning relationship. This reciprocity in students' relationships will encourage true friendships. Even the teacher may become "guest" to the host-student who has a disability, as individual talents and strengths on the part of the disabled student are recognized and utilized in the classroom situation. Consequently, the hospitable teacher will actively encourage new relationships among the students to promote learning and friendships. The ability of each partner to become host or guest, depending on the situation, will both deepen and maintain the relationship.

Friendship is indeed at the heart of what we all need from one another. Our friendships enable us to be active and protected members of the community. Friendships help ensure that being a part of the community, rather than just being in the community, is really for everyone! (Strully & Strully, 1996, p. 154)

## Teacher Growth

A good host seeks to provide for his or her guests, to seek their comfort, and provide for their immediate needs while in the host's care. In the context of the inclusive classroom, this means that the teacher-host will be aware of the special needs of the student-guest. He will not be satisfied with simply learning the general needs that characterize a particular disability (e.g., Down Syndrome or cerebral palsy), but will want to become cognizant of the specific limitations and strengths of the individual student with whom he is working. The teacher will become an expert "child-watcher," seeking to learn from the student's response whether the approach being used is effective, and whether the student is actively engaged in the learning. The observations will lead to alterations in approach or materials as necessary, either through the teacher's own creativity and imagination, through research, or through consultation with the special education service providers. Hospitable teachers will not assume the child is at fault if he or she does not grasp the concepts being taught, but will examine their methods and techniques, or the materials themselves, anticipating that such reflection will lead to their own professional development.

# Kindness

Nicolas Long (1997) states that "kindness gives meaning to our lives and make[s] the lives of others more hopeful and satisfying" (p. 246). He speaks within the context of therapeutic work with troubled students and describes kindness as arising from a feeling of compassion. He emphasizes the establishment of a trusting relationship between the teacher and the student. Several of Long's principles of kindness, with slight modification or expansion to make them applicable to students with various disabling conditions, are appropriate to operationalizing the concept of hospitable classrooms:

- *Protection*—providing a physically and psychologically safe classroom environment. Safety and security are communicated to students who have a disability by an attitude of acceptance and welcome, and through an affirmation of their dignity as persons created in God's image. This also involves an intolerance of teasing, etc., as mentioned previously.

- *Emotional support*—the ability to stand with, rather than against the student. This would is based on the teacher's understanding of how the disability impacts the student's learning and performance, and her making the necessary accommodations to promote student learning.

- *Empowerment*—enabling students who have a disability to participate as fully as possible in all appropriate activities, to make their own decisions when appropriate (rather than having things done for or to them), to be respected as individuals, and to be encouraged to exercise personal talents and abilities both to their own benefit and as "host" in the host-guest relationship.

- *Personal commitment*—unconditional acceptance of the student and a commitment to helping each student in the classroom develop academically, socially, physically, and emotionally to the fullest extent possible. This personal commitment may be the most essential element of a hospitable classroom.

## Who Benefits from Hospitable Classrooms?

The specific focus in this chapter is on students with disabilities. However, the principle of hospitable classrooms has broader application that encompasses all students who might be considered vulnerable (in reality, we all move in and out of vulnerability at various times or in extraordinary situations during our lives). This includes students who are refugees, recent immigrants, or otherwise new to the school or school district; students from dysfunctional or broken families; students whose families have little external support because of poverty, joblessness, or homelessness; or students who are without adequate protection from physical or emotional harm, exploitation, or neglect. Sapon-Shevin (1999, 2003) broadens the discussion on inclusion from simply a concern of special education to other areas of oppression. Classrooms evincing Christian hospitality should address all of these social issues, potentially challenging and transforming not just the school but society as well. Building relationships across the various lines that divide people into categories (following Jesus's example of crossing barriers) is essential to hospitable classrooms and perhaps to the welfare of the nation.

## Conclusion

Christian apologist R. C. Sproul (1999) stated, "The Gospel calls us to live as obedient servants of Christ and as his emissaries in the world, doing justice, having mercy, and helping all in need, thus seeking to bear witness to the kingdom of Christ" (p. 103). It seems to me that creating and maintaining hospitable classrooms is one way that Christian teachers, regardless of where they are teaching or the level at which they teach, can demonstrate this obedient servanthood. As Pohl (2003) asserts, Christian hospitality is "mediating the love of Christ to persons.… When we offer hospitality …we make a powerful statement to the world about who is interesting, valuable, and important to us" (p. 11).

Hospitality should characterize the Christian's life, as our lives are shared with others. "It involves opening our lives to those who need a place, and making room for those the world often overlooks and undervalues" (Pohl & Buck, 2004, p. 11). That, in my view, makes hospitality an appropriate and necessary element of inclusive classrooms.

## For Further Thought

Readings on Christian hospitality and reflection on its application to inclusive classrooms highlights issues which further challenge ideas about how Christian faith informs the practice of inclusive education. The following questions are raised to encourage others to continue the conversation.

Volf (1996) asked his readers to consider what the cross tells us about the Christian self in relation to others and states that "God's reception of hostile humanity into divine communion is a model for how human beings should relate to the other" (p. 100). His comment relates not only to hospitality within the classroom. What implications are there for all forms of interaction between teachers and students, teachers and their peers, and teachers and administrators?

Hospitality is a means of grace both for the recipient and for the giver of hospitality. Pohl (2004) stated that "giving children opportunities for grace and growth in the context of hospitality is a wonderful gift and a formative experience" (p. 13). This suggests that hospitality can promote spiritual formation. If hospitality is the milieu of the classroom, and students, both disabled and non-disabled, are given opportunities to practice reciprocal hospitality (giving and receiving), what part might this play in the development or "healing" of relationships between students who are able-bodied and students who have a disability (especially an emotional or behavioral disability)?

Sanders (1997) asserted that "the measure of the morality of the nation is how it treats its most vulnerable members" (p. 30). If the same is true for inclusive classrooms, what does this say about the morality of the nation's schools?

According to Reynolds (2006), "The key to unlocking the door of hospitality is maintaining an open and ready heart" (p. 201). Given the current emphasis on inclusion in Western schools, what are teacher-training institutions doing to help make the hearts of teachers "open and ready"?

# CHAPTER NINE

# Biblical Justice and Inclusive Education

Many years ago I wrote an article entitled *The Rights of Children* as a call to Christian schools to open their doors to students with disabilities (Anderson, 1977). The message of that article was needed, but over time I came to feel uncomfortable with its emphasis on "rights." My discontent with use of the term "rights" is because this term often leaves out interpersonal or communal connections. As stated at the beginning of chapter eight, many programs or classrooms which include students with disabilities lack an emphasis on building relationship among the students. Students with disabilities are included because it is a right to which they are entitled, but many teachers remain skeptical or resistant.

Both the disability rights movement and the history of special education in the United States since the 1950s have advocated policy change on behalf of people with disabling conditions based on human-rights arguments and appeals to the Fifth Amendment to the Constitution, which guarantees due process and equal protection. These arguments have successfully brought change in American social and educational policy and have undoubtedly influenced practices in other

"Biblical justice and inclusive education," Anderson, D. W., was originally published in the *Journal of Religion, Disability & Health,* 14, 338–354, 2010. Copyright © Taylor & Francis Group, LLC. Reprinted by permission of Taylor & Francis, http://tandfonline.com

nations around the world. Although the legislative impact on educational policy and the practice of special education is clear, such legislation has not necessarily led to inclusive attitudes on the part of teachers, administrators, or non-disabled peers. Although doors have been opened to allow integrated education for persons with disabilities, creating space in the classroom does not necessarily open *people* to being inclusive. As noted in chapter seven, students with disabling conditions may be physically present in the classroom yet remain "outsiders" (cf. Pavri and Luftig, who reported higher levels of perceived loneliness among students with learning disabilities, seemingly related to "diminished social status," 2000, p. 6). Pohl (1999) concluded that "Inclusion mandated by law and provision gathered through taxes cannot guarantee that people will experience the kind of human connections and rootedness that give us a safe and meaning-filled place in the world" (p. 78).

## The Problem

The emphasis on the "rights" of disabled students may actually contribute to their devaluation and inadvertently reinforce a separation between students with disabilities and students who are temporarily able-bodied by accentuating difference. For some, the use of the term *special* in connection with persons with disabling conditions may suggest inferiority and relative powerlessness or weakness, rather than promoting honor, dignity, and respect. One might even question whether special education as it is presently conceived creates a dependency-fostering "culture" (cf. Swain, French, & Cameron, 2003), as it had been accused of in the past, especially for students with severe or multiple disabilities. Has historic special education done an *injustice* to students with disabilities by segregating them and overly emphasizing difference? Do artificially derived standards and test scores do an *injustice* to students by ignoring individuality and limiting intellectual curiosity through "teaching to the test" and stressing adequate (minimal?) yearly progress? Might inclusive practices, though meant to uphold the rights of students who are disabled, deny their individuality and disregard the fact that they have special needs, which traditional methods of assessment and instruction may overlook? Is there continuing *injustice* even though masked by talk of inclusion? Is the assumption that people with a disability need to be 'normal' (or even *want* to be "normal") actually an *injustice*?

Swain, French, and Cameron (2003) suggest that, "the pressure to be normal is often at the expense of the disabled person's needs and rights" (p. 82). Does emphasis on mainstreaming and inclusion demand that students who have a disability be assimilated into the dominant educational culture by "earning" (cf. Rixford, 1997) the right to be in regular education classrooms?

Gaede's (1993) remark about multiculturalism easily could be descriptive of special education:

> [W]e promote multiculturalism—not as an effort to establish justice based on some moral vision, but simply to achieve indiscriminate inclusion. But what we end up with instead is not tolerance, nor inclusion, and certainly not justice. What we get is … people with power deciding what is best for all and executing their will accordingly (p. 49).

Add to this the observation of Hauerwas (2004):

> [W]e usually associate movement towards justice in our society with the language of equality. We assume to be

> treated equally is to be treated justly, but in reflection
> we may discover that is not the case. Often the language
> of equality only works by reducing us to a common
> denominator that can be repressive or disrespectful ...
> No one wants to pay the price of being treated equally
> if that means they must reject who they are (p. 39).

On a very practical level, do we, as Christian educators, see inclusion as important or necessary because of the Individuals with Disabilities Educational Improvement Act, in which case we comply because we want to be good, law-abiding citizens, even though we are not convinced that inclusion is correct? Do we tolerate inclusion out of fear of legal action being taken against us, or simply to keep our job?

## Toward Answering the Problem

I suggest that the real issue is not *rights,* but *justice,* specifically biblical justice and reconciliation. Senior (1995) commented, "Inclusion within the social and political community is an issue of justice fundamental to the gospel. Exclusion, on the other hand, has an oppressive, dehumanizing impact running contrary to the Christian vision" (p. 6). Although Senior was not specifically addressing educational issues, these words apply to school practices as well, moving the discussion beyond rights as constitutionally delineated.

An understanding of biblical justice and reconciliation provides a stronger basis for education that is truly inclusive. Principles of due process and equal protection can be identified in Scripture, but their basis is in biblical justice, not the US Constitution. While private Christian schools in the United States are not bound by the federal laws that require that students with disabilities be included in general education classroom when appropriate, Christian schools are certainly bound by biblical principles of justice and reconciliation. Promoting inclusion on the basis of biblical justice and reconciliation will not simply result in opening doors and space in the classroom, but will open hearts to include all individuals and appropriately recognize and celebrate differences.

## Understanding Justice

Justice is a term that is frequently used without carefully considering its meaning. Justice can be thought of as a principle or quality by which people are treated fairly. It is often understood as a "thing"—a state or a situation, an entitlement. People may be heard to say, usually with some vehemence, "I demand justice!" or "That's not justice!" In this manner, justice tends to be viewed propositionally, and may actually focus on self-preservation. We are often more concerned with our own experience of justice, sometimes even at the expense of justice for others. We may express a desire for "liberty and justice for all," but only if it does not affect what we perceive as justice for ourselves. Justice, then, is understood as a *noun,* something that resides outside of self.

When thus conceptualized, it is easy for people to think of human rights as something that we accord or withhold from others. Whether or not justice and human rights are granted to an individual becomes dependent on what that person does or can do, and how we perceive that individual rather than recognizing who that individual *is* as created in God's image. In the context of students with disabilities, some may even question whether severely disabled individuals are truly "human." If they are not, then the question of human rights no longer is an issue.

The definition of humanity and the related issue of our creation in the image of God were discussed in earlier chapters. Here, I simply assert that neither the presence nor absence of disability brings into question the humanness of an individual or that person's creation as the image of God. Wolterstorff (2008) argued for a theistic grounding of human rights based on what he called *bestowed worth,* that is, worth bestowed on human beings by the love that God has for them, irrespective of what the person does or can do. Wolterstorff concluded that, "if God loves ... each and every human being equally and permanently, then natural human rights inhere in the worth bestowed on human beings by that love. Natural human rights are what respect for that worth requires" (p. 360).

Wolterstorff defined a *right* as "a normative social relationship; specifically, a right is a legitimate claim to the good of being treated a certain way" (p. 385). This follows whether or not the individual is able-bodied and creates a moral obligation never to treat a person as having less worth, never to under-respect the person, never to demean them (p. 370).

Rather than something external to oneself, biblical justice more properly may be understood as a *verb*, an action. Micah 6:8 says "He has told you, O man, what is good; and what does the Lord require of you but to *do justice*, and to love kindness, and to walk humbly with your God?" (Emphasis added.). In the biblical context, justice is not simply a *thing we experience;* it is an *action to be practiced*, and it is understood as a relational concept. The original Hebrew and Greek words *justice* and *righteousness* were essentially the same and were primarily focused on one's relation to others (Orr, 1939). Biblical justice finds its roots in the nature, or character, of God (Buzzard, 1997; Richards, 1991). But its contemporary usage colors—and limits—our understanding and masks its use in the Bible as a synonym for *righteousness* (Roberts, 2002).

Doing justice has to do with how human beings treat one another, individually and in society. The standard that defines just behavior is a moral and ethical one. It is derived from God's character and is expressed in those commands of the law and expectations of the prophets that reveal how God expects his people to relate lovingly to those around them (Richards, 1991, p. 370)

According to Richards, in the New Testament the concept of justice/righteousness is dynamic and goes beyond simply evaluating one's behavior to examining one's character, "the wellspring of actions" (p. 371). From study of the term *justice* in the Bible, Richards concluded that:

> [W]e are immediately confronted with the importance to God of the way we treat other persons. Justice is a concept that calls us to love and [show] concern for those who are weak and oppressed, not simply to moral action in our interpersonal dealings (Richards, 1991, p. 372).

Buzzard (1997) lamented the fact that justice has lost objective meaning and has become a political slogan oriented toward due process, hearings, public trials, and democratic processes. As a result, justice, instead of being a personal quality, becomes formal or instrumental, the work of courts, lawyers, and the government. Rather than simply a philosophical or legal term, justice is an action. Biblical justice involves not simply granting others their rights, but actively seeking to establish their rights.

Micah 6:8 emphasizes *doing justice,* particularly in regard to those who are vulnerable, oppressed, or in some way disadvantaged by the more powerful in society. Justice becomes a lifestyle, evidenced by a motivation to practice good and to interact in a manner that will establish and maintain just relationships with others. In other words, justice is not merely within the province of the court or legal systems, but is actively working in Christians as we maintain faithfulness to our calling and to God (Buzzard, 1997). Just as God's justice/righteousness is grounded in his nature, that same justice/right behavior must be manifest in the Christian, particularly as we are Christ's representatives and must speak for those who may be granted little or no voice.

## Biblical Justice Versus Social Justice

Biblical justice is not the same as justice in the social/legal scheme: Simply because something is legal does not mean it is also just, as for example, paying high taxes to support military action when many in the world face starvation. Zorrilla (1988) warned that justice must not be seen as a private, abstract issue. When reduced to simple morality, the result is often an imposition on others of the values and actions of the dominant culture. Instead, Christians are to give justice a human form as they address both those who are in need and those who keep people in need. "In the practice of justice, Christians actively take part in the compassionate acts of God" (Zorrilla, 1988, p. 79).

*Justice* is sometimes thought to be a synonym for *fairness,* "but often God's justice equals not what is fair but what is right" (Ryken, Wilhoit, & Longman, 1998, p. 474). Smart (2001) explained three kinds of justice or fairness: (a) everybody receives equal treatment; (b) everybody receives what he or she has earned; and

(c) everybody receives what he or she needs (pp. 129–130). In the first of these views, which seems commonly held by teachers, the word *equal* is understood to mean *the same* and upholds the idea of standardization in testing and programming. This approach, though seeming somewhat pragmatic, denies individuality and disregards diversity in order to promote uniformity. The second view essentially blames the victim, taking an almost fatalistic position that "there are some people who are inferior because they lack the requisite personal characteristics to earn the rewards" (Smart, 2001, p. 129). Smart holds that this view of justice stems from a Darwinistic, survival-of-the-fittest purview.

The third view of justice and fairness presents a more mature understanding (cf. Hersh, Paolitto, & Reamer, 1979; Voltz at al., 2005) and implies a shift from a principle-based ethic, which stresses an abstract ideal of justice, to a value-based ethic of care, which stresses individual and community relationships (Murdick, Gartin, & Crabtree, 2002).

Rather than seeing justice as simply equality, at this level benevolence assumes a greater role as consideration is given to individual differences and the needs of others. Smart (2001) linked this conception of justice with equal outcomes, and argued that "if everyone were to receive what he or she needs from infancy, all types of people would succeed in gaining the rewards of society. Everyone would be earning the same reward, at the same standards, but with differing accommodations" (Smart, 2001, p. 130). This view of justice/fairness seems to accord more with the Bible's declaration that God is impartial (cf. Deuteronomy 19:17, Job 34:19, Acts 10:34, Romans 2:11). God's impartiality does not mean that all people are treated alike. It simply means there is no favoritism: all receive what is needed.

## Practical Implications

If Christians are to make God's justice visible and believable, then our words and actions must demonstrate that by our lifestyle and our teaching practice. Wolterstorff (2002) suggested that Christian educators have paid too little attention to ways in which students are wronged. Wolterstorff also pointed out that the hierarchical arrangements typical of schools have great potential for wrongdoing against those who are lower in the hierarchy by not recognizing the inherent worth of those persons. Because "rights and justice have to do with the recognition of *worth*" (Wolterstorff, 2002, p. 281), if a student has been wronged (treated unjustly), the teacher or school has failed to recognize the worth of the student. I suggest that unnecessary segregation of students with disabilities and resistance of teachers to including these students within the classroom community are examples of how these students have been treated wrongly, rather than justly.

## Justice and Reconciliation

When disability itself and the student who has a disability are not understood and when the interdependence of all people is not recognized, those with disabilities are easily devalued, dismissed, or set aside as "someone else's" responsibility. Micah 6:8 points the way to correcting this situation: "The Lord has told you, human, what is good; he has told you what he wants from you: to do what is right to other people, love being kind to others, and live humbly, obeying your God" (NCV).

This verse highlights the connection between justice and love or mercy and includes an implied warning against a hierarchical view of people (humility before God). It calls attention to the barrier that often exists between persons who are temporarily able-bodied and persons who have a disability, a barrier that necessitates reconciliation so that justice can prevail. "To establish justice is to remove anything that hinders healthy relationships between people. To live out justice has to do with resolving conflict so that a community can experience peace and harmony" (Zorrilla, 1988, p. 38).

As with justice, reconciliation is also relational. The element of personal relationship is evident in what DeYoung (1997) suggested as the three main aspects of reconciliation:

(a) being put into friendship with God and one another,

(b) a radical change or transformation in a relationship, and

(c) a restoration of harmony.

In the case of inclusive education, it is evident that a lack of harmony or friendship often exists between persons with and without disabilities, thereby necessitating a radical transformation based on principles of biblical justice (cf. Anderson, 2003). If inclusion is done on the basis of biblical justice—not simply on the assertion of someone's "rights," which may not promote harmonious relationships—the classroom may become a microcosm of an inclusive community whose effect may eventually be seen in society at large. Like justice, reconciliation also is a lifestyle rather than simply a strategy for human relations (Hines & DeYoung, 2000).

Justice and reconciliation are at the core of community, making them essential to establishing a classroom and school community that is inclusive. But community does not mean uniformity. The Bible is clear in teaching that each person is an individual. Although all are created as God's image, each is uniquely designed, gifted, and purposed. Moltmann's reminder (1988) bears repeating: "Every human life has its limitations, vulnerabilities, and weaknesses. We are born needy, and we die helpless. So in truth there is no such thing as a life without disability" (p. 110). To label and separate ourselves from those who are disabled is to act inhumanely, to practice injustice. Acting justly requires loving mercy or kindness (Micah 6:8). Thus, reconciled attitudes between temporarily able-bodied and disabled persons are needed: "To become a humane people, persons without disabilities must be liberated from their assumption that they are healthy and from their fear of persons with disabilities" (Moltmann, 1988, p. 112). Increased knowledge of disability and opportunity to live in community with persons who are disabled is necessary in order to break down this fear. As friendships develop, we will come to appreciate the gifts that individuals with disabilities have and are. This reconciliation is essential for inclusive education programs to be effective and, at the same time, is the result of effective inclusion.

## Interdependence: The Basis for True Community

A school culture based on a theology of interdependence can promote reconciliation and justice as students with disabilities and those who are temporarily able-bodied are brought together in true community (Anderson, 2006a).

> A theology of interdependence honors the value of all individuals, not by what they do, but by who they are, recognizing that each and every person contributes to the community by being, not by doing. Interdependence acknowledges not only our dependence on God and one another, but also God's dependence on us to be

agents of God's healing compassion in the world (Black, 1996, p. 42).

The deeper intent of the movement toward inclusion, as explained by Mittler (2000), is school change that involves "helping all teachers to accept responsibility for the learning of all children in their school and preparing them to teach children who are currently excluded from their school" (p. vii). Kunc (1992) also addressed an aspect of this change:

> When inclusive education is fully embraced, we abandon the idea that children will have to become "normal" in order to contribute to the world. Instead, we search for and nourish the gifts that are inherent in all people. We begin to look beyond typical ways of becoming valued members of the community, and in doing so, begin to realize the achievable goal of providing all children with an authentic sense of belonging (pp. 38–39).

Classrooms characterized by biblical justice and reconciliation become places where diversity is welcomed, rather than being seen as a threat to community. Relationships between disabled and non-disabled students will be consciously nurtured, and a sense of *belonging* to the classroom community made possible as each person's unique contribution to the community—by *being*, not necessarily by doing—is recognized and valued. Although each person's contribution is different, all contributions are appreciated and celebrated (Walther-Thomas, Korinek, McLaughlin, & Williams, 2000). Biblical justice requires that inclusive classroom communities be characterized by a recognition and encouragement of the gifts and talents of each individual.

Inclusive practices, based on acting justly, loving kindness, and humility (Micah 6:8), promote the goal of establishing reconciled communities. Biblical justice will encourage greater emphasis on providing the instructional accommodations each person needs in order to learn and grow, rather than forcing students with a disability to be assimilated into the dominant classroom culture in a way that denies their individuality and their special needs. Because of the diversity of special needs, there is no standard, and thus no limit, for determining whether something is a reasonable accommodation.

In supportive communities, everyone has responsibilities and plays a role in supporting others. Each individual is an important and worthwhile member of the community and contributes to the group. This involvement helps foster self-esteem, pride in accomplishments, mutual respect, and a sense of belonging among community members. *Such a community cannot occur if certain students are always the receivers of, and never the givers of, support* (Stainback & Stainback, 1996, p. 195, emphasis added).

This statement by Stainback and Stainback (1996) raises another concern related to the justice of inclusion. Although promoting access to the classroom, efforts at inclusive education have not necessarily guaranteed welcome as equal members of the classroom "family" for students with a disability. To some extent, this reflects a tendency to view persons with disabilities through eyes of charity or pity, as *objects* requiring help rather than as *persons* who may have much to offer. The resulting psychological (spiritual) and physical barrier creates a situation of injustice by portraying students with disabilities as people always needing assistance, while at the same time causing those who are non-disabled to see themselves as superior. Instead, we must acknowledge that we all require help from time to time. "No one is really independent, although the myth of 'making it alone' keeps many people from asking for and getting the help they need and deserve" (Sapon-Shevin, 1999, p. 87).

Focusing on the needs of disabled students and the accommodations necessary for them to participate in ongoing instruction or classroom activity is a primary element of special education practice. Yet it still may carry the message that these students are *un*-abled. Commitment on the part of the teacher is necessary to establish a just environment in the classroom, a community of mutual respect where a sense of belonging is felt by all. A primary goal of both general and special education is the promotion of physical, social–emotional, behavioral, and academic development of students. But as Nouwen (1988) stated, that goal remains "secondary to a life lived together in a community of love" (p. 62). Rather than emphasizing the differences or problems of those who require special education, the uniqueness of *all* students must be respected and proper regard given to the abilities and gifts *each* student brings to the classroom. Justice demands that each student's learning characteristics be accommodated, regardless of whether those differences have been highlighted with a label.

## Just Communities: Friendship

Although students with disabilities are more frequently integrated into general education classes than in the past, this is only a means to an end: "*Inclusion* does not refer to a physical space; it refers to a condition or state of being. The concept of inclusion implies a sense of belonging and acceptance" (Voltz, Brazil, & Ford, 2001 p. 24). The concept of biblical justice helps us understand that if classrooms and schools are to become inclusive communities, negative attitudes toward disabilities and persons with disabilities must be removed. Negative attitudes on the part of administrators and teachers, students who are non-disabled,

199

and often, students who have disabilities themselves create barriers to effective inclusion. The attitudes may stem from ignorance, stereotype, or prejudice, or they may be the unintended result of past special education practices. A re-envisioning of all persons, including those with disabilities, based on a scriptural understanding of what it means to be human and to be God's image-bearer, is needed.

In philosophical language, space is a *necessary* but not a *sufficient* condition for inclusion. What enables me to participate in my own social world is not the fact that I am allowed to live my life as I want to (which is what "space" can do for me), but that there are people who are committed to me and want to be part of my life ... Ultimately, human participation does not depend on personal freedom but on shared practices of communion, which is why I believe that the issue of participation must ultimately be construed as an issue about friendship rather than citizenship (Reinders, 2008, pp. 161–162).

Community cannot exist without openness to others (Meininger, 2001). Reconciled relationships and belonging are hallmarks of the type of just community we seek to establish in our classrooms (and which should be modeled in teacher-training through collaborative efforts of general and special educators). The principle of interdependence recognizes that we are not individually in charge of our own destiny, but that each part of the community is important to the other. *Community* refers not to a group but to a way of life in which interconnections pervade. When not built upon principles of biblical justice, what is typically considered an inclusive classroom may instead promote a sense of isolation, distress, or powerlessness (or at least distance, discomfort, and weakness) among students with disabilities, especially if those students are the recipient of "services" or "help" from others which, though well-meaning, emphasize the limitations caused by the disability.

Even the use of peer assistance can have the unwanted effect of accentuating the disability and creating a one-way relationship: The student with a disability is seen only as one in need of assistance and the students without a labeled disability as helpers (cf. Bishop, Jumbala, Stainback, & Stainback, 1996). "An overemphasis on the 'helper–helpee' relationship can easily skew the delicate balance of giving and receiving that is the precursor of true friendship" (Van der Klift & Kunc, 1994).

Applying principles of biblical justice and reconciliation— demonstrating love and kindness and walking humbly before God—can promote reciprocity among all involved in the classroom and school community, countering this outcome. This can result in new appreciation for the abilities and gifts of students with disabilities and encourage welcoming and celebration of difference and the contributions of each member of the community. This can promote a mutual sense of both responsibility to and need of one another—similar to what Paul described as the Body of Christ.

Schaffner and Buswell (1996) described the need for schools to become communities in which all students feel valued, safe, connected, and cared for. They hold that if "the element of community is overlooked or if its importance is underestimated, then students who present various kinds of diversity will continue to be disenfranchised and the school's desired outcomes for all students will continue to miss the mark" (p, 53). Students who feel disconnected from the classroom community (a lack of belonging) are less likely to reach their potential (cf. Kunc, 1992).

A culture of community runs counter to individualism, which is prominent in our society and in classrooms where competition is encouraged rather than cooperative learning. Instead of fostering competition, a just community will provide a common place (the classroom) where members share a common purpose. Frazee (2001) described a true community as "one in which there is a natural, emotional, and interdependent association among people. A contrived community, on the other hand, is characterized by the rational and instrumental association persons create, which can be described as impersonal, alienated, and mobile" (p. 200). Frazee's second example is characteristic of professional associations or relationships between university faculty from different disciplines. The first example is what we would hope to find in our own family and, I believe, is more descriptive of the kind of just community required for inclusive education.

Miles (2000) argued that diversity must be welcomed and relationships between disabled and non-disabled students consciously nurtured if there is to be meaningful change in the educational experience of marginalized students. Valuing the unique contributions of each member of the community facilitates belonging and promotes community well-being (Walther-Thomas, Korinek, McLaughlin, & Williams, 2000). Sands, Kozleski, and French (2000) used the motto "Each Belongs" to assert that all children, disabled and non-disabled, belong in school, and to insist that everyone involved shares responsibility for meeting student needs. They stressed the right of all learners to be involved in school activities, the need for acceptance and welcoming of all students, providing support for student weaknesses while building upon strengths, and establishing a spirit of togetherness "to meet the challenges of learning and living with one another" (p. 25). I believe that biblical justice provides a framework for this to happen.

## Conclusion

"Justice is the moral principle that corresponds most closely to the divine attribute of righteousness. In ethical terms, justice is the imperative to do what is right in a manner that is fair and impartial"

(Sanders, 1997, p. 15). Building inclusive practices from principles of biblical justice will help educators recognize that each student should receive what he or she needs, giving due consideration to each one's strengths and weaknesses, while avoiding negativity that results from focusing attention only on limitations or differences. Strully and Strully (1996) asserted that "inclusion means the process of making whole" and added that "embracing differences rather than avoiding differences is what community is all about" (p. 149).

In the biblical context, wholeness is part of the Hebrew term *shalom,* defined as "universal flourishing, wholeness, and delight—a rich state of affairs in which natural needs are satisfied and natural gifts fruitfully employed, all under the arch of God's love ... in other words ... the way things are supposed to be" (Plantinga, 2002, p. 15). This, coupled with Jesus's call for his disciples to be "peacemakers" has direct relevance to the type of community we wish to establish in our schools and classrooms. Biblical justice establishes a situation in which shalom is possible. But neither biblical justice nor shalom are magical formulas separate from the individuals who must implement them.

The just person is the one who practices justice because the Spirit of Christ is living within him ... From this new life arises the desire to live justly before God and humankind. This living is rooted in a desire to share the love of God, and not in selfish efforts to promote human welfare (Zorrilla, 1988, p. 43).

Just as Jesus broke through barriers of gender, religion, ethnicity, and ability/disability during his earthly ministry, teachers must also challenge practices and ideologies that lead to the exclusion of others. All Christians are to "do what is right to other people, love being kind to others, and live humbly, obeying your God" (Micah 6:8, NCV). Teachers must allow this principle to guide them in creating a classroom community that is truly inclusive, truly *just.*

# CHAPTER TEN

# Special Education
# as Spiritual Formation

I would like to pose a question for the reader: Does the spiritual life of special education teachers grow and deepen in the midst of their work? There are at least two implications in this question: (a) that there is a spirituality to special education, and (b) that our involvement in special education can contribute to our spiritual maturity.

## Spirituality of Special Education

Spirituality is something widely written about, but for which there is an abundance of definitions, some secular or psychological and others religious, though often with overlapping ideas. Human beings are, by definition, *spiritual*. Genesis 2:7 explains that God formed man from the dust of the ground—that's our physical nature. We are then

This chapter incorporates some of what was previously published as "Special Education and Spiritual Formation," Anderson, D. W. (2010), *Journal of the International Christian Community for Teacher Education* 5(2). Available from http://icctejournal.org/issues/v5i2/v5i2 anderson/ Reprinted by permission. The idea of special education and spiritual formation was first presented at the biennial meeting of the International Christian Community for Teacher Education, held at LeTourneau University, Longview, TX (May 2010). The theme of that meeting was "Igniting the Flames of Faith and Learning: Preparing Caring, Competent Teachers."

told that God breathed into man the breath of life so that man became a living "creature." Creature comes from a Hebrew word variously translated as *soul* (in the King James Version), *person* (in the New Living Translation), and *being* (in the New International Version). This term refers to our spiritual nature. The "breath of God" making man a living soul or being is the defining characteristic of personhood and, coupled with the fact that only humankind was created in the image of God, distinguishes humankind from animals and the rest of creation over which humankind was placed as steward. Adam and Eve were given charge over the rest of creation as God's agents, responsible to God as the "owner" of all. Persons, so defined, are not so much physical beings seeking the spiritual, as spiritual beings presently "encased" in the physical. The spiritual nature of persons is what leads people to ask deeply spiritual questions regarding meaning or significance, especially in times of suffering or disability or death. It is what drives us to seek fulfillment, hope, or purpose and fuels our will to live. It creates our need for belief or faith in self and others, and moves us to "search" for something transcendent (God) (Swinton, 2002, 2005).

Spirituality has to do with our relationship with others and with God, but also with God's relationship to us (Coulter, 2001). Because of our creation as "persons" in the image of God, spirituality is a fundamental element of humanity, though it is not necessarily experienced through our physical senses and may not be expressed verbally or coherently. Spirituality is not linked to or equated with intellectual understanding. It is a dimension of life and experience that demands that we respect and honor each individual, regardless of his or her ability or disability.

Spirituality has a place in the special education classroom not in the sense of verbalizing or evangelizing, but through our actions as Christian teachers in creating a classroom community where students with disabilities feel valued, a sense of belonging, and an aura of loving relationships.

Swinton (1997) spoke of spirituality in relation to disability:

> It is my assertion that spirituality has as much to do with *feeling* as with *thinking*. Concrete experience of friendship at a human level reveals the 'inexpressibleness' of the transcendent God of love. The doctrine of incarnation suggests that God is revealed not primarily in ideas, but in concrete reality. It is in the flesh of Jesus that we encounter God most fully ... (God) accommodates Himself in the communication of love to cognitively disabled people through loving relationships ... Simply put, loving attitudes reveal a loving deity, and if cognitively disabled persons' experiences help develop a trusting confidence that they exist in a relationship which is fundamentally loving and accepting, then the Christian gospel has been preached experientially and effectively. (p. 26)

Michael Anthony, professor of Christian Education at Biola University, Talbot School of Theology, defined Christian spirituality as the interaction of our theology and daily experience. In his words, "Christian spirituality is intended to be lived out in the context of community with other believers and also in the midst of the lost" (2006, p. 43). This happens as the Holy Spirit draws us into deeper fellowship with God and enables us to put into practice our Christian commitment.

The relationship between spirituality and special education as practical theology (chapter three) is clear. Spirituality as a lived practice integrates the "spiritual" and "theological" with teaching special education students principally through the teacher's character—the ethic of love and the ethic of care (chapter four)—and the application of Christian values to the classroom. In writing on biblical spirituality, Sandra Schneiders asserted that "Christian spirituality is a self-transcending faith in which union with God in Jesus Christ through the Spirit expresses itself in service of the neighbor and participation in the realization of the reign of God in this world" (2000, p. 134). Her statement shows the link between spirituality and a life of service to others and to God. The intimate relationship between Christian spirituality and the character of the special educator is brought out in these words from Kirkpatrick (2003):

> Grounded in the character of God's holiness, Christian spirituality springs from the reality of faith and a right relationship with God. It is not so much a set body of knowledge as much as it is the ability to determine the right time and place for certain actions that demonstrate the redemptive character of what it means to be related to God.... The spiritual life, its consecration and sanctification, its commitment and devotion, is a life that is lived in response to the divine initiative, and is to be lived so as to demonstrate the character of holiness. (p. 49)

Demonstrating the character of holiness refers to our demeanor and involves our demonstrating *spiritual fruits* such as grace, patience, gentleness, forgiveness, and self-control (Galatians 5:22–23).

Can God be encountered in the special education classroom? Yes, for at least five reasons:

- First, since God is omnipresent, he is present in the classroom in this general sense.
- Second, God is present in the classroom because Christian special educators are in the classroom, and we are "in Christ" (1 Corinthians 1:30; 2 Corinthians 1:21) and Christ is "in us" (Ephesians 3:17; Colossians 1:27; 1 John 5:20). Our relationship is with the Father and the Son (John 17:21; 1 John 2:24), and we are indwelt by the Holy Spirit (John 14:16) who is our teacher (Luke 12:12) and our source of spiritual life (John 3:5–6) and spiritual power (Acts 1:8).
- Third, Christians are the "body of Christ" (Ephesians 1:22–23, 3:17, 4:14–16; Colossians 1:28). This phrase is not simply a descriptor of the church. To be the "body of Christ" means that believers (individually and collectively) are the locus of Jesus's activity today: We are his hands and feet and voice in the world. In that sense, Jesus is "present" in the classroom in us. No one has ever seen God, but they do see us, and we should reflect him in our actions and words.
- Fourth, the words of Jesus in Matthew 25:31–40 ask that we recognize that what we have done to *one of the least of these*—and students who have a disability may still be among this group, despite legal requirements that they be included in the schools—*we have done to Jesus.*
- Fifth, God has a presence in the classroom because we all, teachers and students alike, are created as God's image-bearers.

The spirituality of special education, thus, stems from our understanding of God, ourselves, and our students as his creations, as well as from our desire to honor God and live according to his principles as revealed in the Great Commandment to love God with all our heart and soul and mind and to love our neighbor as ourselves (Matthew 22:37–40).

In a practical sense, the spirituality of special education requires recognition of the spiritual assumptions and imperatives for ethical decision-making in assessment, program planning, and placement issues in special education. Osmer (2008), writing on practical theology, identified two further elements where spirituality and special education intersect, both relating to the attitude of special education teachers: the *spirituality of presence* and the *spirituality of servant-leadership.*

Spirituality of presence refers to maintaining an orientation of openness and attentiveness toward others, even a prayerfulness as we try to understand our students and their needs. A spirituality of servant-leadership is patterned after the example of Jesus, who redefined the nature of power and authority (Mark 10:42–45). This aspect of spirituality involves mutual care and service (as in the "one-another" teachings of the New Testament) and a rejection of the strict hierarchies of status and power seen in the world, and often in the classroom, which rely on violence and retribution.

## Special Education and Spiritual Formation

In chapter one, we examined the meaning of "calling." There, we concluded with Hillman (2008) that our primary call is to a living, dynamic relationship with God, which requires a complete surrender of our life to him. Since our primary call is *to live a life worthy of the Lord,* pleasing him in every way (Colossians 1:10) and bringing him glory (Ephesians 1:14; Philippians 1:11), all our work—all our life—is *spiritual* work. As God's "workmanship" we have been designed and equipped for our walk on this planet and our work as Christians so that we do the good things that "God planned in advance for us to live our lives doing" (Ephesians 2:10, NCV). God's call also involves spiritual transformation, as spoken of in Romans 12:1–2 and 2 Corinthians 3:18. God's call, his will, is that we be transformed into the likeness of Christ. This transformation, as we shall see, is not instantaneous, but is a lifelong process.

Psalm 139:13–16 explains that God knits each individual together in the womb. God's fashioning of every one of us includes our strengths and weaknesses, interests and desires. David declared that God "saw me before I was born. Every day of my life was recorded in your book. Every moment was laid out before a single day had passed" (Psalm 139:16, NLT). Wiersbe (2004) explained that this likely included both the span of our lives and the tasks that God has for us to perform (cf. Ephesians 2:10; Philippians 2:12–13). Because of God's goodness, we know that what he plans comes from a loving heart (Jeremiah 29:11) and will ultimately bring him glory. And because of God's sovereignty, we know that what he plans will ultimately come to pass. Furthermore, given God's sovereignty, which includes his directive will and his permissive will, we recognize that things do not happen completely by accident. Therefore, we can conclude that Christian special educators do not simply meet their students by accident, but by God's design. It is reasonable, therefore, to expect that our work as special education teachers will in some way contribute to our spiritual maturation. This makes it essential that we remain alert to what God might want to teach us through our interaction with each student who has a disability, and consider how these interactions can contribute both to our professional development and our spiritual formation. As Guinness (1998) suggested, our calling to God and to serve God is "key to tracing the storyline of our lives" (p. 181).

Perkins (2003) stated, "God's call to service for my life cannot be separated from God's intention to work in my life" (p. 157). I believe that reflection on biblical themes that inform special education and disability studies (such as those explored in this book), along with our actual interaction with persons who have disabilities, can contribute in a very practical manner to our spiritual maturation. We will come back to this idea later. But first we need to focus more directly on the concept of spiritual formation.

## Understanding Spiritual Formation

Mulholland (1993, 2000, 2006) has written extensively about spiritual formation, primarily focusing on the importance of Scripture to our formation as believers. He carefully pointed out that our reading and study of Scripture should not be just to gather factual information. Since Scripture is a primary means by which God speaks to us, it is important that our reading of his Word be formational, that we remain open to God's shaping us to be like Christ in every aspect of our relating to the world and to others. We must allow the Holy Spirit to work in our hearts and lives "to shape our *being* in the image of Christ" (Mulholland, p. 2000, p. 102; italics in original). Maddix (2010) likewise maintained that studying Scripture has less to do with information-gathering and more to do with our spiritual formation and transformation:

> Christian spirituality focuses on the progressive transformation of the human person into the likeness of Jesus Christ. It is the result of the cooperation of our whole lives with the power and presence of Christ's Spirit, who is alive and working within the whole person—body and soul, thoughts and feelings,

emotions and passions, hopes and fears and dreams. (Maddix, 2010, p. 240)

## The Importance of Spiritual Formation

Mulholland (2000) asserted that "human life is, by its very nature, spiritual formation" (p. 26). The question, then, is not whether to undertake spiritual formation, but in what kind of spiritual formation are we already engaged? Paul's exhortation in Romans 12:2 is that we not be conformed to this world, but be transformed by the renewing of our mind. Christians must resist the pressure to conform to the brokenness and disintegration of the world and, instead, be increasingly conformed to the wholeness and integration of the image of Christ as God's Spirit works within us (Mulholland, 2000, p. 26).

Second Corinthians 5:17 declares that to be in Christ is to be a new creation, a new person. Thus, Paul describes Christians as having "put off the old self" and "put on the new self, which is being renewed in knowledge after the image of its creator" (Colossians 3:9b–10). This renewal, or re-imaging, is an ongoing process: "We are new and continue to become new" (Estep, 2010, p. 14). This transformation in our very nature is a central feature of our Christian faith. Mulholland (2000) put it succinctly: "We are all pilgrims on the way toward the wholeness God has for us in Christ" (p. 15).

## Defining Spiritual Formation

Mulholland (1993) defined spiritual formation as a "journey into becoming persons of compassion, persons who forgive, persons who care deeply for others and the world' (p. 25). It is a process whereby we are continually being conformed to the image of Christ *"for the sake of others"* and is *"inseparable from our relationships with others"* (Mulholland, 2000, pp. 25, 28; emphasis added). This service orientation is particularly relevant to special education, wherein we serve the students directly and serve their families and society indirectly.

Spiritual formation differs from regeneration in that regeneration is a gift from and entirely carried out by God, and is instantaneous and complete. Spiritual formation, on the other hand, requires our cooperation with God, is progressive and incomplete in this lifetime, and involves obedience and faithfulness to God (Carlson, 2010). Spiritual formation involves being formed in Christ (Christlikeness) *and* having Christ formed in us, allowing Paul to say "I have been crucified with Christ. It is no longer I who live, but Christ who lives in me. And the life I now live in the flesh I live by faith in the Son of God, who loved me and gave himself for me" (Galatians 2:20). Galatians 4:19 is Paul's prayer that the believers in Galatia would become so like Christ that it could be said that Christ has been formed in them (Maddix, 2010, pp. 240–241). Thus, we conclude that spiritual formation involves taking on the qualities or characteristics of Jesus Christ.

The Apostle Paul said in Romans 12:2 that we are not to be conformed to, or fashioned like the world, but to be transformed by the renewal of our minds. This spiritual formation, or inward renovation, brought about by the Spirit of God should be outwardly demonstrated in our lifestyle, actions, motives, and words. The dual actions of renunciation and renewal is the outworking of the decisive commitment urged in Romans 12:1 where Paul exhorts believers to completely surrender their entire person to God as a living sacrifice. For special education teachers, this should impact who we are, how we view our students, and how we "do" special education.

Paul's teaching in 2 Corinthians 3:18 speaks to spiritual formation:

> And we all, with unveiled face, beholding the glory of the Lord, are being transformed into the same image from one degree of glory to another. For this comes from the Lord who is the Spirit.

Three implications from this passage help us understand that spiritual formation:

- It is a lifelong process of change from the inside out, which affects the whole person (not just the mind).
- The formation is into the likeness of Christ (yet without losing our personal identity).
- Transformation is the result of the action of the Holy Spirit.

Second Corinthians 3 speaks of the ministry of the Spirit as being superior to the ministry of law in the Old Testament. Paul describes the ministry of the Spirit as bringing confident hope (3:4), life (3:6), liberty (3:17), and transformation (3:18). In contrast to Moses's *reflecting* the glory of God when he descended Mount Sinai (a result of his having been speaking with God, but something that did not continue), Paul says that believers *radiate* the glory of God. As the Spirit of God works to transform us, to move us closer in spirit and character to the image of Christ, this "radiated glory" continues to increase as our "lowly body" is transformed to be like Jesus's "glorious body" (Philippians 3:21). Whereas Old Testament law can lead us to Christ (Galatians 3:24), only grace can make us *like* Christ, as the Holy Spirit opens our mind and heart to God's truth and transforms us, allowing Christ to shine through us. The Greek word rendered as "transformation" is *metamorphoô*, which gives us the English word metamorphosis, used to describe the change from caterpillar to butterfly. It refers to a process

215

of change from the inside out that results in the character of Jesus emerging in the life of believers. This process continues throughout our lifetime as the Holy Spirit works to change and shape our being so that the glory of God becomes more evident in believers.

"Spiritual growth is movement into a deeper and closer relationship with God. As this occurs, our wills and character are increasingly conformed to God's will and character, and we become more whole" (Benner, 1988, p. 90). This relationship with God results in a desire to more closely follow Christ, and the process continues: "As we continually reflect the glory of the Lord, we are continually being transformed into the image of the one whose glory we are reflecting" (Hoekema, 1986, p. 24). We do not simply wait for the Spirit of God to transform us, however. Romans 12:2 urges that we not be conformed to the world, that we adopt a posture toward life that seeks transformation, and that we respond positively to the prompting of the Spirit in our lives. As the "agent of our transformation" (Bridges, 2012), the Holy Spirit works in us to convict us of sin, to help us see the connection between Scripture and specific issues in our lives, to awaken and sensitize our conscience, to create a desire to conform to the will of God, and to enable us respond and to do the works that God has prepared beforehand for us to engage in (Ephesians 2:10). Sometimes God will even use adversity or suffering in our lives to bring about this transformation.

Bridges (2012) wrote about the dual actions of not being conformed to the world but being transformed by the renewal of our mind using the term "dependent responsibility" (pp. 98). Drawing from Philippians 2:12–13—"Work out your own salvation with fear and trembling, for it is God who works in you, both to will and to work for his good pleasure"—Bridges explained that believers are responsible for working out in their lives that which was implanted in them when they were saved, but we are able to do this because God, through his Spirit, is at work within us. Hence, "we are both fully responsible and fully dependent" (Bridges, p. 106).

## The Effect of Spiritual Formation

The direction of our transformation is established in Romans 8:29 where Paul indicates that God has determined beforehand that we be conformed to the likeness of Christ: "For those whom he foreknew he also predestined to be conformed to the image of his Son, in order that he might be the firstborn among many brothers." In practical terms, this means being like Jesus in his faithful commitment to fulfilling the Great Commandment to love God and love one's neighbor (Matthew 33:37–39) and in his desire to please the Father through obedience to God's will (John 5:30, 6:38, 8:29). Being spiritually transformed means that these characteristics must become primary in our lives as well. Our desire to be conformed to the character of Christ must manifest in an equal desire to know and do the will of God (Bridges, 2012).

Colossians 1:9–10 describes the process and outcome of spiritual formation:

> And so, from the day we heard, we have not ceased to pray for you, asking that you may be filled with the knowledge of his will in all spiritual wisdom and understanding, so as to walk in a manner worthy of the Lord, fully pleasing to him, bearing fruit in every good work and increasing in the knowledge of God.

Paul's prayer is that believers be completely sated with the knowledge of God's will. "In the language of the New Testament, to be filled means to be 'controlled by'" (Wiersbe, 2001, *Colossians 1:9)*. Paul asks that believers be controlled by the full knowledge of God's will by means of spiritual wisdom and understanding. This is the desired result of studying God's Word and receiving illumination from the Holy Spirit. Thus, spiritual intelligence—growing in the will of God by knowing the Word of God—is the first step toward fullness of life. The result of this "filling" is practical and four-fold:

- walking in a manner worthy of the Lord,
- fully pleasing God,
- bearing fruit in every good work,
- and increasing in experiential and relational knowledge of God.

Thus, we conclude with Bridges (2012):

> This transformation into the image of Jesus is much more than a change in outward conduct; rather, it is a deep penetrating work of the Holy Spirit in the very core of our being, what the Bible calls the heart—the center of our intellect, affections, and will. (p. 12)

Rather than simply a change in behavior or morality, the transformation spoken of in Romans 12:2 and 2 Corinthians 3:18 results from the work of the Holy Spirit in shaping us to Christ's image. But we are to actively participate in this process as we strive not to be conformed to the world, and respond appropriately to the moral exhortations and commands of Scripture. The Holy Spirit is the "agent of transformation" who works in believers and enables us to do what God has prepared for us to do (Bridges, 2012). God equips us to do his will and works in us what is pleasing in his sight (Hebrews 13:21). This mutuality of relationship—God's working in us and our obedience to him—is also seen in Philippians 2:12-13 where we are told to work out our own salvation with fear and trembling, recognizing that it is God who works in us both to will and to work for his good pleasure. That is, we are to be focused and diligent in living out our new life (salvation life), acknowledging the importance of living in a way that will please God. At the same time, however, God works in us "to will and to work for his good pleasure."

There is a tension, then, between our need to labor faithfully and our "dependent responsibility" to God (Bridges, p. 105). Further evidence of the tension is found in Philippians 4:13 ("I can do all things through him who strengthens me") and Colossians 1:29 ("For this I toil, struggling with all his energy that he powerfully works within me").

## Spiritual Formation and Special Education

Thus, spiritual formation is not something we *do* ourselves; it is something which is done in us by the Holy Spirit, though not without our cooperation and submission. Certainly, Scripture is a key element used by the Holy Spirit to bring about our transformation. We must allow God to speak to us, to reveal his truth as we meditate on and study God's Word. But I suggest that we also must be open to what God may show us about himself, ourselves, and the Christian life through our encounters with students who have disabilities. In this section, I want to stress God's Spirit "speaking" to us through our experiences with disability and with students who have a disability. This does not negate the need to study the Scriptures, God's primary way of revealing himself and his will to us. But as we reflect biblically on our encounters with students, God will help us to see our students and ourselves though his eyes.

We are told that "the word of God is living and active, sharper than any two-edged sword, piercing to the division of soul and of spirit, of joints and of marrow, and discerning the thoughts and intentions of the heart" (Hebrews 4:12–13). Looking biblically at our interactions with students who have special needs and at ourselves can open areas where God's Word needs to teach, reprove, correct, and train us in righteousness (2 Timothy 3:16), specifically in relation to our work as special educators. Just as we study Scriptures seeking to allow God is open us to "its deeper dimensions, its multiple layers of meaning" (Mulholland, 2000, p. 56), so we must reflect on our experiences with students for deeper, spiritual meaning—such as how we view humanity in general, how we understand ourselves and our need to grow spiritually, what needs to change in our behavior, and so forth. Just as we are the object that is shaped by God's Word, God can use our encounters with students as a means to further develop us in the image of Christ.

Paul commanded that we be imitators and followers of God as his beloved children (Ephesians 5:1). Mulholland (2000) said that "for those who have set their feet upon the journey into wholeness in Christ, an essential part of that journey is becoming the agent of God's wholeness into the broken life of the world" (p. 79). As we live out our Christian faith with students and families affected by disability, we become that agent. This is a journey in which we become persons of compassion, forgiveness, and deep caring for others (Mulholland, 1993, p. 25).

Paul captured another aspect of our spiritual formation when instructing believers to "put off the old self" and "put on the new self" (Colossians 3:9–10; Ephesians 4:22, 24), to "put on Christ"

(Galatians 3:27; Romans 13:14), and to "put to death" the sinful, worldly desires (Colossians 3:5). Our study of and meditation on the Word of God, coupled with the Holy Spirit's acting in our lives (and our submission to the Spirit of God), furthers the process of "putting off" and "putting to death." Our classroom experiences with students with disabilities then provides an opportunity to demonstrate that spiritual growth.

Reflecting on our interactions with children who have disabilities can, with the Spirit's illumination of our mind and heart, help us to identify what may yet need to be "killed" and what needs to be nurtured in our lives (e.g., the fruits of the Spirit). With each encounter with students with disabilities, we must consider what God wants to teach us or break us from. Keeping a journal of reflections on student encounters (both positive and negative) and on the search for Scriptural insight can foster the teacher's spiritual development while promoting professional development. Such journaling is something I encouraged students to do when completing their student teaching/practicum assignments. Those who took to heart this task and shared their journals with me showed keen perception of the students, their teaching, and themselves.

Mulholland (2000) stated, "The core of spiritual formation is breaking the crust of self and bringing forth a new creation in the image of Christ" (p. 113). This "breaking the crust" comes as God's Spirit helps us see Scriptural truths applied to life as the Holy Spirit guides our reflection on encounters with students who have a disability and makes us aware of areas in our lives and character that need to be changed, and as we remain open to "receiving the message" of the students. Students may respond or react because of limitations related to their disability or out of frustration, but we must also consider that God may be "allowing" this encounter in order to teach us something. If that is the case, we must not waste the opportunity to learn and grow.

When reflecting on negative or positive student encounters, therefore, we need to stand back and evaluate the situation. We must not simply ask what we can learn about teaching; we need to ask how is God meeting us (and the student) in this encounter. What does God want us to learn from this encounter about himself, about humanity, about ourselves, about living as an example of Christ, about grace, forgiveness, compassion, etc.? We need to evaluate the encounter spiritually, not just cognitively. It is important that we guard against making quick judgments based on what we think we know about the student or on our prejudices and habits, and reflect deeply, seeking spiritual significance.

Spiritual formation is a lifelong process of growing into the image of Christ (Mulholland, 2000). It is not something only for the "super religious." Rather, it is …

> *the primal reality of human existence.* Every act of life is an experience of spiritual formation. Every action taken, every response made, every dynamic of relationship, every thought held, every emotion allowed: These are the minuscule arenas where, bit by bit, infinitesimal piece by infinitesimal piece, we are shaped into some kind of being. We are being shaped either toward the wholeness of the image of Christ or toward a horribly destructive caricature of that image. (pp. 25–26, emphasis in original)

Maddix (2010) stated that "acts of Christian service keep us in the presence of Christ where the Holy Spirit has an opportunity to go on transforming us" (p. 242). Special education is such an act of Christian service. As we reflect on our work with students who are disabled, trying to view the students and the task of teaching through the eyes of God, we allow God's Spirit to have a transforming effect on us. We need to heighten our senses to see the presence of Christ in our classroom experience and in the students with whom we work. Colossians 3:17 says that whatever we do, in word or deed, is to be done in the name of the Lord Jesus. Wiersbe (2001) explained this to mean that all we say and do should be associated with the name of Jesus Christ; our words and our works should glorify Jesus's name. To do things "in the name of Jesus" connotes identification—we belong to him and we have authority in his name. This provides motivation for godly living and for continued growth toward Christlikeness. We bring the presence of Christ into the classroom. But more than this, we need to look upon our students as described in Matthew 25:37–40,

> Then the righteous will answer him, saying, 'Lord, when did we see you hungry and feed you, or thirsty and give you drink? And when did we see you a stranger and welcome you, or naked and clothe you? And when did we see you sick or in prison and visit you?' And the King will answer them, 'Truly, I say to you, as you did it to one of the least of these my brothers, you did it to me.'

We need to ask ourselves several questions: Do we see and treat our students in the manner we would see and treat Jesus? Do we see our involvement in special education as opportunities to love God and our neighbors—those who might elsewhere be called "stakeholders": the students and their families, our faculty associates, the administrators, and so on? Do we keep the idea of bringing glory to God at the forefront of our activity and our being?

Becoming Christlike is not something personal but is to be lived out before the world. Said Mulholland (2006):

> Union with God results in our being a person through whom God's presence touches the world with forgiving, cleansing, healing, liberating and transforming grace ... To be like Jesus, then, as it is portrayed in the New Testament, is a matter of both "being" and "doing." It is being in a relationship of loving union with God that manifests itself in Christlike living in the world. (p. 16)

## Teaching for Spiritual Formation in the University

How do Christian university faculty teach students preparing to be special education teachers in a way that communicates our own wrestling with and understanding of the integration of our faith with the discipline? How do we stimulate students to reflect on this important area on their own? Is it sufficient to give them an assignment to write about integrating faith and learning? Are we, as Christian teacher-trainers, able to trace how our professional study and experience has contributed to our own spiritual formation?

Spiritual transformation is something the Holy Spirit accomplishes, but not without the witness of others (such as Christian faculty) and not without effort on our part. As we have already seen, Romans 12:2 indicates that there is both an active (do not be conformed to this world) and a passive (but be transformed by the renewal of your mind) aspect to our spiritual formation. The end result of this transformation is that we are able to *test* and *discern* God's will. This transformation and renewal results in a new way of seeing and being in God's world: to "see the world through God's eyes" (Swinton, 1999). This includes how we perceive, value, and respond to persons who are disabled, how we view our professional activity and responsibility, and how we see our place in God's mission.

The facts taught in special education are no different in a Christian university than in a secular training program. Christian faculty seeking to prepare special education teachers need to consider how to keep our presentation from being "just the facts" but not the Spirit. Our own understanding of faith-learning integration must become evident to our students, both in teaching about the topics and in how we relate to our students. Education is about change and growth. University professors need to reflect on how we can promote both professional development and spiritual development through our teaching. Are there specific ways the curriculum can contribute to the students' spiritual formation? How can we encourage in students our own reflection on the integration of faith and learning that has contributed—and continues to contribute—to our development of a theology of disability or hermeneutic of special education?

If special education professors seek to "ignite the flames of faith and learning" in our students, more is involved than simply helping students master the knowledge-base and skills of teaching. Students must also be helped to think biblically and critically about the discipline of special education. Reflection on biblical themes that inform special education/disability studies contributes in a very practical manner to the special educator's spiritual maturation. For faculty to share our own journeys toward Christlikeness with our students, and invite or challenge them to move forward in their own journey becomes critical. As college and university faculty share our journey toward Christlikeness with students studying to become special educators, we invite or challenge our students to move forward in their own spiritual development as well as in their professional knowledge and skills.

Rather than considering how God fits into the discipline of special education, it is necessary to ask how special education fits into God's mission. Moreland (1999) spoke of a spiritual dimension to integration of faith with one's professional discipline. He described integration as a spiritual activity that has as its goal structuring the mind and strengthening the belief structure that informs a life of Christian discipleship. Considering the spiritual dimension of faith-learning integration requires that faculty explore with their students what light God's Word sheds on the field of special education. Becoming like Christ, having the mind of Christ, does not mean that we quote Scripture whenever we believe it to apply to what is being taught, but that scriptural truth shapes our thinking, valuing, and doing.

"A Christian mind … must take captive and subordinate scientific, technical, legal or other perspectives to the theological perspective" (Gill, 1989, p. 66). Having the mind of Christ means allowing God to illuminate facts, values, meanings, and the context in which these have significance. This allows us to reflect on special education, disability, and persons with disabilities within the context of biblical revelation, going beyond the medical model upon which much of special education has been based, and going beyond the disability studies model, with its focus on social and cultural aspects. Such a biblical focus frees us to go "beyond the narrow field of vision in the world around us, crossing boundaries, exploring new possibilities" (Gill, 1989, p. 68).

Fundamental to spiritual formation and understanding how the Christian faith informs the discipline and practice in special education is recognizing the Bible's emphasis on Christians being called to serve others. Faculty need to help our students broaden their conception of special education from simply a career to understanding it as a ministry (as discussed in chapter one).

To have the mind of Christ is to be especially concerned with people who are in some way disenfranchised, as in the history of exclusion of persons with disabilities from education and community life (cf. Perkins, 2007). "The constant message of the Scriptures buttressed by the stunning example of Jesus is that God's kingdom people are to use their authority, power, and prestige to help and serve, never to hurt, those without authority, power, and prestige" (Kraft, 1996, p. 313). As Farnsworth (1985) asserted, "From a Christian perspective, one's career emerges out of and is committed to seeking first the kingdom of God (Mt. 6:33)" (p. 101). His point is that focus must be on the kingdom, not on the career, and what we do must be seen within the sphere of stewardship. "The emphasis must be on giving, not taking, on furthering the kingdom through service to others, not advancing oneself by furthering one's career" (Farnsworth, 1985, p. 101).

Being a special educator must be understood as a way of living out the gospel in daily life as special education teachers seek to bring reconciliation between persons with disabilities and those who are temporarily able-bodied, as they promote justice and equality through advocating and practicing inclusive education, as they interact with families affected by disability and professionals who work with them, and as they seek optimal development of students with special needs—cognitively, physically, emotionally, and socially.

## My Spiritual Formation

How does this apply to our role as special educators? The obvious implication is that we need to study Scripture *at least* as diligently as we studied to become a special education teacher in the first place, and we need to study it *more* than our efforts to continue our education and remain current in the field. Scriptural truth not only applies to what God requires in terms of our character, but it helps us see the world, ourselves, and our students more biblically (refer to chapters two and four). Paul said that "All Scripture is breathed out by God and profitable for teaching, for reproof, for correction, and for training in righteousness, that the man of God may be complete, equipped for every good work" (2 Timothy 3:16–17). God has given us his Spirit who will teach us all things and bring to remembrance all that Jesus has said (John 14:26; 16:13). As we look intently into God's word and listen to the prompting of the Holy Spirit, God will further the process of our transformation.

But I propose that God also uses our activity as special education teachers and how we engage with students who have a disability to shape us to be like Christ. In chapter three I spoke of learning from students who have disabilities and shared the examples of several individuals who worked with or parented children with disabilities. Understanding how my faith integrates with or informs special education (perhaps I should say informs me as a special educator) has been an ongoing process of shaping and broadening my worldview as a Christian. Noll (1985) remarked that "Christian world views are always in the process of reformation" (p. 31). This reformation of our worldview parallels our own transformation as we are caught up in the process of being remade in the image of Christ.

Here, I summarize what I have learned through my work with children in general and special education, and through my study of scriptural principals in relation to special education/disability studies. These experiences and the children themselves have helped me to grow spiritually in several ways. They have:

- helped me to appreciate God's heart for people who are disenfranchised;
- encouraged development of the fruits of the Spirit (Galatians 5:22–23), especially compassion, patience, kindness, goodness, gentleness, and self-control;
- increased my understanding and appreciation of biblical concepts of justice and hospitality as they inform special education practice;
- broadened my understanding of what it means to be created in (as) God's image;
- led to a greater awareness of God's mysterious ways and infinite wisdom;
- deepened my respect for and acceptance of differences, specifically differences associated with disability, helping me to see the beauty of each individual despite severe or profound disability;
- brought recognition that human weakness provides an avenue for God's strength to shine (2 Corinthians 12:7–10);
- encouraged greater dependence upon God, following the example of persons with disabilities;
- strengthened my appreciation for the eternal, when disability will be done away with;
- heightened a sense of my own shortcomings and God's greatness, sovereignty, and grace;
- advanced my understanding of the character and love of the God we serve;
- altered my view of personal affliction, both by putting my own afflictions or suffering in perspective, and by recognizing true grace under fire as I watch people with disabilities struggle daily

with their impairment along with negative and condescending attitudes of many who are temporarily able-bodied.

It is necessary that we maintain a teachable attitude, which "begins with a spirit of humility that recognizes that we know so little of God's Word and apply even less of what we know" (Bridges, 2012, p. 108). It can be easy for a special education teacher to act out of a prideful position, assuming they know all the answers and have nothing to learn from their students. This reflects a failure to connect what God reveals in his Word about ourselves, humanity, our students, and our work in the classroom.

For example, though we have *head* knowledge of the fruits of the Spirit—love, joy, peace, patience, kindness, faithfulness, gentleness, self-control (Galatians 5:22–23)—we often fail to understand how these principles are to be worked out in our professional (or personal) lives. As the Spirit of God works from within to form us into the image of Jesus, and as we seek to apply God's Word to our life and work, we will become more able to demonstrate the spirituality of presence and of servant-leadership as we work with students who have special needs. We will be better able to create classrooms that are hospitable, promote interdependence, and operate on the principle of biblical justice. We will be enabled to give character witness of our faith as we provide an appropriate education, and an appropriate educational environment to the students God has placed before us.

# Moving Forward

When preparing university students to become special education teachers, it is always my desire to challenge them to move beyond a narrow focus on skills, techniques, and legal responsibilities required of the profession and to think about disability and special education *Christianly*. My colleagues and I have sought to integrate this thinking within the entire program of studies, but I often thought it would be appropriate to offer a *capstone* course that would help students uncover biblical and theological teaching integral to understanding special education as ministry. This book is an attempt to present the essence of such a course.

## Agents of Change

Christians who teach basic education, special education, or higher education are in a position to minister to the intellectual, developmental, and spiritual needs of others. As representatives of Jesus, we are to declare by word and deed Christian truth and to work toward reconciliation with God and with one another. It is my belief that education is fundamental to that ministry of reconciliation, whether it is education about the world and its people as created by God, about redemption through Christ, or about helping people with disabilities to reach their potential and become fully integrated in schools and society. Christians need to view special education as a response to God's call to join his mission of restoration, renewal, and reconciliation by establishing classrooms based on principles of biblical justice and the freedom of responsible interdependence, with the hope that changes among people of school age will spread into the world.

As agents of change, teachers foster changes in the students with whom they work and changes in schools for the betterment of the students they serve (cf. Fullan, 1993), and special education teachers and researchers have helped bring changes in federal law regarding education of students with disabilities. But Christians are also called to be agents of change in society and culture. A biblical understanding of disability, students with disabilities, and our teaching interactions fostered by practical theology can help identify practices and situations within schools and society that need to be changed in light of God's concern for the oppressed and disenfranchised. This is part of our being the *light and salt in the earth*.

## Calling Revisited

Guinness (1998) defined calling as "the truth that God calls us to himself so decisively that everything we are, everything we do, and everything we have is invested with a special devotion and dynamism lived out as a response to his summons and service" (p. 4). He further clarified that a Christian's calling is to be a follower of Jesus and a follower of "the Way" (John 14:6). To follow Jesus is to adjust our thinking and behavior to conform to his way of life (cf. Romans 12:2; 2 Corinthians 3:18). In Guinness's words, "We leave all other allegiances behind and walk after him, *doing what he says and living as he requires*" (p. 110, emphasis added).

Incarnational teaching is part of this following, or living, in "the Way." Jesus said "*As* the Father has sent me, even *so* I am sending you"(John 20:21, emphasis added). Our "sending" is to model that of

Jesus. We want to incarnate Jesus among those with whom we work, to incarnate the message of hope and peace which he proclaimed, to seek opportunity to serve others as Jesus did, to come alongside others, to manifest the spirituality of presence and the spirituality of servant-leadership. Given Jesus's orientation toward the poor, widows, orphans, diseased, disabled persons—those considered nobodies or outsiders of his society—the way we relate to such people today is not simply concern for social justice, but lies at the heart of our response to the gospel itself (cf. Peskett & Ramachandra (2003, p. 166). Those affected by disability need to see evidence of Christ's life in our lives, personal and professional.

It bears repeating, one's *calling* is not restricted to what some think of as their "spiritual life" (after all, *all* of life is spiritual). Nor is God's call focused on our vocation. Calling provides "the storyline for our lives" (Guinness, 1998) allowing a sense of continuity and coherence that helps us through times of turbulence. "The truth of calling is as vital to our ending as to our beginning," said Guinness (p. 241), and explained that calling gives us purpose in our life-journey, helps us understand that retirement from a job does not mean termination of our vocation (involvement in God's mission), and encourages recognition that the outcome of our lives is in God's hands.

All Christians are called to servanthood and stewardship. Becoming a special education teacher places one in a field of service that can bring us much blessing and can be used by God to form us into the kind of persons he intended. We serve God and others using the gifts and talents he designed into us. This is done out of responsible stewardship of what God has given us as his creation, and stewardship of others whom God created and has brought into relationship with us. As Hazle (2003) reminded us, "The church does not exist primarily to maintain itself but to serve the world around it; it is the world that God loves and for which God in Christ died" (p. 353). All believers, but especially those involved in special education, need to keep this servant mentality in the forefront of their thinking.

When teaching at the university, I sought to help my students grow and develop "wholly." My desire was to fulfill my calling through faithful stewardship of what God has entrusted to me, while helping my students to become faithful stewards as well. My concern went beyond helping students to develop professional attitudes and competencies. There was also concern for their development as mature, thinking, responsible Christian world citizens. My hope for my students and for this book is to motivate individuals to evaluate their own walk with Christ, their reasons for choosing special education as a profession, how they see Scriptural truth relating to teaching, and how they can be salt and light while teaching in public or private schools. I encourage all who are involved with special education or disability students to reflect on the discipline and how it dovetails with their Christian worldview (in the process, asking them to become more aware of their own worldview, and to critique it from a biblical perspective). The place to begin this process is with God, the sovereign Creator and Lord, and with mankind as created in (as) God's image.

## Kingdom Thinking

Chapter one spoke of serving in God's kingdom and how, through the ministry of Jesus, the kingdom of God broke through into the world. But for many, the kingdom of God brings only thoughts of a heavenly afterlife in the presence of God. Actually, the Bible gives little information about heaven. Jesus did speak of the kingdom of heaven/ kingdom of God, but mostly focused on its growth, and almost always referred to the kingdom as "near," "here," or "within" (Mark 1:15; Luke

10:9–11, 17:21). One reason for this is that we are still here. Jesus did not simply remove us to heaven at the time of our salvation; he left us on Earth so that we can participate with him as he builds his church. We have been left behind—on purpose, for a purpose. Chan (1998) asserted:

> The Christian story is not primarily about how God in Jesus came to rescue sinners from some impending disaster. It is about God's work of initiating us into a fellowship and making us true conversational partners with the Father and the Son through the Spirit and, hence, with each other (1 John 1:1–4). (p. 78)

Though the biblical authors do not provide details about the hereafter, Chan observed that "they have bequeathed to us a rich vocabulary describing the nature of the life of fellowship (justification, regeneration, reconciliation, and so on)" (p. 78). The purpose for which we have been left behind includes being salt and light in the world (Matthew 5:12–13), proclaiming the gospel in word and deed (Matthew 28:18–20), and doing that for which humankind was originally created, designed, and gifted: bringing glory to God. Ephesians 2:8–10 declares that we have been saved by God's grace, not by works of our own.

The Bible teaches that no one can please God and earn a place in God's kingdom by his own doing. But many Christians stop with thanking God for his gift of grace that saves. They rest (and sometimes stagnate) without recognizing that God saved us for a purpose. It is not that God is a nice guy and took pity on us. We are not saved just so we can go to heaven with the expectation of a reward (for what?). Chan held that we must understand grace to be an "empowering gift" (1998,

p. 83). Jesus has given us an assignment. As we work, grace empowers us to respond in a changed life that will glorify and praise God—a life that will display God to the world.

We are now part of God's army and engage in spiritual warfare by bringing, verbally and through demonstration, the message of freedom, release, restoration, peace, and hope. The kingdom of God is here *now*, though not yet fully here. We need to put our talent to work so that God is glorified, not bury it in the backyard as the wicked and lazy servant did in Jesus's parable in Matthew 25:14–30. This is part of our calling.

Stearns (2010) maintained that Jesus's view of the gospel "embraced a revolutionary new view of the world, an earth transformed by transformed people ... the *whole* gospel means much more than the personal salvation of individuals. It means a *social revolution*" (p. 20, emphasis in original). Obedience to the will of God is the primary motive for engaging in any social ministry—such as special education. We serve our students and their families as an instrument of God's compassion—the same compassion as Jesus demonstrated when confronted with the wearied and troubled crowds who came to him for relief and release. This can be taxing on our abilities and passion, but as Jesus's representatives, "we depend upon God's capacity to help us help others" (Watkins, 2004, p. xiii).

In his book, *God is Up to Something Good*, Evans (2002) stated "Through His magnificent grace, God can take the good, the bad, and the ugly experiences in your life and use them to make you unbelievably better at what He's created you for" (pp. 11–12). For the most part, our work in special education is "good," though there are times when there are bad days and "ugly experiences" (not necessarily the fault of the students, however), but the promise is that God can use these experiences to instruct, strengthen, and refine us so that we are transformed to be like Christ.

## Moving Forward at Last

I have titled this last section *Moving Forward* rather than "conclusion" for two reasons. First, because the topic, a theology of special education, is far from exhausted. There is more to be said about theology and special education, and readers are encouraged to continue the discussion from their own study of God's Word as the Spirit of God helps them to see further biblical and theological concepts that relate to our work as special educators. In my own study of the Scriptures, God continues to open my mind to biblical themes that inform a Christian understanding of special education and take me beyond what has been expressed in this book and my other writings on reconciliation, interdependence, hospitality, and biblical justice. What I have attempted to convey in this book is that there is a stronger basis for Christians to be involved in special education than simply altruism, or as a means of earning a living and paying the bills.

This leads to the second reason for calling this "Moving Forward." It is my prayer that readers will be able to integrate the theological and biblical ideas presented in this volume into their lives and practice, giving them a greater sense of the importance of their work with students who have disabilities and their role as representatives and advocates of God's kingdom.

Virginia Breen, mother of two children affected by autism, drew from her experience seeking services for her children and described two types of people: *Why* people, who look backward and are caught in "why me?" questions, and *How* people, who focus on moving forward. Applying this to teachers, Breen commented,

> Over the years I've learned there are two types of
> teachers, perhaps driven by their personality as much as
> their professional history. One type will generally view
> special-needs children as problems to be endured. The
> other will see them as treasures waiting to be unearthed.
> (Bonker & Breen, 2011, p. 39)

"How teachers," said Breen, "see the treasures and have the strength and courage to go digging" (p.39). And to these teachers, she and other parents of children with disabilities are eternally grateful.

How teachers are able to see beyond the limitations caused by a student's disability and view their students with a biblically informed vision of what it means to flourish as a human being. Jesus did not simply give theological lectures about the kingdom of God. He demonstrated its meaning in actions of healing, reconciliation, restoration, and compassionate love. Our vocation as Christians is to be the Body of Christ in action today, wherever God has placed us and in whatever occupation we find ourselves. God wants our lives to count, to bring him glory. The ministry of special education gives us opportunity to bring to families affected by disability the same love and hope as Jesus demonstrated.

Zorrilla (1988) asserted that "Living obediently in God's kingdom causes changes in human relations—the kingdom introduces a new order of values and attitudes that contrast sharply with those of the world" (p. 59). What a privilege to be a part of what God is doing through us as we engage in special education. Can we say that as special educators we are a prophetic instrument in the hands of God?

# References

Albert, B. (2004, September). *Briefing note: The social model of disability, human rights and development:* Disability Knowledge and Research Project: Enabling Disabled People to Reduce Poverty. Retrieved from http://www.handicap-international.fr/bibliographie-handicap/1Handicap/ModelesComprehension/socialModel.pdf

Anderson, D. W. & Pudlas, K. A. (2000). *Special education: Apologetic and methodological issues.* Paper presented at the 4th Biennial Symposium of the Coalition of Christian Teacher Educators at Covenant College, Lookout Mountain, GA., May 2000).

Anderson, D. W. (1977). The rights of children. *Christian Educators Journal,* 17(2), 7–10.

Anderson, D. W. (1997). The teacher as servant-leader. In H. Van Brummelen & D. Elliot (Eds.), *Nurturing Christians as reflective educators. Proceedings of the second biennial symposium for Christian professional education faculty* (pp. 23–38). San Demas, CA: Learning Light Educational Publishing and Consulting.

Anderson, D. W. (1998). The integration of faith and leaning in special education. *Perspectives: An Academic Journal of Daystar University,* 2(1), 30–45.

Anderson, D. W. (2003). Special education as reconciliation. *Journal of Education and Christian Belief,* 7 (1), 23–35.

Anderson, D. W. (2005, January). *Christian education as transformation.* Paper presented at The Stapleford Centre Annual Theology and

Theory of Education Conference. The Hayes Conference Centre, Swanick, Derbyshire, England.

Anderson, D. W. (2006a). Inclusion and interdependence: Students with special needs in the regular classroom. *Journal of Education and Christian Belief.* 10 (1), 43–49.

Anderson, D. W. (2006b). Special education as spiritual warfare. *Journal of the International Community of Christians in Teacher Education,* 2(1). Retrieved from http://icctejournal.org/ICTEJournal/vol2issue1andersond

Anderson, G. (1985). Christian mission and human transformation: Toward century 21. *Mission Studies,* 2(1), 52–65.

Anderson, R. S. (2001). *The shape of practical theology: Empowering ministry with theological praxis.* Downers Grove, IL: InterVarsity Press.

Anthony, M. J. (2006). *Perspectives on children's spiritual formation: Four views.* Nashville: B & H Academic.

Ariel, A. (1992). *Education of children and adolescents with learning disabilities.* Columbus, OH: Merrill.

Barnes, A. (n.d.; originally published 1832). Acts—Chapter 17. In R. Frew (Ed.), *Barnes's notes on the New Testament—Explanatory and practical.* Colorado Springs, CO: WORDsearch CROSS e-book.

Bartel, M. J. (2001). *What it means to be human: Living with others before God.* Louisville, KY: Geneva Press.

Beasley-Murray, G. R. (1992). The kingdom of God in the teaching of Jesus. *Journal of the Evangelical Theological Society, 35*(1), 19–30.

Beck, M., & Malley, J. (2003, March). A pedagogy of belonging. *The International Child and Youth Care Network, 50.* Retrieved from http://www.cyc-net.org/cyc-online/cycol-0303-belonging.html

Benner, D. G. (1988). *Care of souls: Revisioning Christian nurture and counsel.* Grand Rapids, MI: Baker Books.

Betenbaugh, H., & Procter-Smith. M. (1998). Disabling the lie: Prayers of truth and transformation. In Eiesland, N. L. & Saliers, D. S., (Eds) *Human disability and the service of God: Reassessing religious practice* (pp. 281–303). Nashville: Abingdon Press.

Billings, J. T. (2004). Incarnational ministry and Christology: A reappropriation of the way of lowliness. *Missiology: An International Review,* 32(3), 187–199.

Bishop, K. D., Jubala, K. A., Stainback, W., & Stainback, S. (1996). Facilitating friendships. In S. Stainback & W. Stainback (Eds.), *Inclusion: A guide for educators* (pp. 155–169). Baltimore, MD: Paul H. Brookes.

Black, K. (1996). *A healing homiletic: Preaching and disability.* Nashville: Abingdon.

Block, J. W. (2002). *Copious hosting: A theology of access for people with disabilities.* New York: Continuum International Publishing Group.

Bonker, E. M., & Breen, V. G. (2011). *I am in here: The journey of a child with autism who cannot speak but finds her voice.* Grand Rapids, MI: Revell.

Boyd, G. A. (1997). *God at war: The Bible and spiritual conflict.* Downers Grove, IL: InterVarsity Press.

Bridges, J. (2012). *The transforming power of the gospel.* Colorado Springs, CO: NavPress.

Brown, C. (1996, 2003). *I am what I am by the grace of God.* Warsaw, OH: Echoing Hills Village Foundation.

Browne, E. J. (1997). *The disabled disciple: Ministering in a church without barriers.* Ligouri, MO: Ligouri Publications.

Brownell, M. T., & Walther-Thomas, C. (2002). An interview with Marilyn Friend. *Intervention in School and Clinic,* 37(4), 223–228.

Browning, D. S. (1981). Toward a practical theology of care. *Union Seminary Quarterly Review,* 36(2–3), 159–172.

Browning, D. S. (1991). *A fundamental practical theology.* Minneapolis: Fortress Press.

Bruneau-Balderrama, O. (1997). Inclusion: Making it work for teachers, too. *The Clearinghouse,* 70(6), 328–330.

Buzzard, L. (1997). Justice. In R. Banks & P. Stevens (Eds.), *The complete book of everyday Christianity.* Downers Grove, IL: InterVarsity Press. WORDsearch CROSS e-book.

Carlson, G. C. (2010). Adult development and Christian formation. In J. R. Estep & J. H. Kim (Eds.), *Christian formation: Integrating theology and human development* (pp. 209–235). Nashville: B & H Academic.

Chan, S. (1998). *Spiritual theology: A systematic study of the Christian life.* Downers Grove, IL: InterVarsity Press.

Clark, D., & Emmett, P. (1998). *When someone you love is dying: Making wise decisions at the end of life.* Minneapolis: Bethany House.

Colson, C. W. (2010). Epilogue: Learning to love. In E. Colson (Ed.), *Dancing with Max* (pp. 186–197). Grand Rapids, MI: Zondervan.

Colton, A. B., & Sparks-Langer, G. M. (1993). A conceptual framework to guide the development of teacher reflection and decision making. *Journal of Teacher Education,* 44(1), 45–54.

Conn, H. M., & Ortiz, M. (2001). *Urban ministry: The kingdom, the city, and the people of God.* Downers Grove, IL: InterVarsity Press.

Cooling, T. (2010). *Doing God in education.* London: Theos.

Cope, M. (2011). *Megan's secrets: What my mentally disabled daughter taught me about life.* Abilene, TX: Leafwood Publishers

Coulter, D. L. (2001). Recognition of spirituality in health care: Personal and universal implications. In W. C. Gaventa & D. L.

Coulter (Eds.), *Spirituality and intellectual disability: International perspectives on the effect of culture and religion on healing body, mind, and soul* (pp. 1–11). New York: Haworth Pastoral Press.

Council for Exceptional Children. (2005). *Universal design for learning: A guide for teachers and education professionals.* Columbus, OH: Merrill/Prentice Hall.

Dahlstrom, R. (2011). *The color of hope: Becoming people of mercy, justice, and love.* Grand Rapids, MI: Baker Books.

DeYoung, C. P. (1997). *Reconciliation: Our greatest challenge, Our only hope.* Valley Forge, PA: Judson Press.

Dudley-Marling, C. (2001). Reconceptualizing learning disabilities by reconceptualizing education. In Denti, L., & Tefft-Cousin, P (Eds.), *New Ways of Looking at Learning Disabilities: Connections to Classroom Practice* (pp. 5–17). Denver: Love Publishing.

Dunavant, D. (2009, October). Man—Made in the image of God. *Journal of the Southern Baptist Convention, 10.* Retrieve from: http://www.sbclife.org/articles/2009/10/sla6.asp

Eggen, P., & Kauchak, D. P. (2009). *Educational psychology: Windows on classrooms* (8th ed.). Upper Saddle River, NJ: Prentice Hall.

Ellsworth, P., & Sindt, V. (1992). *What every teacher should know about how students think: A survival guide for adults.* Eau Clair, WI: Thinking Publications.

English, D. (1992). *The message of Mark: The mystery of faith.* Downers Grove, IL: InterVarsity Press.

Estep, J. R. (2010). Christian anthropology: Humanity as the Imago Dei. In J. R. Estep & J. H. Kim (Eds.), *Christian formation: Integrating theology and human development* (pp. 9–36). Nashville: B & H Academic.

Estep, J. R. (2010). Moral development and Christian formation. In J. R. Estep & J. H. Kim (Eds.), *Christian formation: Integrating theology and human development* (pp. 123–159). Nashville: B & H Academic.

Estep, J. R., Anthony, M. J., & Allison, G. R. (2008). *A theology of Christian education.* Nashville, TN: B & H Publishing Group. WORDSearch CROSS e-book.

Evans, T. (1998). *The battle is the Lord's.* Chicago: Moody Press.

Evans, T. (2002). *God is up to something good.* Sisters, OR: Multnomah Publishers.

Farnsworth, K. E. (1985). Furthering the kingdom in psychology. In A. Holmes (Ed.), *The making of a Christian mind: A Christian world view and the academic enterprise* (pp. 81–103). Downers Grove: IL: InterVarsity Press.

Ferguson, D. L. (1995). The real challenge of inclusion: Confessions of a "rabid inclusionist." *Phi Delta Kappan, 77,* 281–287.

Frangipane, F. (1989). *The three battlegrounds.* Cedar Rapids, IA: Arrow Publications.

Frazee, R. (2001). *The connecting church: Beyond small groups and authentic community.* Grand Rapids: Zondervan.

Fullan, M. G. (1993). Why teachers must become change agents. *Educational Leadership, 50*(6), 12–17. Available: http://www. michaelfullan.ca/Articles_98-99/03_93.pdf

Gaede, S. D. (1993). *When tolerance is no virtue.* Downers Grove, IL: InterVarsity.

Galindo, I. (1998). *The craft of Christian teaching: Essentials for becoming a very good teacher.* Valley Forge, PA: Judson Press.

Gargiulo, R. M., & Metcalf, D. (2010). *Teaching in today's inclusive classrooms: A universal design for learning approach.* Belmont, CA: Wadsworth.

Gill, D. W. (1989). *The opening of the Christian mind: Taking every thought captive to Christ.* Downers Grove, IL: InterVarsity Press.

Glanzer, P. L. (2012, March). The missing factor in higher education. *Christianity Today,* 56, 18–23.

Glasser, A. F. (2006). Introduction to missiology. In D. Horton & R. Horton (Eds.), *The portable seminary: A master's level overview in one volume.* Grand Rapids, MI: Bethany House. WORDsearh CROSS e-book.

Graham, D. (2003). *Teaching redemptively: Bringing race and truth into your classroom.* Colorado Springs, CO: Purposeful Design Publications.

Grant, C. C. (1998). Reinterpreting the healing narratives. In Eiesland, N. L. & Saliers, D. S., (Eds) *Human disability and the service of God: Reassessing religious practice* (pp. 72–87). Nashville: Abingdon Press.

Guinness, O. (1998). *The call: Finding and fulfilling the central purpose of your life.* Nashville, TN: Word Publishing.

Habermas, R. T. (1993). Practical dimensions of Imago Dei. *Christian Education Journal,* 13(2), 83–92.

Harrison, T. (1979). *Disability: Rights and wrongs.* Oxford: Lion Publishing.

Harshaw, J. R. (2010). Prophetic voices, silent words: The prophetic role of persons with profound intellectual disabilities in contemporary Christianity. *Practical Theology,* 3(3), 311–329.

Hauerwas, S. (2004). Community and diversity: The tyranny of normality. In J. Swinton (Ed.), *Critical reflections of Stanley Hauerwas' theology of disability: Disabling society, enabling theology* (pp. 37–43). Binghamton, NY: Haworth Pastoral Press.

Hauerwas, S., & Willimon, W. (1989) *Resident aliens: Life in the Christian colony.* Nashville, TN: Abingdon Press.

Hazle, D. (2003). Practical theology and the implications for mission. *International Review of Mission,* 92(366), 345–355.

Hersh, R. H., Paolitto, D. P., & Reimer, J. (1979), *Promoting moral growth: From Piaget to Kohlberg.* New York: Longman.

Hill, B. V. (1976). Teaching as reconciliation. *Journal of Christian Education Papers* 56, 8–16.

Hillman, G. (2008). Calling and spiritual formation. In P. Pettit (Ed.), *Foundations of spiritual formation: A community approach to becoming like Christ* (pp. 195–216). Grand Rapids, MI: Kregel Publications.

Hines, S. G., & DeYoung, C. P. (2000). *Beyond rhetoric: Reconciliation as a way of life.* Valley Forge: Judson Press.

Hodge, C. (1871). *Systematic Theology.* New York: Charles Scribner and Co., WORDsearch CROSS e-book.

Hoekema, A. A. (1986). *Created in God's image.* Grand Rapids, MI: Eerdmans.

Holmes, A. (1985). Toward a Christian world view of things. In A. Holmes (Ed.), *The making of a Christian mind: A Christian world view and the academic enterprise* (pp. 11–28). Downers Grove, IL: InterVarsity Press.

Johnson, D. E. (2002). Spiritual antithesis: Common grace, and practical theology. *Westminster Theological Journal, 63,* 73–94.

Keefe, E. B., Moore, V., & Duff, F. (2004). The four "knows" of collaborative teaching. *Teaching Exceptional Children, 35*(5), 36–42.

Keller, T. (2010). *Generous justice: How God's grace makes us just.* New York: Dutton.

Kim, H.-S. (2007). The hermeneutical-praxis paradigm and practical theology. *Religious Education, 102*(4), 419–436.

Kirkpatrick, W. D. (2003). The Trinity and Christian spirituality. *Southwestern Journal of Theology, 45*(2), 48–63.

Kraft, C. H. (1996). *Anthropology for Christian witness.* Maryknoll, NY: Orbis Books.

Kunc, N. (1992). The need to belong: Rediscovering Maslow's hierarchy of needs. In R. A. Villa, J. S. Thousand, W. Stainback & S. Stainback (Eds.), *Restructuring for caring and effective education: An administrative guide to creating heterogenous schools* (pp. 24–39). Baltimore: Paul H. Brookes.

Lederhouse, J. (1999). Peace-keeper vs. peacemaker: A conception of classroom ethos for Christian teachers. In Daniel C. Elliott & Steven D. Holtrop (Eds.), *Nurturing and reflective teachers: A Christian approach for the 21st century* (pp. 69–76). Claremont, CA: Learning Light Educational Publishing.

Lerner, J. W., & Johns, B. (2009). *Learning disabilities and related mild disabilities* (11th ed.). Boston: Houghton Mifflin Harcourt Publishing Company.

Long, N. J. (1997). The therapeutic power of kindness. *Reclaiming Children and Youth,* 5(4), 242–246.

Longchar, W. (2011). Collective resistance as prophetic witness: Mission from the margin's perspective. *Ecumenical Disability Advocates Network Quarterly Newsletter* (January–March), 4–8.

Macquarrie, J. (1995). Theological reflections on disability. In Bishop, M. E. (Ed.) *Religion and disability: Essays in scripture, theology and ethics* (pp. 27–45). Kansas City, MO: Sheed and Ward.

Maddix, M. A. (2010). Spiritual formation and Christian formation. In J. R. Estep & J. H. Kim (Eds.), *Christian formation: Integrating theology and human development* (pp. 237–271.). Nashville: B & H Academic.

Mades, S. (2001). Are people with disabilities made in the image of God? *Minnesota Association for the Education of Young Children Views* (Spring 2001), 11–12, 19.

Marsden, G. M. (1997). *The outrageous idea of Christian scholarship.* New York: Oxford.

McCollum, A. B. (1998). Tradition, folklore, and disability: A heritage of inclusion. In Eiesland, L. & Saliers, D. E. (Eds.), *Human disability and the service of God: Reassessing religious practice* (pp. 167–186). Nashville: Abingdon.

McKinley, D. (2003). *Christian community hospitality.* Paper presented at Presbyterian Pastoral Care Network National Gathering, October 20–23, 2003. Retrieved from http://www.pastoralcarenetwork.org/resources.html

Meininger, H. P. (2001). Authenticity in community: Theory and practice of an inclusive anthropology in care for persons with intellectual disabilities. In W. C. Gaventa, Jr. & D. L. Coulter (Eds.), *Spirituality and intellectual disability: International perspectives on the effect of culture and religion on healing body, mind, and soul* (pp. 13–28). Binghamton, NY: Haworth Pastoral Press.

Migliore, D. L. (2004). *Faith seeking understanding: An introduction to Christian theology* (2nd ed.). Grand Rapids, MI: Eerdmans.

Miles, S. (2000). Enabling inclusive education: Challenges and dilemmas. Paper presented at the symposium "Children with Disabilities and the Convention on the Rights of the Child," Gustav Stresemann Institute, Bonn, Germany, 27-29 October 2000. Available from http://www.eenet.org.uk/resources/docs/bonn_2.php

Miller, D. L. (1998). *Discipling nations: The power of truth to transform cultures.* Seattle, WA: YWAM Publishing.

Miller, D. L. (2009). *LifeWork: A biblical theology for what you do every day.* Seattle, WA: YWAM Publishing.

Mittler, P. (2000). *Working toward inclusive education: Social contexts.* London: David Fulton Publishers.

Moltmann, J. (1998). Liberate yourselves by accepting one another. In Eiesland, N. L. & Saliers, D. S., (Eds) *Human disability and the service of God: Reassessing religious practice* (pp. 105–122). Nashville: Abingdon Press.

Moore, V., & Keefe, E. B. (Eds.). (2001, April 18–21). *Encouraging educators to continue team teaching in inclusive classrooms.* Paper presented at the Council for Exceptional Children Conference, Kansas City, MO, USA.

Moreland, J. P. (1999). *Integration and the Christian scholar.* Paper presented at the Christian Scholarship Conference, Ohio State University, October 22, 1999. Columbus, OH. Retrieved from http://www.leaderu.com/aip/docs/moreland2b.html

Morris, J. (2001). Impairment and disability: Constructing an ethics of care that promotes human rights. *Hypatia,* 16(4), 1–16.

Mulholland, M. R. (1993). *Invitation to a journey: A road map for spiritual formation.* Downers Grove, IL: InterVarsity Press.

Mulholland, M. R. (2000). *Shaped by the Word: The power of scripture in spiritual formation* (revised ed.). Nashville: Upper Room Books.

Mulholland, M. R. (2006). *The deeper journey: The spirituality of discovering your true self.* Downers Grove, IL: InterVarsity Press.

Murdick, N., Gartin, B., & Crabtree, T. (2002). *Special education law.* Upper Saddle River, NJ: Merrill/Prentice Hall.

Newman, E. (2007). *Untamed hospitality.* Waco, TX: Center for Christian Ethics at Baylor University.

Noll, M. A. (1985). Christian world views and some lessons in history. In A. Holmes (Ed.), *The making of a Christian mind: A Christian world view and the academic enterprise* (pp. 29–54). Downers Grove, IL: InterVarsity.

Nouwen, H. J. M. (1974). *Out of solitude: Three meditations on the Christian life.* Notre Dame, IN: Ave Maria.

Nouwen, H. J. M. (1975). *Reaching out: Three movements of the spiritual life*. New York: Image Books/Doubleday.

Nouwen, H. J. M. (1988). *The road to Daybreak: A spiritual journey.* New York: Image Books/Doubleday.

Nouwen, H. J. M. (1997). *Adam: God's beloved.* Maryknoll, NY: Orbis Books.

Nouwen, H. J. M. (2003). *Creative ministry.* New York: Image Books/Doubleday.

Nuffer, P. (2010). Towards a Lutheran ethic of disability: Theological reality that embraces differences. *Missio Apostolica,* 18(2), 104–105.

Oden, A. (Ed.). (2001). *And you welcomed me: A sourcebook on hospitality and early Christianity.* Nashville: Abingdon Press.

Orr, J. (1939). *International standard Bible encyclopedia.* Retrieved from http://www.bible-history.com/isbe/J/JUSTICE

Osmer, R. R. (2008). *Practical theology: An introduction.* Grand Rapids, MI: Eerdmans.

Page, F. (2008). *The Nehemiah factor: 16 characteristics of a missional leader.* Birmingham, AL: New Hope Publishers.

Palau, L. (1999). *Where is God when bad things happen?* New York: Doubleday.

Patterson, B. A. B. (1998). Redeemed bodies: Fullness of life. In Eiesland, N. L. & Saliers, D. (Eds.), *Human disability in the service of God: Reassessing religious practice* (pp. 123–143), Nashville: Abingdon.

Pavri, S., & Luftig, R. (2000). The social face of inclusive education: Are students with learning disabilities really included in the classroom? *Preventing School Failure,* 45(1), 8–14.

Perkins, J. (2003). *Beyond charity: The call to Christian community development.* Grand Rapids, MI: Baker Books.

Perkins, J. (2007). *With justice for all* (3rd ed.). Ventura, CA: Regal.

Peskett, H., & Ramachandra, V. (2003). *The message of mission: The glory of Christ in all time and space.* Downers Grove, IL: InterVarsity.

Petersen, J. (1993). *Lifestyle discipleship: The challenge of following Jesus in today's world.* Colorado Springs, CO: NavPress.

Piper, J. (1998). *God's passion for his glory.* Wheaton, IL: Crossways Books.

Piper, J. (2012). *The pleasures of God: Meditations on God's delight in being God* (revised ed.). Colorado Springs, CO: Multnomah Books.

Pivik, J., McComas, J., & LaFlamme, M. (2002). Barriers and facilitators to inclusive education. *Exceptional Children, 69*(1), 97–107.

Plantinga, C. (2002). *Engaging God's world: A vision of faith, learning, and living.* Grand Rapids: Eerdmans.

Pohl, C. D. (1995). Hospitality from the edge: The significance of marginality in the practice of welcome. *The Annual of the Society of Christian Ethics,* 121–136.

Pohl, C. D. (1999). *Making room: Recovering hospitality as a Christian tradition.* Grand Rapids, MI: Eerdmans.

Pohl, C. D. (2002, Spring). Hospitality, a practice and a way of life. *Vision,* 34–43.

Pohl, C. D. (2003). Biblical issues in mission and migration. *Missiology: An International Review, 31*(1), 1–15.

Pohl, C. D. (2003-2004, Winter). Hospitality: Mysterious and mundane. *Reformed Review, 57*(2), 1–14.

Pohl, C. D., & Buck, P. J. (2004). Hospitality and family life. *Family Ministry,* 18(3), 11–25.

Praisner, C. L. (2003). Attitudes of elementary school principals toward the inclusion of students with disabilities. *Exceptional Children,* 69(2), 135–145.

Pudlas, K. A. (1995). Reflection on exceptionality: Toward an inclusive world view. In Elliott, D. (Ed.) *Nurturing reflective Christians to teach: A valiant role for the nation's Christian colleges and universities* (pp. 63–73). Lanham, MD: University Press of America.

Pudlas, K. A. (1997). Beyond reflection: Preparing teachers for inclusion. In Van Brummelen, H. & Elliott, D. C. (Eds.), *Nurturing Christians as reflective educators* (pp. 171–180). San Dimas, CA: Learning Light Educational Consulting and Publishing.

Pudlas, K. A. (June, 1999). *Are we practicing what we preach? Inclusion, self-concept, and professional efficacy.* Paper presented to the Canadian Association for Educational Psychology at the XXVI Annual General Conference of the Canadian Society for Studies in Education at University of Sherbrooke, Sherbrooke, Quebec.

Reinders, H. (2008). *Receiving the gift of friendship: Profound disability, theological anthropology and ethics.* Grand Rapids: Eerdmans.

Reynolds, T. E. (2006). Welcoming without reserve? A case in Christian hospitality. *Theology Today, 6*(3), 191–202.

Reynolds, T. E. (2008). *Vulnerable communion: A theology of disability and hospitality.* Grand Rapids, MI: Brazos Press.

Richards, L. O. (1991). *Encyclopedia of Bible words.* Grand Rapids, MI: Zondervan.

Rixford, M. E. (1997). From the walls of the city: Disabilities as culture. *Journal of Pastoral Care, 51*(2), 151–164.

Roberts, J. D. (2002). Reconciliation with justice. *Perspectives in Religious Studies, 29*(4), 401–409.

Robinson, D. W. (2010). Book review: Paul D. Spears & Steven R. Loomis, Education for human flourishing: A Christian perspective. *Journal of the International Community of Christians in Teacher Education, 5*(1), retrieved from http://icctejournal.org/issues/v5i1-review

Rogers, J. (1993). The inclusion revolution. *Phi Delta Kappa Research Bulletin, 11,* 5.

Rose, D. H., & Meyer, A. (2006). *A practical reader in universal design for learning.* Cambridge, MN: Harvard Education Press.

Rowland, C., & Bennet, Z. (2006). "Action is the life of all": The Bible and practical theology. *Contact* (150), 8–17.

Ryken, L., Wilhoit, J. C., & Longman III, T. (Eds.). (1998). *Dictionary of biblical imagery.* Downers Grove, IL: InterVarsity Press.

Sailhamer, J. H. (1998). Genesis. In Barker, K. L. & Kohlenberger, J. R. III (Eds.) *Zondervan NIV Bible Commentary. Volume 1: Old Testament* (pp. 1–63). Grand Rapids, MI: Zondervan.

Saliers, D. E. (1998). Toward a spirituality of inclusiveness. In Eiesland, N. L. & Saliers, D. E. (Eds.), *Human disability in the service of God: Reassessing religious practice* (pp. 19–31). Nashville: Abingdon.

Sanders, C. J. (1997). *Ministry at the margins: The prophetic mission of women, youth and the poor.* Downers Grove, IL: InterVarsity Press.

Sands, D. J., Kozleski, E. B., & French, N. K. (2000). *Inclusive education for the 21st century.* Belmont, CA: Wadsworth.

Sapon-Shevin, M. (1999). *Because we can change the world: A practical guide to building cooperative, inclusive communities.* Boston: Allyn and Bacon.

Sapon-Shevin, M. (2003). Inclusion: A matter of social justice. *Educational Leadership, 61*(2), 25–28.

Schaeffer, G. E. (1996). Peace. In Elwell, W. A. (Ed.), *Baker's evangelical dictionary of biblical theology.* Grand Rapids, MI: Baker Book House.

Schaffner, C. B., & Buswell, B. E. (1996). Ten critical elements for creating inclusive and effective communities. In Stainback, S. & Stainback, W (eds.), *Inclusion: A guide for educators* (pp. 49–65). Baltimore: Paul H. Brookes.

Schneiders, S. M. (2002). Biblical spirituality. Interpretation, 56(2), 133–142.

Schon, D. A. (1987). *Educating the reflective practitioner.* San Francisco: Josses-Bass

Senior, D. (1995). Beware of the Canaanite woman: Disabilities and the Bible. In Bishop, M. E. (Ed.) *Religion and disability: Essays in scripture, theology and ethics* (pp. 1–26). Kansas City, MO: Sheed and Ward.

Seymore, J. L. (2004, Summer). The clue to Christian religious education: Uniting theology and education, 1950 to the present. *Religious Education,* 99(3), 272–286.

Shelly, J. A., & Miller, A. B. (1999). *Called to care: A Christian theology of nursing.* Downers Grove, IL: InterVarsity Press.

Shults, F. L., & Sandage, S. J. (2006). *Transforming spirituality: Integrating theology and psychology.* Grand Rapids, MI: Baker Academic.

Sire, K. W. (1997). *The universe next door: A basic worldview catalog* (revised ed.). Downers Grove, IL: InterVarsity Press.

Smart, J. (2001). *Disability, society, and the individual.* Austin, TX: ProEd.

Smith, D. I., & Carvill, B. (2000). *The gift of the stranger: Faith, hospitality and language learning.* Grand Rapids, MI: Eerdmans.

Smith, G. T. (1999). *Courage and calling: Embracing your God-given potential.* Downers Grove, IL: InterVarsity Press.

Smith, J. D. (2003) *In search of better angels: Stories of disability in the human family.* Thousand Oaks, CA: Corwin Press.

Smith, P. (Ed.). (2010). *Whatever happened to inclusion? The place of students with intellectual disabilities in education.* New York: Peter Lang.

Snyder, H. A. (2004). *The community of the king.* Downers Grove, IL: InterVarsity Press.

Sproul, R. C. (1999). *Getting the gospel right: The tie that binds evangelicals together.* Grand Rapids, MI: Baker Books.

Stainback, W., & Stainback, S. (1996). Collaboration, support networking, and community building. In Stainback, S. & Stainback, W. (Eds.), *Inclusion: A guide for educators* (pp. 193–199). Baltimore: Paul H. Brookes.

Stearns, R. (2010). *The hole in our gospel.* Nashville, TN: Thomas Nelson.

Steele, R. B. (1994). Accessibility or hospitality? Reflections and experiences of a father and theologian. *Journal of Religion in Disability and Rehabilitation,* 1(1), 20.

Steensma, G. (1971). *To those who teach: Keys for decision making.* Signal Mountain, TN: Signal Publication/Consulting Corporation.

Stevens, D. C. (1992). The theology of Christian education. In M. J. Anthony (Ed.), *Foundations of ministry: An introduction to Christian education for a new generation* (pp. 24–36). Grand Rapids, MI: Baker Elementary.

Stewart, M. Y. (2012). The ethic of love in ancient Judaism and early Christianity. *Proceedings of the Second Nishan Forum on World Civilizations,* 3, 821–854.

Strully, J. L., & Strully, C. (1996). Friendships as an educational goal: What we have learned and where we are headed. In Stainback, S. & Stainback, W (Eds.), *Inclusion: A guide for educators* (pp. 141–154). Baltimore: Paul H. Brookes.

Swain, J., French, S., & Cameron, C. (2003). *Controversial issues in a disabling society.* Buckingham, UK: Open University Press.

Swinton, J. (1997). Restoring the image: Spirituality, faith, and cognitive disability. Journal of Religion and Health, 36(1), 21–27.

Swinton, J. (1999). The politics of caring: Pastoral theology in an age of conflict and change. *Scottish Journal of Healthcare Chaplaincy,* *2*(2), 25–30.

Swinton, J. (2000). *From bedlam to shalom: Towards a practical theology of human nature, interpersonal relationships and mental health care.* New York: Peter Lang.

Swinton, J. (2001). *Spirituality and mental health care: Rediscovering a "forgotten" dimension.* London: Jessica Kingsley Publishers.

Swinton, J. (2002). Spirituality and the lives of people with learning disabilities. *Tizard Learning Disability Review, 7*(4), 29–35.

Swinton, J. (2005). *Why psychiatry needs spirituality.* Paper presented to the Royal College of Psychiatrists AGM. Edinburgh, June 22, 2005. Available: http://www.rcpsych.ac.uk/pdf/ATT89153.ATT.pdf

*The American Heritage Dictionary* (2nd college edition). (1982). Boston: Houghton Mifflin Company.

Thorsos, N. (2012). Christian special educators responding to the call to serve: The perception of disability with a Christian worldview lens. *Journal of the International Christian Community for Teacher Education, 7*(1), retrieved from http://icctejournal.org/v7i1/v7i1-thorsos/

Tomlinson, C. A. (1999). *The differentiated classroom: Responding to the needs of all learners.* Alexandria, VA: ASCD.

Tomlinson, C. A. (2005). *An educator's guide to differentiating instruction.* Boston: Houghton-Mifflin.

Tucker, J. A. (1996). Training Christian special educators. *Journal of Adventist Education, 58*(3), 29–33. Available: http://circle.advantist.org//files/jae/en/jae199658032905.pdf

U.S. Department of Education (2003). *No child left behind: A parents' guide.* Washington, DC: U.S. Department of Education.

Van Brummelen, H. (1997). Postmodernism and teacher education programs in Christian colleges. In H. Van Brummelen & D. C. Elliot (Eds.), *Nurturing Christians as reflective educators: Proceedings of the second biennial symposium for Christian professional education faculty* (pp. 91–111). San Demas, CA: Learning Light Educational Consulting and Publishing

Van Brummelen, H. (2002). *Stepping stones to curriculum: A biblical path (2nd ed.)*. Colorado Springs, CO: Purposeful Design Publications.

Van der Klift, E., & Kunc, N. (1994). Beyond benevolence: Friendship and the politics of help. In Thousand, J. S., Villa, R. A. & Nevin, A. I. (Eds.) *Creativity and collaborative learning: A practical guide to empowering students and teachers* (pp. 391–401). Baltimore: Paul H. Brookes.

Vanier, J. (1992). *From brokenness to community.* Mahwah, NJ: Paulist Press.

Vanier, J. (1998) *Becoming human.* Mahwah, NJ: Paulist Press.

Volf, M. (1996). *Exclusion and embrace: A theological exploration of identity, otherness, and reconciliation.* Nashville: Abingdon.

Voltz, D. L., Brazil, N., & Ford, A. (2001). What matters most in inclusive education: A practical guide for moving forward. *Intervention in School and Clinic, 37*(1), 23–30.

Voltz, D. L., Sims, M. J., Nelson, B., & Bivens, C. (2005). M2ECCA: A framework for inclusion in the context of standards–based reform. *Teaching Exceptional Children, 37*(5), 14–19.

Walsh, B. J., & Middleton, J. R. (1984). *The transforming vision: Shaping a Christian world view.* Downers Grove, IL: InterVarsity Press.

Walsh, J. M., & Jones, B. (2004). New models of cooperative teaching. *Teaching Exceptional Children, 36*(5), 14–20.

Walther-Thomas, C., Korinek, L., McLaughlin, V. I., & Williams, B. T. (2000). *Collaboration for inclusive education: Developing successful programs.* Boston: Allyn and Bacon.

Washington, R., & Kehrein, G. (1996). Where are my ambassadors of reconciliation? In Clark, D. K. & Rakestraw, R. V. (Eds.) *Readings in Christian ethics—Volume 2: Issues and applications* (pp. 280–287). Grand Rapids: Baker Books.

Watkins, D. R. (2004). *Christian social ministry: An introduction.* Nashville: Broadman & Holman Publishers.

Webb-Mitchell, B. (1993). *God plays piano, too: The spiritual lives of disabled children.* New York: Crossroads Publishers.

Webb-Mitchell, B. (1994). *Unexpected guests at God's banquet table: Welcoming people with disabilities into the church.* New York: Crossroads Publishers.

Wiersbe, W. W. (2001). *The Bible exposition commentary—New Testament, Volume 2.* Colorado Springs, CO: Victor. WORDsearch CROSS e-book.

Wiersbe, W. W. (2004). *The Bible exposition commentary—Wisdom and poetry.* Colorado Springs, CO: Victor. WORDsearch CROSS e-book.

Winn, J., & Blanton, L.(1997). The call for collaboration in teacher education. In Blanton, L., et al. (Eds.) *Teacher education in transition: Collaborative programs to prepare general and special educators* (pp. 1–17). Denver: Love Publishing Co.

Wolfensberger, W. (2001). The prophetic voice and presence of mentally retarded people in the world today. In W. C. Gaventa & D. L. Coulter (Eds.), *The theological voice of Wolf Wolfensberger* (pp. 11–18). New York: Haworth Pastoral Press.

Wolfteich, C. (2000). Graceful work: Practical theological study of spirituality. *Horizons, 27*(1), 7–27.ong, A. (2007). *Theology and*

*Down syndrome: Reimagining disability in late modernity.* Waco, TX: Baylor University Press.

Wolterstorff, N. P. (1976). *Reason within the bounds of religion.* Grand Rapids, MI: Eerdmans.

Wolterstorff, N. P. (2002). *Educating for life: Reflections on Christian teaching and learning.* Grand Rapids, MI: Baker Academic.

Wolterstorff, N. P. (2004). *Educating for shalom: Essays on Christian higher education* (C. W. Joldersma & G. S. Stronks, eds.). Grand Rapids, MI: Eerdmans.

Wolterstorff, N. P. (2008). *Justice: Rights and wrongs.* Princeton, NJ: Princeton University Press.

Womack, M. M. (1998). *The college press NIV commentary—1,2,& 3 John.* In J. Cottrell, Ph.D. & T. Ash, Ph.D. (Eds.). Joplin, MO: College Press Publishing Co. WORDsearch CROSS e-book.

Yong, A. (2007a). *Theology and Down syndrome: Reimagining disability in late modernity.* Waco, TX: Baylor University Press.

Yong, A. (2007b). The Spirit of hospitality: Pentecostal perspectives toward a performative theology of interreligious encounter. *Missiology: An International Review,* 25(1), 55–73.

Zacharias, R. (2007). *The grand weaver: How God shapes us through the events of our lives.* Grand Rapids, MI: Zondervan.

Zorrilla, H. (1988). *The good news of justice. Share the gospel: Live justly.* Scottsdale, PA: Herald Press.